Stewards in the Kingdom

A Theology of Life in All Its Fullness

R. Scott Rodin

InterVarsity Press
Downers Grove, Illinois

InterVarsity Press
P.O. Box 1400, Downers Grove, IL 60515
World Wide Web: www.ivpress.com
E-mail: mail@ivpress.com

InterVarsity Press® is the book-publishing division of InterVarsity Christian Fellowship/USA®, a student movement active on campus at hundreds of universities, colleges and schools of nursing in the United States of America, and a member movement of the International Fellowship of Evangelical Students. For information about local and regional activities, write Public Relations Dept., InterVarsity Christian Fellowship/USA, 6400 Schroeder Rd., P.O. Box 7895, Madison, WI 53707-7895.

Cover illustration: Craig Tuttle/The Stock Market

ISBN 0-8308-1576-7

Printed in the United States of America ∞

Library of Congress Cataloging-in-Publication Data

Rodin, R. Scott, 1957-
  Stewards in the kingdom : a theology of life in all its fullness / R. Scott Rodin.
     p. cm.
  Includes bibliographical references.
  ISBN 0-8308-1576-7 (pbk. : alk. paper)
  1. Christian ethics. 2. Stewardship, Christian. I. Title.

BJ1275 .R55 2000
248'.6—dc21

                                                                          99-053609

20	19	18	17	16	15	14	13	12	11	10	9	8	7	6	5	4	3	2	1
16	15	14	13	12	11	10	09	08	07	06	05	04	03	02	01	00			

Dedication and Acknowledgments

This book is dedicated to all of my colleagues
in Christian ministry who have been called to positions that require them
to be godly stewards of the riches of the kingdom of God.

I wish to thank so many of you who have shared your frustrations,
your successes and your insights with me,
and who have encouraged me in the writing of this book.

I pray that this book will be a blessing to pastors, lay leaders,
Christian fundraisers, parachurch ministry leaders and Christian school,
college and seminary faculty, students and leadership.
You were in my thoughts and prayers as I wrote.

Finally, I want to acknowledge my family who created the time
in our lives for me to complete this book.
To my wife, Linda, and my children,
Anthony, Ryan and Lindsay, thank you for supporting me
in such a loving way!

CONTENTS

Introduction
9

1 Docking the *Ship*
15

2 Knowing the Triune God of Grace
32

3 Knowing God the Creator as the Triune God of Grace
58

4 The Sin of the Steward
84

5 The Faithful Steward
104

6 The Myth of the Two Kingdoms
122

7 The One Kingdom of the Steward
152

8 The Family, the Church & the Future of Stewardship
175

9 A Theology of Asking & Giving
194

Bibliography
217

Indexes
219

Introduction

When people read my curriculum vitae, they usually look confused and ask something like, "What does a fundraiser do with a Ph.D. in theology?" Or they ask the converse, "What does a theologian do with fifteen years of fundraising experience?" Good questions. The odd combination that marks my spiritual journey has brought me to this book out of a love for my profession and a deep desire to help undergird it with sound theology.

Research and experience has brought me to the conclusion that the church has lost its passion for stewardship and that theologians have not provided a compelling theology to help the church regain it. To some extent, the whole discussion of godly stewardship has been taken off the table in most churches and ministries. Pastors do not like to preach about it, nor do parishioners like to hear about it; few people write about it, and even less read about it. An effective wedge has been driven between the spiritual and the material. We do not talk about religion at social gatherings and we do not talk about money in the church.

The results of this deepening gulf are found in the rise of ineffective and un-Christian fundraising practices that have led to the growing number of financially strapped churches and ministries. The continuing fear and consequent disaffection by churches to the whole subject of stewardship has opened the door for the stranglehold that materialism and consumerism now have on God's people. Studies continue to show that the spending practices of self-professing, born-again Christians vary little from those who claim no role for religion in their lives.[1]

---

[1]George Barna, *The Second Coming of the Church* (Nashville: Word, 1997). See chap. 1, especially pp. 4-6.

The place to begin to turn the tide is in the education of our pastors, lay leaders and ministry professionals. It must happen in our seminaries, in trustee- and deacon-training sessions, in para-church development departments, in home Bible study groups and in the pastor's study. It must start with a reeducated and transformed Christian leadership. It must be built on a sound and compelling theology, and it must return the concept of the godly steward to the daily vocabulary of Christian life and worship. The purpose of this book is to start us in this direction by providing us with a *theology of the steward.*

There is a second and equally compelling reason for this study. The Christian life is to stand out in the world, marked by the attributes of peace, purpose, wholeness, fruitfulness and joy. Jesus promised us that in him we may have "life in all its fullness." That is, in Christ we may know the life of freedom and joy for which we were created and redeemed. However, for an increasing number of Christians today, that full and joyous life is being strangled by the trials and temptations of daily life. It is my contention that the loss of a theology of the steward has not only damaged our ministries, it has robbed us of the rich, full and fruitful life that God intends for us. For so many reasons that we will discuss in this book, the Christian life has been stripped of these kingdom characteristics, replacing them with just as much anxiety, stress, despair, frustration, depression and fear as is known by those in the world around us. The thesis of this book is that by reclaiming the central motif of the steward, and building it on a sound theological and biblical base, we will be freed and empowered to live as joyous children in the kingdom of God. For that reason, the subtitle of this book is *A Theology of Life in All Its Fullness.* That is the life God desires for us. That is the life for which Christ died. That is the life that will shine like a light set on a hill, drawing to it all who are lost. That is the life lived by stewards in the kingdom of the triune God of grace.

This "life in all its fullness" is not some new prosperity gospel, nor does it come from a naive disregard for the evil in the world nor from a theology of escapism. It comes from a theology of the steward that calls us into the most intense engagement with the lostness and brokenness of our age. It comes through sacrifice, selflessness, giving and compassion, but it comes through a radical reinterpretation of what each of these means in light of our understanding of who God is and who we are as stewards in his kingdom. For this reason, the full, rich and abundant life in Christ *is* the life of the steward in the kingdom of God. That is why a theology of the steward is the foundation for recapturing for every Christian that "life in all its fullness." That is the purpose of this book.

The Steward as Christian Ethic

The theology of the steward belongs to the field of Christian ethics. This simple statement introduces us to a terrain within Christian theology that is both imbued with opportunities and littered with land mines. The opportunities that lay before us are the possibilities for a study of the steward that is uniquely and truly Christian. Such an ethic will be characterized by our participation in Christ, the Christian life as joyous response, embracing the radical new values of the kingdom of God and a return to evangelical obedience all within the context of Christian ethics as doxology (worship and praise).

In the study of Christian ethics where you start determines where you will end up. For the Christian, our ethics are our responses to the command of the God who has saved us in Jesus Christ. Therefore, they are both freely given and an act of obedience to the commands of the gracious God who calls us into a new life in Christ. As response our ethics are wholly dependent upon what comes before. They are conditioned by that which calls us to response. The first critical distinction we must make in this study is that for the Christian, what motivates our response is not *what* but *who*. We are not motivated by guilt, by altruism, by seeking after a greater good, by pressure to conform to standards of acceptable behavior, nor by a set of biblical or ecclesiastical rules. Christian ethics is nothing less than the study of doxology! It is our freely given yet directly commanded act. Therefore it unfolds in our life as both our obligation and our only possibility.

The study of ethics must recognize its place in the process of the calling of the Christian and the Christian's response. This process can be described in three acts. The first, and this will be the subject of much of our study, is that the Creator *acts*. God takes the initiative that is unmerited and merciful. God acts in the sending of the Son to speak a word to us that we could not hear on our own. He reveals himself, his grace, his loving intent and his righteousness to us and makes us capable by the Spirit to hear and see and understand. Therefore, the self-revelation of the Creator is the beginning point of all Christian ethics. We can go no further until we are absolutely certain who our God is. Without this understanding, Christian ethics is impossible.

Second, in revealing himself to us in Jesus Christ, our Creator also reveals to us who we *really* are. Jesus Christ ushered in a new reality called the kingdom of God and called us into it as God's children. If this is who God is, then our understanding of who we are is radically changed at its most fundamental level. We have become something new. Our existence in this world is now defined in different terms. We are worshipers, disciples, neighbors. This too is determined solely by the Creator who acts, who speaks, who calls, who saves, who reveals and who commands. And that Creator also calls us, commands us and frees us to respond.

Only upon the foundation of these first two acts of God toward us and for us can the study of Christian ethics be built. John Calvin put it this way in speaking of true spiritual insight, "This spiritual insight consists chiefly in three things: (1) knowing God, (2) knowing his fatherly favor in our behalf, in which our salvation consists, and (3) knowing how to frame our life according to the rule of his law."[2] Only after understanding and acknowledging the first two acts of God can we begin to ask the questions of what "framing our life" looks like. Only here are we able to speak of *our* acts in response to God's great act for us. Only here can we begin to speak of worshiping, for we have become worshipers *in Christ*. Only here can we begin to speak of disciple*ship*, for we have become disciples *in Christ*. And only here can we begin to talk about steward*ship*, for we have become stewards *in Christ*. The same is true for all of the categories that describe our response. What we are to do is wholly dependent upon whom we have become. And whom we have become is seen and known and understood solely in God's gracious actions toward us. Emil Brunner summed up Christian ethics as, "the science of human conduct as it is determined by Divine conduct."[3] That divine conduct is the gracious act of God toward us in Jesus Christ, the unveiling of the heart of God that calls us into a life of free response.

> Because only conduct which takes place on the basis of this faith can be "good conduct," in the sense of the Christian ethic, therefore, the science of good conduct, of ethics, is possible only within that other science which speaks of the Divine act of revelation, that is, within dogmatics.[4]

---

[2]John Calvin, *Institutes of the Christian Religion* (Philadelphia: Westminster Press, 1960), p. 277.
[3]Emil Brunner, *The Divine Imperative* (London: Lutterworth Press, 1942), p. 86.
[4]Ibid., p. 84.

This is the only possible approach to Christian ethics if our ethics are not to drift aimlessly, to become stratified into either a grace-less list of do's and don'ts, or an equally dogmatic adherence to a tolerance of everything and a devotion to nothing. When ethics are cut loose from a doctrine of God, they can lead us into wrong notions of ethical behavior that are based more on the world's standards than anything remotely Christian.

The land mines strewn before us in this terrain of Christian ethics represent false starts that lead us to flawed conclusions and inevitably to counterfeit ethics. The most nefarious of these land mines is the temptation to begin the study or discussion of any Christian ethic at someplace other than at the beginning. This may seem obnoxiously obvious, but in practice it is the downfall of too many efforts in Christian ethics. Divisive denominational issues, "how to live the Christian life" topical books, sermons and even scholarly attempts at a truly theological approach to the ethical issues of our day, all start falsely when they start by asking, "How are we to live?" instead of asking, "Who are we in Christ?" and even more importantly, "Who is this God who has acted graciously toward us?" We too easily can become obsessed with "doing" over "being," and so we seek solutions that involve us only superficially but require no permanent change. The evidence of this obsession comes at the point where ethical discussions begin with a focus on the issues of *how, when, where* and *why*. That is, they focus on the third act, assuming everyone has started at the same place or that the starting place need play no role in the real issues that are here at the end of the process.

If a study of Christian ethics in any area is to avoid this significant land mine, it must begin at the beginning. It must not assume that everyone has started at the same place, and it must lay out the foundation upon which its conclusions will be built. The same must hold for those involved in debate and discussion on ethical issues. The discussion must begin at determining if there is common ground at the foundational level. Otherwise, there is no chance for consensus to be found in the implications that follow.

This book then is about making a right start and building a solid theological justification for placing the motif of the steward at the center of Christian life and worship. Its focus will be on *who* we are and *whose* we are before defining *how* we are to live. It attempts to put first things first and to champion the call to center all of our ethical discussions on the reality of God for us in Jesus Christ. It will lead us to the full, joyous and meaningful life for which we were created, the life of the steward in God's kingdom.

The final chapter of this book is a theology of asking and giving. It is written for everyone who is responsible to raise money, for everyone who gives money to the work of God's kingdom, and for all Christian leaders who have to deal with issues of money and stewardship. I hope it will serve to inspire further dialogue and study in this important sphere of Christian mission. I also hope that it will raise the profile and highlight the crucial role that this most noble Christian ministry plays in the furthering of the gospel of Jesus Christ.

Chapter 1

Docking the *Ship*

ON JULY 29, 1996, BRITISH OLYMPIC SPRINTING CHAMPION LINFORD Christie walked off the track at the Atlanta Summer Olympic Games having failed to defend his 1992 gold medal Olympic title as the fastest man in the world. His failure did not come at the hands of a faster man, as the result of a stumble or because of illness or injury. After four years of tenacious preparation and a worldwide media frenzy in anticipation of the single greatest ten seconds in sports, Christie left the track having never gotten out of the starting blacks. He had done the unimaginable. At the greatest moment in his athletic career, with the world holding its breath and watching, Christie made a false start. Not once, but twice. An official's red card confirmed the incredible.

In a matter of a few moments Linford Christie was disqualified from the one event that defined him as an Olympian. All the speed, strength, training and mental preparation that led to that critical moment had been wasted. The hopes of the British people and the prospects of a new Olympic record were dashed. Christie would leave a broken man and a brilliant career would forever be remembered for that one infamous moment of failure. All because of a false start.

Avoiding a False Start

The history of the church's handling of issues regarding stewardship is laden with false starts. The task in this first chapter will be to negotiate our way around the land mines that have disabled so many other works on this subject. We will attempt to make a right start and build a theology of the steward on a sound theological foundation. We will move from the *who* question of theology to the *how* question of Christians ethics and discipleship, and we will see the damage caused whenever we switch this direction around. Therefore, this book is not only an attempt at a new and fresh understanding of the call to be stewards, it is a methodology for doing Christian ethics. In attempting to achieve both, how we start will determine where we will end up. As the history of Christian theology and ethics has proven all too well, everything depends upon making a right start.

Docking the *Ship*

In order to assure that we make the right start, we must immediately change our language. For too long, attempts to undergird Christian tithing and fundraising with some sort of theology have employed the term *stewardship*. The problem that should be immediately apparent is that this focus indicates a classic false start. Steward*ship* is the practice, the work, the vocation of a steward. It is the "how-to," the ethical imperatives of the call to be a steward. The very term indicates that we can move past the whole discussion of what it means to *be a steward* and focus on the practice of steward*ship*. This is a false start.

A subtler form of this false start is seen in some of the better books on stewardship that seem genuinely to seek to ask the more fundamental and all-determining questions about being a steward. However, a close examination exposes a methodology that first lays out what a steward does and then attempts to support that view with an a posteriori analysis of the meaning of steward. This too is a false start.

This false start is also prevalent in the teaching and sermonizing on Christian giving. Sermons focus on the biblical support for the tithe, on the evils of money and materialism, and on exegeting and contextualizing the stories of the widow's mite, the rich young ruler, Paul's example of the Macedonian church and Jesus' commands on cheerful giving. Parishioners are challenged, pleaded with, reasoned with, cajoled, shamed and even threatened into practicing better stewardship. Denominations produce programs that organize campaigns, train solicitors and provide appeal letters all under the banner of better biblical stewardship. And books are written on stewardship that spend countless pages detailing all the Bible verses commanding us how and why to give, focusing us solely on the *practice* of stewardship.

In all of these ways while we have produced resources for understanding what stewardship looks like, we have failed to raise up stewards. The result is the continual need to develop new fundraising strategies and undertake innovative approaches and clever campaigns to balance the budget and further the work of the church. This must indicate that we are not preparing our people to be informed, committed, godly stewards. This false start assumes that unchanged hearts will follow the radical new ethics of the kingdom of God. It assumes that somehow repentance, conversion and the new life in Christ does not include a fundamental redemption of our attitudes toward possessions. And it assumes that the call to be people of the kingdom of God does not call us simultaneously to a radical new relationship with creation as well as with God and our neighbor. It assumes, falsely, that the call to be a steward is not the necessary prerequisite to the life of biblical stewardship. This is indeed a false start!

In this false start the church is really only following the world. We are a society in search of quick solutions. We want solutions on the how-to level rather than the more fundamental *who* level. Tell us *how* to lose weight, not that *we must change* who we are—that is, our habits, our lifestyle and our attitudes. That is the hard work that our society holds in such disdain. And so the solution to obesity is sought in pills, in electroshock belts that burn fat while we watch TV, in blitz-diets and even in prayer. We want ten minutes a day on an Aerobisizer II Deluxe Gliding Absflexing Weight Machine to undo twenty-three hours and fifty minutes of overeating and laziness. We want to fix things. We want formulas that tell us what do to but never mention who we must *become* in order to accomplish what we want.

So we start at the end. Starting with the *how* questions in Christian ethics is akin to the person who sits down toward the end of a movie and asks, "Why did she say that?" "What did all that mean?" or "How come they did that?" Aside from the strong urge to physically assault someone like this, it is clear quite quickly that by missing the start, the ending will make little sense. If one gives in to the further temptation to try to figure it out anyway, it will become apparent that the answers to the *why, what* and *how* questions vary radically with the answers from those who have watched the entire movie. Imagine the absurdity of the "drop-in" movie watcher arguing over the meaning of the dialogue or the direction of the plot with those who have watched the film from the beginning. Yet that is exactly what we do when we seek to find unity on the pressing issues of our day without first seeking unity on the foundations from which those pressing issues have emerged!

The ethics that result from the overemphasis on *doing* and the absence of *being* have beleaguered the church in its teaching of biblical stewardship. Robert Wuthnow spells this out in uncompromising clarity in speaking of the status of the average churchgoer:

> We pray that things will go well for us, we hear sermons counseling us to work hard and to be good stewards, and many of us give lip service to the idea that greed is sin or that God is concerned about the poor. For millions of us, faith nudges our attitudes and our economic behavior in one direction or another. It does so, however, in ways that are seldom as powerful as religious leaders would like and that do little to challenge the status quo. Religion is thus an ambiguous presence in our society. It sends mixed signals about our work, telling us to work hard but not too hard. It counsels us to be diligent with our money but seldom instructs us in how to be diligent. It raises our anxieties about money and discourages us from talking openly about them. It warns us against the excessive materialism that pervades our society but offers little to keep us from the temptations of materialism. Feeling ambivalent about the role of faith, we therefore go about our lives pretty much the same as those who have no faith at all.[1]

To avoid this lethal land mine, we must set aside all discussion of steward*ship* and discipline ourselves to start at the beginning, on the call to be stewards. By setting aside the imperatives of the vocation of the steward until its proper place—at the end—we can free this study from the tentacles that bind so many other noble efforts, and we can focus our attention on the *who* question—the heart of all Christian ethics. If we will be true to the call to begin at the beginning, we can be prepared to talk about the practical imperatives of stewardship in a truly informed theological way.

The dichotomy between the question of *what* we should do—Christian ethics—and *who* we are—Christian theology—has a long and sad history in the church. For too long we have divided our theology and ethics in

---

[1]Robert Wuthnow, *God and Mammon in America* (New York: Free Press, 1994), p. 5.

our formal studies and in our more topical writings. In seminary we have separate disciplines and faculties for "systematic theology" and "practical theology"—as if systematic theology is not practical (which is too often the case by the way it is presented), and practical theology has no systematic basis. Both disciplines suffer if the study of the practice of Christian ministry is not built on a sound theological base. Brunner reminds us, "The attempt to make a clear-cut distinction between dogmatics and ethics from the point of view that one is concerned with Divine and the other with human action spoils both dogmatics and ethics."[2] Such a division between dogmatics and ethics causes us to lose our focus and creates a weak and impotent ethic. Speaking of our ethical responsibilities with respect to the poor, Ron Sider remarks, "Our problem is not primarily one of ethics. It is not that we have failed to live what our teachers have taught. It is that our theology itself has been unbiblical."[3] Our call then is to build the right theology of the steward upon which we can develop a credible ethic of stewardship. That is the order we must discipline ourselves to maintain if we are to make a right start.

Stewards in the Kingdom of the Triune God of Grace

Throughout this book we shall use the phrase "stewards in the kingdom of the triune God of grace," which will provide us with the process under which this study must be taken if it is to avoid a false start. To unpack that process we must understand that Christian ethics is the study of the imperatives of the Christian life (how we should live) that by definition follow from the indicatives of the Christian faith (what we believe). That is the order that must be maintained! Everything we say and do as Christians depends on this ordering, and once this process gets out of order, our ethics cease being Christian. As such they lose all authority and influence. They become nothing more than directionless discussions of various opinions and testimonies of individual experiences. They become as relative as the situational ethics of the world around us. God's command on our lives as his redeemed people are then reduced to a shopping list of do's and don'ts that can be heeded or ignored depending on one's context, history and biblical interpretation. The distinction between church and world becomes blurred to insignificance. The church becomes pallid

---

[2]Emil Brunner, *The Divine Imperative* (London: Lutterworth Press, 1942), p. 84.
[3]Ronald J. Sider, *Rich Christians in an Age of Hunger* (Dallas: Word, 1997), p. 64.

and ineffective. And our witness as light in a world of darkness illumi-
nates a path that leads to nowhere. What is perhaps worse is that each
individual Christian life, and therefore the collective witness of the community of believers, loses its vitality, its power, its zeal and its joy. When
we lose our direction through such a flawed approach to the ethical concerns of our day, our people are left to struggle on their own with only a
future hope of escape from a life lived in no qualitatively different way
than their secular neighbor. The "life in all its fullness" promised us by
Jesus is replaced by a life lived in all its freneticness, stress and anxiety.
This is what is at stake in choosing how we are to study Christian ethics.

The process offered in the phrase "stewards in the kingdom of the triune God of grace" is to be read backwards. Our end goal is to build a
credible Christian ethic of the theology of the steward from which we can
then speak of our response of steward*ship*. To reach this point we must
first understand fully what it means to be a steward. We know we are
called to be stewards, but we cannot begin at this call. By definition, a
steward is under the command of one who owns the resources that are to
be stewarded. *Steward* is a title of a servant, one hired to undertake this
activity on behalf of the owner. Therefore, we must move the ethical question back one step and ask, "Whose steward are we? To whom do we owe
allegiance in our work?"

The answer we find is shaped by our status as *children in the kingdom of
God*. When we examine the life of the Christian in Scripture, it is marked
at every point by its membership in the kingdom of God. We are first and
foremost God's children and people of his kingdom. Our call to be stewards then is a call that originates solely from our status as children of the
kingdom of God. Our being as stewards is inseparable from our being as
children of the kingdom of God. Therefore, if we are to understand what
it means to be a steward, we must move the ethical question back to the
question of what it means to be a child in the kingdom of God.

But we cannot start here either. For this kingdom is defined by the God
who has established it and called us into it. It is *this* God's kingdom, and
we are *this* God's children. Therefore, the ethical question of living as a
steward must move back another step, to the *who* question. Who is this
God in whose kingdom we live, whose children we are and to whom we
are to be stewards? This is the question that must undergird every Christian ethic, and if you have reached this question, you have almost assur-
edly avoided a false start. Knowing the God in whose kingdom we live as

his children is the basis of all Christian ethics. Yet how many discussions on major ethical issues in the church, how many sermons on "how you should live," and how many "how-to" books on every aspect of "godly living" begin here? Indeed, how many books on stewardship begin at the beginning with a thorough treatment of the doctrine of God and how that understanding of who God is informs us of who we are, which leads us to the answers of the focus of this study, "How then should we live as stewards?" Any treatment of Christian ethics that does not start here starts falsely and will end almost certainly with an uneven and ineffectual ethic. Yet as we see in the phrase, we have not yet captured the whole of the proper starting point. We still stand the chance of falling victim to a false start if we do not press this discussion back one final step.

Knowing the God in whose kingdom we live as his children requires one additional and all-important move. Our knowledge of God is only true knowledge, effectual knowledge, "sufficient" as Karl Barth rightly defines it, if it is knowledge that has been revealed to us. It is not a human knowledge dreamed up from our own philosophies, fabricated from a selection of our individual experiences or constructed from the reasonableness of the "human come of age." The Christian faith is distinctly a revealed faith. Therefore, the only truly Christian ethic is the ethic built on a Christocentric epistemology; that is, a Christ-centered way of knowing who our God is and who we are as his children. If the only God we know is the God revealed to us in Jesus Christ, then we must let this God and no other direct our ethics. What we find in this Christ-centered way of knowing is that the Son came to reveal to us the Father and to establish his kingdom filled with the Holy Spirit. The God revealed to us in Christ is known to us in three persons: Father, Son and Holy Spirit. The God of the kingdom in which we live as children is the triune God revealed to us in Christ—and no other. We are children in the kingdom of the triune God. That is the truth of our being. That is the reality of our existence. It all begins with knowing God with certainty as the triune God who has revealed himself to us in Jesus Christ.

Finally, it is not enough to understand this God only as the triune God. The very fact that he has chosen to reveal himself to us, to come to us in Jesus Christ, to die for us and to call us his children in Christ, reveals something even greater about this triune God. It revels to us that this God is *for us*. This is the God we can call Abba, Father. This God is our creator, sustainer, redeemer and friend. And by this knowledge of who our creator God is, we come to a real knowledge of who we are. It is here and only here that our knowledge of ourselves has validity. This self-knowledge is as Christocentric as our knowledge of God. Therefore, the real *who* question that abides at the heart of all valid Christian ethics is the dual question, "Who is this God we know in Jesus Christ?" and "Who are we, as children of this God?" From the answers to these two questions will emerge a powerful, effectual Christian ethic.

The answers will also have a distinguishing mark. They will testify that this is the God of grace. It is only by grace that we have knowledge of God. It is only by grace that we know God as Father, Jesus as Savior and Spirit as Comforter. It is only by grace that we know ourselves as created for relationship with this God, as redeemed by the precious blood of this Savior, and as participants in the life of God and mission of God's people through the movement of this Spirit. And our lives as children in the kingdom of this God must reflect that grace in every ethical act and decision.

This is the right start we must make. We must dock the *ship* that would want us to look at the imperatives of the faith before the indicatives of grace. We must ask what it means that we are stewards in the kingdom of the triune God of grace. We must begin at the beginning, and that leads us to ask first the epistemological question, "Who is this God, and how do we know?" It leads us to the starting point for every Christian ethic, every Christian doctrine, every Christian creed, and every attempt to know and understand ourselves and our world as Christians. It leads us to Jesus Christ.

Ask the Epistemological Question

In teaching theology classes at Eastern Baptist Theological Seminary I am constantly trying to provide students with the tools they will need as pastors to interpret the issues of the day in truly Christian terms and make the results usable for the laity. To that end we spend a great deal of time learning the process of "thinking theologically" and applying our thinking through the use of test cases as we develop our own personal theological positions. The recurring theme I press home at every possible opportunity is the importance of understanding the way in which we can know anything of certain about God. This theme is critical for theological reflection as theology is the study (*logia*) of God (*theos*). This casts the theological enterprise in a wholly distinctive light in comparison to the other *logia* in academia. There is a clear subject-object dichotomy in the fields of *bio-logia*, *zoo-logia, psyche-logia, physio-logia, socio-logia* and so forth. In these fields the subject, namely the investigator, (therefore, the "ist"—biolog*ist*, zoolog*ist*, psycholog*ist*, etc.) stands over against the object of inquiry: life, animals, the mind, etc. The investigator seeks objectivity, a detachment that will allow for unbiased investigation. From this investigation, conclusions can be drawn from theory, hypothesis and experimentation. In the process it is crucial that the object remain object and the subject remain subject. This is the basis for all good scientific investigation.[4]

What happens though when we deal with *theo-logia?* The roles of subject-object become rearranged, for we as theologians are both and at once subject and object. It is God who stands over against us. And therefore, the focus of our study is always subject and never only object. We have no place where we can stand over against God and gain a detached, objective perspective. God is not available to us for our occasional probing, experimentation and investigation. And most problematic, he is not knowable through human cognition, sensation or even imagination. Scripture testifies that it is sin that prohibits us from having a natural knowledge of God. Sin has made it impossible for us to know God in and of ourselves. We may know some things *about* God from creation, and we can speculate on what God might be like based on experience and reason, but we are wholly prohibited from direct, reliable knowledge of God by the brokenness of our sin and sinful world. How then do we properly carry out our work of studying God?

Theology, properly done, is wholly dependent upon our understanding that the Christian faith is a revealed faith, and that revelation is a self-revelation of a God who desires us to know him, that we may know ourselves as his children. Therefore, true, reliable and sufficient knowledge of God is not impossible; indeed, it is the great gift of the grace of God.[5] God has revealed himself to us through the incarnation. That is the truth

---

[4]It would be wrong to say that scientific investigation achieves its goal of detached objectivity. Michael Polanyi, in his attack on this presupposition, reminds us that "even the most strictly mechanized procedure leaves something to personal skill in the exercise of which an individual bias may enter" (Michael Polanyi, *Personal Knowledge* [London: Routledge Kegan Paul, 1958], p. 16). For Polanyi, every act of knowing is an action that requires involvement on some level, mitigating against the absolute objectivity sought by the researcher. However, the subject-object classification does not break down in the way that we experience in the work of *theo-logia.*

[5]See the treatment of the first chapter of John in chapter two of this book. Or better yet, read

upon which our faith depends. In Jesus Christ we have the only direct, true and reliable knowledge of who our God is. That is the truth upon which all Christian theology depends. This self-revealing of God is our starting place for faith, theology and ethics. Again this is the only valid place where we as Christians can start. "Theology is a joyful intellectual task because the source of its task is the source of the profoundest joy."[6] That is not a popular word to those in the church who wish to let experience, culture and reason share equally in revealing God to us, but it is the unshakable ground that cannot be yielded if we are to continue to be the church of Jesus Christ.

How we know God and how we can be certain we know is the stuff of epistemology. And epistemology simply must gain a greater place in our theology and our ethics today. So for my students, my rallying cry to them and to you is, "Ask the epistemological question!" By this I mean that every doctrine, creed and ethic has an epistemological base. And that base has already determined to a great degree the force and direction of the doctrine, creed and ethic. The discussions we must have around the issues that divide us inside and outside the church must begin and focus on the epistemological roots of each position. Let me illustrate.

One assignment I have for my class is to read a booklet put out by the Jehovah's Witnesses debunking the doctrine of the Trinity. The booklet carries the subtitle "Is Jesus Christ the Almighty God?" The booklet is well argued, thorough and historically fairly accurate. I ask my students to respond to a fictional parishioner who has been disturbed by the booklet. I ask them to read the pamphlet and respond at a lay level, indicating that they understand the core problem with the theology behind the pamphlet's prodigious use of Bible verses, history and Christian doctrine. What I am looking for is whether the students can ask the right questions. If they approach the Jehovah's Witnesses' challenge to the Trinity with a Bible-verse-by-Bible-verse exegetical attack, or if the students take on the Jehovah's Witnesses over their historical inaccuracy, their misunderstanding of church doctrine or their theological simplicity, the students demonstrate that they themselves have missed the point (and failed the exam!). Even worse, they will end up arguing over issues that cannot be resolved because these issues are

---

the entire book of John, looking and listening to the text as it speaks of how Jesus reveals to us the heart of the Father *with certainty!*

[6]Thomas C. Oden, *The Living God* (San Francisco: Harper Collins, 1961), p. 377.

constructed on radically different epistemologies.

The key is in the language of the title. The question I want students to ask the Jehovah's Witnesses is, "Who is the almighty God?" And further, "How do you know?" If there is disagreement on who God is and how we know for certain who God is, then every creed, doctrine and ethic will follow suit. For the Jehovah's Witnesses, the nature, will and work of God is not in any way dependent upon the revelatory work of Christ. Their epistemology is a priori to the work of Christ, stemming instead from select Old Testament interpretation, human reason, experience and a strong dose of Arianism[7] that rears its ugly head in every century in one form or another. Therefore, for the Jehovah's Witnesses, the claims of Christ must be interpreted in a way to fit into the frame of the God whom they have already constructed from their anthropocentric (human-centered) epistemology. Simply put, if this is who God is (indivisible, unchangeable, unmovable, etc.) then Jesus Christ cannot be "the almighty God." So the claims of Jesus' deity and his revelation of the nature of God as Trinity must be rejected. From this false start they construct an entire theology based on fitting a deconstructed Jesus into this epistemologically flawed frame. The main problem between the Christian faith and the Jehovah's Witnesses' then is primarily epistemological, and that is the key to being able to talk with them about our faith. That is the tool I try to teach my students.

This important theological tool is critical for our discussion of the theology of the steward. As with all ethical questions of the faith, the framing of the questions is vital. The example can be further illustrated by the current divisions in many denominations over the issue of homosexuality. The false start being promoted by some in leadership is the focus on the unity of the church. Now this may seem strange to call Christian unity a false start, but such is the subtle deception of the enemy that would have us produce an ineffectual ethic on such a critical issue. The problem again is that unity is the ethical imperative that can only be the product of the indicatives of grace. That is, unity comes from a people who have been redeemed and changed and who find their unity in that common transformation. If there is a lack of unity evidenced by deep divisions over

---

[7]Arianism follows the teaching of Arius, who held that the Son was not equal to the Father and therefore denied the Christian view of the Trinity. It set up a hierarchy within the Godhead and subordinated the Son to the status of a created heavenly being that served God but was not equal to God nor coeternal with the Father.

major ethical issues, it likely stems from a lack of unity at the foundational level. The problem in many denominations is not the lack of unity, nor even the issues that seemingly have caused division. The problem is in the membership's multifarious understandings of the God they worship. Ethical divisions with the strength and passion evidenced in this debate can only be based on more fundamental differences in the perception of who God is and therefore who we are and what we are called to do. That is where the discussion must begin. To attempt to paste over these fundamental differences in the name of unity is to start falsely. It leaves us to seek after a false unity, a unity that must be conjured up, a unity to which people adhere because of guilt, peer pressure or the threat of denominational estrangement. It witnesses to a lack of understanding of unity in Christ as our response to the God who called us out of the world as his people. It is tearing up many denominations, eating at the heart of the church, and it is a false start that must be recognized by our leadership if we are to begin the arduous task of moving back and beginning at the beginning.

This same mistake can be seen over and over again in how the church handles other ethical divisions and divisive issues that confront us. We are forever making false starts. How can we discuss euthanasia, capital punishment, abortion or biomedical ethics without a thorough study of the meaning of life in light of who we are as the children of the kingdom of the God who was revealed to us in Jesus Christ? How can we rightly discuss issues of oppression, justice, racism and discrimination without a thorough study of what it means that all humanity is created for relationships, and therefore is created in the image of the trinitarian God revealed to us in Jesus Christ? How can we rightly discuss the problem of evil and suffering without a thorough study of the nature of God that points us to the heart of a loving Father revealed to us in Jesus Christ? How can we discuss the challenges of multiculturalism and pluralism rightly without a thorough study of the purpose of God the Creator to call all humanity to himself through the redemptive work of the Son that is revealed to us in Jesus Christ? How can we rightly discuss human sexuality and homosexuality without a thorough study of the command of God the Creator who made us male and female for relationships that reflect the glory of the trinitarian God who is revealed to us in Jesus Christ? And how can we discuss money, ownership, giving and asking rightly without a thorough study of the meaning of creation, fall and redemption for those who are called as stewards and for creation itself, in light of our status as children in the kingdom of the God who has revealed himself in Jesus Christ? All of these questions must be framed in thoroughly epistemological language. This is not a panacea for all that divides us, but it is a prerequisite for substantive dialogue that will have a chance to lead to consensus and the long sought after unity of the church.

The Theology of the Steward

This study starts at the beginning and seeks to avoid the temptations to make a false start, that is, to talk about stewardship before developing a theology of the steward. We will work through the process laid out earlier, beginning with the epistemological question, constructing from there a doctrine of God, moving to an understanding of the kingdom of this God and who we are as children of this God in this kingdom, and finally asking what it means to be called to be stewards. Before we begin, we must be sure of our language and decide if a right start includes the use of the term *steward*.

Theologians, I am convinced, are professional term-creators. We are applauded for our ability to make up new words that supposedly better capture the true meaning of our brilliant insights and keen analysis. Conveniently, these terms also serve to keep the uninformed at arm's length, for we have created our own vocabulary that one must decipher to unlock the secrets of the theological enterprise. While some new terms have proven helpful, especially with the need to be gender inclusive, most are too indicative of arrogance and a certain pompousness that seems grossly out of place in a field in which we are called humbly before God in the attempt to speak about him. Therefore, I am reluctant to offer new terms for our study. Yet I believe we must also understand the limitations of the language we will adopt.

The term *steward* is misunderstood and even foreign in our society. We do not have any terms in our modern vocabulary that carry the richness of this term. *Caretaker* fails to capture the responsibility laid on the steward. *Manager* seems inadequate to describe the relationship between the owner and the steward. *Custodian* is too passive a term. *Agent* is too self-serving in our day. *Ambassador* is too political, and it lacks the servant aspect. *Warden* is too administrative and loses the sense of the personal. *Guardian* is too closely tied solely to parental responsibilities.

Vocationally, perhaps the director of a charitable foundation may be the closest image we have today as one to whom resources are entrusted for the purposes described by the rightful owner. However, even here there is a purely financial tone to the term. There is also a definite sense of distance between steward and owner that is antithetical to the biblical understanding of our vocation as stewards.

Without a clearly better term in our modern vernacular, we return again to the term *steward*. But before adopting it, we must look at the pros and cons of the term and see if we can accept it for our use in this study.

The negative images come almost solely from the church's use of the biblical symbol. Doug Hall points out that the term has historically described giving as the means to achieve the *real* mission of the church. Therefore, stewardship has no real value in and of itself but only in relationship to its ability to help the church achieve its goals.

> So thoroughly is the term associated with church management and finances; so demeaned is it by the implicitly unfavorable comparison with the spiritual end (mission) for which it is only the means, that it will require a great deal of critical thought and work to bring the stewardship idea to the prominence that its biblical background warrants and the times demand.[8]

Because of the lack of sound teaching on stewardship, the image of the steward offered by the church has become blurred. Perhaps the primary understanding today of the term *steward* is one who shares one's own resources with others. Here the characteristic mark of the biblical steward—handling with integrity the resources *of another*—is completely lost. Being a godly steward has been reduced to nothing more than being a good investor or philanthropist or business owner. While these are all vestiges of what being a steward might look like, they miss the mark by staying in an "ownership frame" that is completely foreign to the biblical notion of *steward*. This is an image that will be hard to unseat in the church.

The image is further tarnished by its association with the purely financial aspect of its meaning. When the call to be a steward is equated only with one's finances, then the role can be fulfilled by tithing to the church,

---

[8]Douglas John Hall, *The Steward* (Grand Rapids, Mich.: Eerdmans, 1990), p. 13. He goes on to say, "It would not be an exaggeration, I think, even to say that stewardship has a distasteful connotation for the majority of churchfolk, including clergy."

while our use of time, our relationships with others, our care for the environment and our care for ourselves remain our own concern detached from the "spiritual" part of our lives. This attitude, as we will see in chapter six, leads to the myth of the two kingdoms in which there is a kingdom of that which is "ours" side by side with the kingdom of God, or the spiritual things in our lives. To be a steward in this limited sense is to deal with our financial obligations in the spiritual realm, while leaving all else under the auspices of our own control in our worldly kingdom. This bifurcation of the role of the steward is prevalent in the church, and it poses a major challenge to the teaching of stewardship and the raising up of committed, godly stewards.

Finally, because the term is so associated with the finances in the church, it also carries the baggage of the myriad of negative images of the church's involvement with money and fundraising. By putting the word *steward* in the title of this book, I was cautioned that many would see it as another attempt to get more money from people for the church. The very word smacks of tawdry fundraising schemes, heavy-handed techniques, poor stewardship sermons, guilt giving and ecclesiastical graft. It brings to mind the charge "the church only wants my money" and all the variants on that theme. Robert Wood Lynn laments that the term *stewardship*

> has been used to describe all manner of different Christian concerns. But amidst all the popular new talk about stewardship, I don't see anything in the stewardship teachings of the last twenty-five or thirty years that brings distinctively new and powerful meanings to the act of giving.[9]

This inertia, too, will be difficult to overcome in the church.

The positive reasons to use the term include its biblical foundation. While many terms are used in Scripture, the image of the steward emerges to take a special place in the teaching of Godly living as children in the kingdom of God. Hall also concludes, "The metaphor of the steward is conspicuously present in the biblical tradition, even though it has never been consistently or profoundly appropriated by evolving church doctrine."[10]

The term is also rich in its ability to demonstrate its relational character. We have said that *steward* is a wholly relational term, and we will

---

[9]Robert Wood Lynn, "Faith and Money," in *Inside Information,* spring 1997, p. 6.
[10]Hall, *Steward,* p. 76.

develop this idea on four levels. First, *the term immediately identifies the steward as one who is not the rightful owner of that which is to be stewarded.* Stewards are by definition not owners, but they have a relationship with the owner in order to be a faithful steward. This steward-owner relationship is of primary importance in a study of the theology of the steward.

Second, *the term denotes a relationship between the steward who cares for the resources of the owner and those for whom those resources are meant.* The biblical steward invested the resources in the lives of those to whom the owner was inclined. Therefore, there is a necessary relationship between the steward and the recipients of the resources being stewarded.

Third, *there is a relationship between the steward and the steward's own needs.* That is, while the resources are not owned by the steward, the steward is expected to live from the resources and in that way be a steward to himself or herself. There is a self-stewardship implied in the term.

Fourth, *there is a relationship between the steward and the resources themselves.* Here issues of control, power, materialism, exploitation, waste, harvest and domination need to be discussed. Here the steward faces the temptation to act the part of the owner. Here is where the dark side of ownership is manifested, and stewardship is abandoned. The term *steward* carries the identification of one who draws clear lines between investing and exploitation, between management and control, between caretaking and domination, between use and waste. Here the term *steward* is most poignant and most challenging.

These four relationships will be key in our development of the theology of the steward, for while here they depict the positive relational aspects of the term, they will also be the foci of the effects of the fall, which brought brokenness to each. Van Dyke, Mahan, Sheldon and Brand pointed this out with clarity in speaking of the four great separations of sin and judgment,

> First came a separation of humans from God. . . . Second the Fall created a separation of human beings from each other. . . . Third, each human became divided in and separated from the self. . . . Fourth humans were separated from creation.[11]

Clearly the terms *steward* and *stewardship* can be both helpful and prob-

---

[11]Fred Van Dyke, David Mahan, Joseph Sheldon and Raymond Brand, *Redeeming Creation: The Biblical Basis for Environmental Stewardship* (Downers Grove, Ill.: InterVarsity Press, 1996), p. 69.

lematic to this study. We must recognize at the beginning that many may have trouble embracing the theology that will be presented because of their reaction to the terms used. However, it may be for these very reasons that we should cleave to these terms and seek to resurrect their proper meaning rather than create a new vocabulary. It is the harder way, but the term *steward* is too appropriate to abandon as useless. Instead we will attempt to recapture its meaning for the church by building a proper theology upon which it can stand. We will begin at the primary relationship of the steward—the relationship between the steward and the rightful owner of the resources to be stewarded. This is both the first and primary relationship, and as we have argued, it is the only proper starting point for a credible and valid Christian ethic. Therefore, we will begin this study with a doctrine of God based on a Christocentric epistemology. In other words, we will start with the *who* question.

Chapter 2

Knowing the
Triune God of Grace

KNOWING INFORMATION ABOUT A PERSON AND KNOWING A PERson are two entirely different things. One day I was walking through a train station and a man stopped me and said, "I know you. You spoke at our church last week." To be accurate, this man was right and wrong. He did know *who I was*, but he certainly did not *know* me. At one level we are known through our relationships with a large group of people who we may call acquaintances or casual friends. These people may know things about us: where we live, what we do for a living, how many children we have, even our interests and dislikes. But the form of the relationship, the frequency of interaction and the level to which the conversation is allowed to go indicate that this knowledge is still a *knowing about* and not a true *knowing*. This may seem like splitting hairs, but in the field of epistemology this distinction is crucial. If we are to know the God to whom we have been called as stewards, we must be sure that such knowledge is dependable, certain and sufficient.

In the early part of the twentieth century as the Pacific Northwest was being settled, there was a need to find wives for the lumberjacks working there. So a system of "mail-order brides" was established whereby men could write for a wife, naming certain desirable characteristics. The potential groom received information, perhaps a letter and a photograph from the bride-to-be, and from that information major life decisions were to be made. At this point there was certainly knowledge *about* one's prospective mate. However, it was not until the train arrived and the woman in the blurry photo stepped off that true knowledge could begin to be gained. Unfortunately, too often this truer knowing stood in sharp contradiction to the knowledge *about*, and many a potential bride returned home on the next train! Clearly the requirements for direct knowledge are distinct from those that provide us with knowledge about the other.

Knowing About God

Romans 1 tells us that there is ample evidence in the world around us to proclaim the glory of God. Speaking to the Gentiles in Rome specifically but all humankind in a broader sense, Paul warns,

> The wrath of God is being revealed from heaven against all the godlessness and wickedness of men who suppress the truth by their wickedness, since what may be known about God is plain to them, because God made it plain to them. For since the creation of the world God's invisible qualities—his eternal power and divine nature—have been clearly seen, being understood from what he has made, so that men are without excuse. (1:18-20)

Paul makes it clear that there is a level of knowledge about God that comes from the witness of his creation, and that knowledge carries with it a responsibility for all humankind. What can be known from this general revelation is the deity and power of God. This general revelation is so clear that people everywhere, regardless of cultural context or individual experience stand accountable for their response. Calvin writes, "There is . . . no nation so barbarous, no people so savage, that they have not a deep-seated conviction that there is a God." He concludes, "There lies in this a tacit confession of a sense of deity inscribed in the hearts of all."[1]

Paul is attacking idolatry that places a human-crafted object in the place of the God who is sufficiently revealed in creation to, at the very least, summon the worship of the creature. Idolatry is a lie, and by its

---

[1] John Calvin, *Institutes of the Christian Religion* (Philadelphia: Westminster Press, 1960), p. 44. Calvin goes on to say, however, that of the seed sown in the hearts of men "scarcely one man in a hundred is met with who fosters it, once received, in his heart, and none in whom it ripens—much less shows fruit in season" (p. 47).

practice we have become fools and have "exchanged the glory of the immortal God for images made to look like mortal man and birds and animals and reptiles" (1:23).

For Paul, God's general revelation of his deity and power in creation is sufficient to warrant the worship of God alone. We must be clear in our understanding of Paul's intent here. He is not saying that true, personal, saving knowledge of God is accessible to us in God's creation. General revelation can provide us with knowledge about God, his power and deity, and that knowledge requires certain responses from us. However, this is not the personal knowledge of God as the father of Jesus Christ, to whom we too cry, "Abba, Father." Paul does not expect that the general revelation in creation will show us the heart of the father nor will it reveal his saving intent in the sending of his son. Nevertheless, it does proclaim the existence of a God who has created the world in orderliness, and who reigns over the world, sustaining and nurturing it, and us in it. In response to this general revelation we are obligated to pay homage.

General knowledge of this sort—knowledge *about* God—can be gained from many sources. Paul is speaking of a kind of cosmological knowledge of God revealed in creation. This can be taken a step further in the knowledge of God gained from the understanding of our creation in the image of God. If we are created in God's image, or if we were before the fall and if the image has not been completely lost through sin, then we can learn something of the creator by looking at his image in us. Here we may find that reason, love, creativity, joy and devotion are attributes that may attain to the creator, since they are among the best attributes of humanity.

In addition to this general cosmological knowledge there is phenomenological or existential knowledge that can come from our experience of God in our lives and the collective experience of the community of faith. There is philosophical knowledge that is produced through our logic and reason, thinking through the things of God and making sense and semblance of the world around us.

Historically, knowledge of God has been sought through negation (the *via negativa*). Early church theologians reasoned that we as humans with finite minds can never know anything absolute about who God is, so the only knowledge available to us is to discover God by what he is not. Therefore, according to the *via negativa*, we can say that if God is God, he is not limited in power and so he must be omnipotent. Similarly, he is not able to be divided and so he is indivisible. Reason and experience tell us

God is not limited in space (omnipresent), he is not contingent (impass-able), he is not changeable (immutable), his knowledge is not limited (omniscient), he is not understandable to human minds (incomprehensi-ble) and so on. The church constructed a prodigious list of all that God "is" based on our ability to identify the things he is not.

In all these ways and more we have been given glimpses of who God is, and these pieces of information are not invalid or useless. Indeed, they obligate us even further to seek after true knowledge of this God who has created and sustained us for some purpose. The problem with general revelation is its severe limitations if it alone is the sole source of knowl-edge of God.

The first of these limitations is the distortion of sin in creation. No mat-ter how glorious the manifestation of God appears in our world, it is seri-ously marred by sin, and through that sin it is open to serious deception by the enemy. That is, general revelation is always open for question and is never, finally, a reliable form of knowledge. The creation is in chaos and decline, and vestiges of the glory of God are harder and harder to find. Our experience of God is severely tarnished by our own sin and the deceptions that still plague our lives. Human reason and logic have failed us repeatedly in our effort to make sense of our world. And we, as the image of God, bear in us only fleeting glances of the true image bestowed before the fall. Calvin's sad conclusion is on the mark:

> It is therefore in vain that so many burning lamps shine for us in the work-manship of the universe to show forth the glory of its Author. Although they bathe us wholly in their radiance, yet they can of themselves in no way lead us into the right path.[2]

The second limitation is that whatever knowledge may be accessible to us in general revelation must depend upon our perception and interpre-tation of that knowledge, and that makes this form of knowledge wholly subjective. There is no objectivity possible in general revelation, and so we are thrown back upon ourselves to try to figure out who God is and what he wants of us by piecing together strands and bits of information and synthesizing them into some form of personal religion and experi-ence. When knowledge of God becomes ours to assemble as we see fit, we do not resist the temptation to project our own biases, prejudices, fears and misperceptions into our own image of God who, after all, we create.

---

[2]Ibid., p. 68.

God becomes "man shouted in a loud voice." What we are left with is a more insidious idol than the golden calf or the statue of Baal, for it bears our own image, and we end up worshiping a deification of ourselves, the ultimate idolatry. This yields any possible worship from this general revelation equally distorted, with the result that "whatever they afterward attempt by way of worship or service of God, they cannot bring as tribute to him, for they are worshipping not God but a figment and a dream of their own heart."[3]

This scenario reaffirms the importance of making a right start in Christian ethics. It must be absolutely clear that general knowledge *about* God is wholly insufficient on its own to inform a Christian ethic. If our knowledge of God is relative, subjective and human-centered, then our ethics can never be more than purely situational. If we cannot know anything of God for certain, then we cannot live any life for God with certainty. The Christian faith can only be one of many religions seeking to provide some level of god-experience that helps people cope with life.

This depiction of the anemic Christian faith built only on general revelation is not such a foreign one. Today the pressure to be sensitive to religious pluralism and the inculturalization of our understanding of God has raised up (once again) human experience as the locus of credible God-knowledge. We are moving away from the demands of a faith founded on special revelation and are moving toward a new image of God in which everyone can find themselves and be comfortable. Notice how theology begins taking on the framework of the subject-object dichotomy of the sciences. God is ceasing to be the subject. We, in our exalted position of "humanity come of age" are able to investigate God through the use of the tools of personal experience, scholarship and preference. We stand over against God, and together with every voice heard and every experience represented, we reconstruct God in our image, according to our likeness. The syncretic, postmodern God that is emerging is looking so much like everyone that she/he/it is becoming superfluous. What then is the alternative to the hedonism that lies at the end of general revelation?

Knowing God as Self-Revealer
In any relationship, true knowledge requires self-disclosure, and self-dis-

---

[3]Ibid., p. 48.

closure at the most meaningful levels only occurs within the confines of intimate relationship. There exists a great divide among theologians over the issue of our innate ability to know God. Issues of original sin, the *imago Dei* (image of God) and the Fall, and the nature of God cause significant disagreement at this most critical point.

Early in the twentieth century Karl Barth undertook the task of reclaiming for the church the sense of God's "wholly otherness." Barth was intent on reestablishing the "infinite qualitative distinction" (from Søren Kierkegaard) between the holy God and fallen humanity. The failure of nineteenth century liberal Protestantism was manifest for Barth in its teaching of an immanent continuity between God and man. From Kant and Schleiermacher through Ritschl and von Harnack, humanity had traveled the way of the *analogia entis* (analogy of being) where the creature was of the same ontology (nature or essence) as the creator. The Enlightenment was the catalyst for this shift in Protestant epistemology. There were three distinguishing marks of this theology. Each of these sounds disturbingly familiar today, and each is being challenged and supplanted by a postmodern philosophy that is even further from the truth.

The first was the new realization that there was a continuity in the nature or essence of God and creation. God was defined as that which is sublime in the world, not in distinction from the created world but by extension of it. Therefore, to know God we must know ourselves and what is the best in us. Sin is overcome through our quest for self-understanding. Thus direct knowledge of God was ours by virtue of our creation, for as the *imago Dei*, God was not too far distant from us. The sovereignty of God, the transcendence of God and the need for special revelation were sacrificed at the foot of this humanistic idol. The Christian life became a striving after moral goodness in a general, utilitarian sense, with Jesus as our example. Thus the "quest for the historical Jesus" was undertaken with much enthusiasm. If we can understand the human Jesus, stripped from the mythology of the supernatural, we can see who we can become and how we are to live.

Second, the human being that was now the center of the universe was imbued with a divine autonomy. It was believed that we have within ourselves the innate ability to govern and judge rightly and justly, to know truth and to apply our reason to move humanity to the highest possible plane of existence. We are not in need of anything from outside ourselves.

God has nothing more to say to us, for all we need, we have within us. The idea of special revelation, of the miraculous, the supernatural, the "need" for God, for repentance, dying to sin, etc., were but sad vestiges of the dark, unenlightened Middle Ages. Through the work of Copernicus, Descartes and Newton, humanity had come of age!

Third, there was a dynamism in liberal Protestantism that sought to replace the dead orthodoxy of the sixteenth and seventeenth century with a realized eschatology. The kingdom of God was here. The Enlightenment had ushered it in, and now there was every reason to expect that humanity would create heaven on earth. The new utopia would be the result of a humanity that sought after the social good for everyone, which dedicated itself to progress, change and self-actualization. The gospel became a manual for doing good works, while the idea of an individualistic faith and the need of salvation from sin and damnation faded into near extinction. To know God was to know oneself, for as Leo Tolstoy's 1894 book title reminded us, "the kingdom of heaven is within you."

In response to this emerging secular humanism Barth sought to turn the ship of church theology around 180 degrees. He did so by reclaiming for the church the wholly otherness of God, and he vigorously attacked the *analogia entis*, replacing it with the *analogia fidei* (analogy of faith) as the reality of our existence before God. That is, our relationship with God is solely through faith, and that faith is made possible not by our innate human ability or inborn receptivity to God but by virtue of God's ability and desire to cross the great divide that separates us from God and to reveal himself to us. The two pictures cannot be more distinct. For Barth, the activity of God amongst us creates a crisis in our existence. God is God, and we are humans who cannot bear to stand in the presence of the holy God. God's presence among us shines a white-hot light on our sin and need for redemption.

It also places us in a paradox, for we are called to be people of God and therefore to speak about God. That is our obligation. Yet as sinful humanity we cannot speak of God in and of ourselves. As the famous maxim goes, "The finite cannot conceive of the infinite" (*Finitum non capax infiniti*). To speak of God from true knowledge of God is impossible. Therefore, we are caught in an "impossible possibility." The solution to this paradox is not found in human ingenuity, moral atonement theory or the optimism of modernity. It is also not found in the prospects of technology, nor in postmodernism's abandonment of truth or its demands for tolerance of the various deities and goddesses of our pluralistic world. It is found in "the absolutely *new* event."[4] It is found in God's gracious coming to us in Jesus Christ, the one and only place where God and humanity can be considered together, the only place where theology is possible. In this event God gives the definitive word about himself, and our only possible role is to hear and respond in gratitude and worship.

The *good news* is, this event has happened; it is the defining moment in our human history. For this reason, our knowledge of God is not only reliable and sufficient, but it is entirely a knowing through God's action. We know God as the God who acts, and all we can know of God is revealed in his activity toward us. To seek knowledge of God "in and behind" his gracious activity toward us in Jesus Christ is yet again to start falsely. The very being of God must be understood in the activity of God toward us.

In Christian theology we must always move from the concrete to the abstract. We start with what is revealed to us, and from there we ask the difficult theological and ethical questions. Too many ethics are written backward. They begin with what we do not know; they construct a system of beliefs, laws and regulations based on experience, and they project them back into God. Therefore, what is up for grabs is our understanding of God, driven by our own passion to justify ourselves and our sin. We again create God in our own image.

This mistake is found in the great debates of our day over the nature of truth, over the exclusiveness of the gospel, over the moral issues of homosexuality, euthanasia and abortion, and in our discussions of stewardship. When books and sermons on stewardship begin with attempts to relate and apply select biblical texts to our need to give, or when stewardship discussions revolve around the questions of defining the tithe, demythologizing Jesus' command to the rich young ruler, or deciphering the role of faith in our personal giving, then we have fallen into this trap, and we have started falsely. We have begun with the abstract ethical question and attempted to work our way back to the reality of who we are in Jesus Christ. And we never get there. We stop at one of countless places along

---

[4]Karl Barth, "The Task of Ministry," in *The Word of God and the Word of Man* (London: Hodder & Stoughton, 1928), p. 197. "God stands in contrast to man as the *impossible* in contrast to the possible, as *death* in contrast to life, as *eternity* in contrast to time. The solution of the riddle, the answer to the question, the satisfaction of our need is the absolutely *new* event whereby the impossible *of itself* becomes possible, *death* becomes life, *eternity* time, and *God* man" (emphasis in original text).

the way where we become "satisfied" with our ethic because it sounds so Christian, seems so biblical, makes so much sense and fits so comfortably with our experience and our worldview. If we start with our experience, with the abstract question, with a desire to create a comfortable ethic or with the need for our conclusions to conform to the rigors of human logic and worldly reason, then our ethics will be counterfeit.

God, whose being is in his activity toward us in his self-revealing and coming to us, has not left us to our own devices. In terms of knowledge of God, we are not outside but inside. We no longer stand far off and seek knowledge of God, but in Jesus Christ we are given direct access to the heart of God. It is not ours to accept or reject, for it is the reality of our existence. We can reject it only in a denial of who we are in Christ. But we can do this. We can resurrect the god made in our own image and worship the creature instead of the Creator. We can deceive ourselves into thinking that this is a sign of our enlightenment. We can exchange the truth of God for a lie. We can go this way through a denial of our God-given freedom to choose for him. We can do this. But we cannot change the ontological reality of the incarnation. God has come to us in Jesus Christ, revealing his will and calling us into participation in the fellowship with God made possible in and through Jesus Christ.

If we are to construct a truly Christian ethic, then we must avoid these distractions and false starts and seek knowledge of God only through a participation in the life of the Son's revelation of the Father in the power of the Holy Spirit. We must discipline ourselves to seek knowledge of God only in God's self-revelation to us. We must speak theologically only as we are informed and inspired by the truth of the incarnation that is God with us. Only in Jesus Christ will we find true knowledge of God, for he is true God. Only in Jesus Christ will we find true knowledge of ourselves, for he is true Man. Only in Jesus Christ will we find a relationship with God, for "God was in Christ, reconciling the world to himself." Only in Jesus Christ will we find the answers to the ethical questions of our day, for to know him is to know the truth that sets us free.

If we are God's stewards, called according to his command and empowered for his service, then we can look nowhere else for the answer to our questions about what that service looks like or what is expected of us. To look elsewhere, to the standards of the world, to our own experiences or preferences, to reason and logic, to technology or philosophy, to New Age spiritualism or postmodern deconstructionism, or even to the

CALLED ACCORDING TO HIS COMMAND
EMPOWERED FOR SERVICE

church's interpretation or the writings of theologians, to look for our marching orders from any other source is to start falsely from which can only come a counterfeit ethic. This is the land mine we must continue to avoid if we are to know what it means to be called to be stewards in the kingdom of the triune God of grace.

John 1: God's Great Self-Disclosure

The message of God's self-revelation to us is laid out in its fullest in the Gospel of John. Here we have a text that stands out against flawed episte-mologies and provides us with the clearest explanation of God's revela-tory intent in the incarnation and work of Jesus Christ.

The book of John begins with the loaded statement that in the begin-ning there was the Word, which was both with God *(pros ton theon)* and which was God *(theos en ho logos)*. The *logos* of God is defined as being both coeternal with God, and therefore not less than God as a created entity must be, and who also is God, and therefore who is capable of revealing God. It would not be an overstatement to say that the entire Christian faith depends on the validity of this truth that the *logos* of God is truly God himself.

Having established this truth, John tells us that the Word of God was active in creation, that indeed all things that were made were made by him and through him. He is the author of life, and that life is the source of our being. Everything we are we owe to the Word for whom, through whom and by whom we were created. The reason for our existence, the sought-after "meaning of life" is found in our oneness with the Word. John then reveals the absurdity of the world's rejection of the one who created us and to whom we owe our existence. For when he came to the world, the world did not recognize him. When he came to those chosen as his people, they rejected him. But those who did see and believe and accept he claimed as his own, as ones born of God.

John turns us then to the revelatory work of the Word of God. In verse 14 we have the great incarnation announcement, that the Word became flesh and dwelt among us. Immediately John switches from the language of God and *logos* and introduces the relational language that will dominate his Gospel. For the Word now becomes the one sent by the Father, full of grace and truth. We must pause here and seek to understand why grace and truth are so vital to this incarnational announcement.

Grace and Truth

If we return to our earlier discussion, we will remember that the movement of God toward us was a movement of grace. It was unmerited, unexpected and perhaps even unreasonable. Why would God continue to love us in the face of our outright rejection of him as creator and sustainer? Why would God respond to stubborn defiance with anything but wrath that means annihilation? What kind of God sacrifices for the salvation of a recalcitrant and rebellious creation? The grace of God revealed in Christ is the hallmark of our faith. It defines who our God is and who we are in him. That the Word made flesh is described as "full of grace" is a signifier that the very act of incarnation is a gracious, saving event, and in that way it is the earliest self-revelation of the heart of God. To say "the Word was made flesh" is to say "grace." That is the first thing that must be grasped in this text.

The second pronouncement is that the Word made flesh is full of truth. This is supported later in John when we are told if you know and believe this Jesus "You will know the truth, and the truth will set you free" (Jn 8:32). And this is possible because Jesus himself proclaimed, "I am the way and the truth and the life. No one comes to the Father except through me" (14:6). How are we to understand Jesus as the truth? In the ministry of Jesus there is the pronouncement of the presence of the kingdom of God. It is a kingdom with a unique set of values, with its own ethic, its own reason for being and its own *telos* (end). The struggle for Jesus' followers, then and now, is how the kingdom of God fits into the reality of the world around us. How do we square the often radical disparity between "kingdom of God" values and the acceptable standards of our world? How could we survive if we constantly forgave, loved our enemies, walked the extra mile, gave the extra cloak, gave all we had to the poor, put God before family, job and self? Surely there must be some way to synthesize the teachings of Jesus about this kingdom of God and the *reality* of the world in which we must live and survive. This desire for synthesis is yet another temptation for any Christian ethic, another land mine that lies in our path. And nowhere is this temptation greater than in the ethic of the steward.

By claiming not just to be the bringer of truth but to actually *be* the truth, Jesus is introducing his people to a new reality. The coming of the kingdom of God is the ushering into our existence of a fundamentally new sense of what is real and what is counterfeit. The claims of Jesus call

RED
NO GOD

GOD FOR US
BLUE

god in us
RED

Knowing the Triune God of Grace   43

us to see God, the world and ourselves through an entirely new set of lenses. It is the ultimate shift of paradigms. In it, all that we have been taught to believe that is real is seen for what it is—grass that withers and blows away. The things of this world are temporary trappings that have no future. Money, fame, health, security, all the *real* things we pursue in life are in and of themselves facades. They can be used by the kingdom, but they have no reality apart from Jesus Christ. The same is true for evil. Evil has a reality in that it is present and active, and it effects our lives every day. It is not illusory, it is not "all in our heads." But even the bitterness and horror of the absolute evil we see around us and experience is not ultimately real. It is passing; it is defeated; it has no reality in the kingdom of God except as that which is no longer enigmatic. The world outside the kingdom of God takes on the transparency that C. S. Lewis describes of hell in *The Great Divorce*. It has existence, but it has no substance. It is passing away.

The incarnation announced in the book of John is the coming of a new reality in the midst of the substancelessness of our world. It does not give us freedom to abandon the world but just the opposite. It calls us into a life of committed engagement with the world so that the world may be drawn through our witness into the kingdom through grace. This is the truth of the reality of the world in which we live. This is the answer to where truth is to be found. Not in a church, a religion or a doctrine but in Jesus Christ.

This claim to truth also points to the exclusive revelatory claims of Jesus. If he is the truth made flesh, then his revelation of the heart of God is true and certain and sufficient. We can trust that the God revealed to us in Jesus Christ is really the God we serve. In verse 18 John tells us that the Word has seen God and knows God and therefore is able to make him known to us. The rest of the book of John is filled with Jesus' revelation of the heart of God. And because he is the truth, this revelation is trustworthy.

Grace and the "Heart of God"

Further in John, and built on this dual notion of grace and truth, we come to 3:16, the "gospel in a nutshell." Jesus proclaims that the coming of the Son into the world was the act of God motivated by love. If Jesus is "full of grace and truth," then we have revealed to us a God who is *for us*. And if this revelation is trustworthy, then we do not fear that there is another nature in God, a hidden God who is other than this God. That is not to say that God's self-revelation in Jesus Christ revealed the entirety of God. *Finitum non capax infiniti* (the finite cannot contain the infinite)! What it does assure us of is that the revelation we have of God is accurate and reliable. While God is infinitely more than we can ever know of him, we have full assurance that nothing in that infinite nature runs contrary to the nature revealed to us in Jesus Christ. That is the assurance we must have if Jesus Christ is the self-revelation of God, full of grace and truth. John 3:16 is that certainty, and that is why it is such a beloved and comforting text.

The Triune God Revealed

Finally we turn to John 17, which is the pinnacle in Scripture's description of the revelatory work of the Son, and therefore the self-revelatory work of God. This chapter should be read and reread by all who want to understand the incarnation and the nature of the work of Christ.

In verse 1 we are invited into the intimate prayer of the Son to the Father through the Spirit. This simple prayer serves a revelatory function. It reveals the undeniable trinitarian form in which we know God. It is a revelation that must be embraced by faith. It defies logic and explanation, but it is the centerpiece of the doctrine of God. Who is the Christian God? He is the Father, Son and Holy Spirit, three persons yet one God. How do we know? Because that is the God revealed to us in Jesus Christ and no other.

In verse 6 Jesus goes on to give us assurance of this revelation. Those to whom the revelation of God was intended have heard and seen and believed. God's intentions are not contingent. Despite the dilemmas of election, free will and predestination, we must hold here that those who were called to hear have heard. That is our assurance that God's revelatory work is efficacious. God can be known in a way that is sufficient for our salvation, even through the distortion of our sinfulness. That is the grace of God coming to us where we are. That is the truth of God calling us out into the kingdom of God. That is the work of the Son in revealing the Father.

In verse 10 the true nature of the Trinity is revealed further by the audacious claim that all that belongs and pertains to God is consequently that of the Son. "All I have is yours, and all you have is mine." What an incredible statement! It was these sorts of statements that were such a challenge for the early church. Having evolved from a strictly monotheis-

tic Hebraic faith, the concept of a man claiming unity with God was
wholly problematic. Even if the divinity of Jesus was affirmed, the implications for a slide into polytheism on the one side or abstraction on the
other caused great concern. As a result, the challenge of how to speak of
the deity of Christ was one of the earliest challenges of the church. The
Council of Nicaea in A.D. 325 provided us with language that attempted
to give clarity on how we can claim both monotheism and trinity. By
adopting gnostic language and "Christianizing" it, the early fathers at
Nicaea gave the best account to date of how we must speak about the
implications of John 17. Among the terms they employed was the rich
and image-filled word *perichoresis*. The Nicene fathers used this term to
describe the unity of the persons of the Trinity that so bound them
together that we could and must speak of "one God" but which also left
room for the distinction of persons and preserved the deity of Christ.

This *perichoretic* unity can be described as a mutual indwelling, a oneness in which a different entity emerges while maintaining the distinction
of the parties. *Perichoresis* means there can be Father in heaven and Son in
our midst without ever needing to talk about a split in the Godhead. It
also means that the divinity of Son and Spirit are not dependent upon
proximity to God the Father, and so Jesus can call the Father "the only
true God" without diminishing his own divinity. It does not solve the logical problem, and nothing ever will, but it does give us the relational language with which we can discuss the God who is revealed to us in Jesus
Christ.

It is important language for another reason. There are two other
places in Scripture where there is talk of a *perichoretic* type of unity. One
deals with marriage where "the two shall become one flesh." Here there
is a vestige of the Trinity where man and woman continue to be distinct
people, and yet through marriage before God, they form a new entity in
their unity. This is the "one flesh," which is a sacred gift from the God
who is by nature three-in-one. It is here that the ethics of human sexuality must begin if that explosive issue is to be discussed within in a truly
Christian frame! Similarly the church is "many parts but one body." Our
unity takes the form of a new entity, the body of Christ, yet without losing the distinction of the persons in the church. This is hard to do to say
the least. But the Spirit who empowers us is able to lead us into this
kind of unity if we will submit ourselves to that power. What a challenge for the church!

UNITY
DIVERSITY

These two images of unity and diversity, not as mutually exclusive but as together each in their fullness without diluting the fullness of the other, are useful for the church only when they are based on the Trinity that they reflect. Looking first to their meaning in the self-revelation of God in Jesus Christ is the only possible starting place in our ethical discussions, and our theological anthropology (study of humanity) and ecclesiology (study of the church) will stand or fall on whether we make this right start.

Verses 20-26 are the climax of the chapter. The language here is rich with images of whole relationships, unity and participation. Jesus is praying for us that we might experience the unity of the Godhead as we participate in the Son's relationship with the Father in the Spirit. James Torrance has long championed the rich nature of our participation into which we are called in Christ. Of the work of Christ for us he proclaims, "He lifts us up out of ourselves to participate in the very life and communion for which we were created."[5] We participate in mission (v. 21), in glory (v. 22), in unity (v. 23), in eternity (v. 24) and in love (v. 26). In Ephesians Paul proclaims, "God raised us up with Christ and seated us with him in the heavenly realms in Christ Jesus" (2:6). Calvin notes that the language of the Son's seeming subordination to the Father denotes instead that because Jesus is endowed with heavenly glory, "he gathers believers into participation in the Father."[6]

Participation is the form of our relationship with God in our new reality as Christians. It characterizes our worship together as the body of Christ. "As in worship, so also in our personal relationships with one another, we are given the gift of participating through the Spirit in the incarnate Son's communion with the Father."[7] The result of our participation in this intimate way is a call to active mission and the living out of the ethical imperatives of this phenomenal act of grace. As F. F. Bruce points out,

> It is no invisible unity that is prayed for here. "I in them," says Jesus—but they are also in him (15:4). "Thou in me"—but he is also in the Father (14:10). If the Father is in him and he is in them, then the Father is in them:

---

[5]James B. Torrance, *Worship, Community and the Triune God of Grace* (Carlisle, U.K.: Paternoster Press, 1996), p. 9.
[6]John Calvin, *Institutes of the Christian Religion* (Philadelphia: Westminster Press, 1960), p. 155.
[7]Torrance, *Worship*, p. 28.

they are drawn into the very life of God, and the life of God is perfect love.[8]

We are now called to live as people who are one in Christ. Not "as if" we were, but because we *actually are!* This is the new reality of our existence, this is the kingdom of God into which we have been called as children, and it changes everything.

We must ask what it means now that we are called stewards in this kingdom. We must ask what it means that we are called as stewards to participate through and by and in our stewardship in the Son's worship of the Father in the Spirit. We must seek to understand the Scriptures that speak of giving all we have to those in need in light of our new status in a kingdom that we are to seek with our whole hearts, trusting that "all these things will be given to you as well" (Mt 6:33). We must ask the ethical questions of living as stewards in this kingdom with an unmitigated commitment to understand the meaning of our vocation as stewards whose existence is marked both before and after by our participation in the very life of God. Hall was on the right track when we commented, "The christological assumption of Christian stewardship is that as those who are 'in Christ' we are taken up into his stewardship."[9] This is the task that we must pursue if we are to build a wholly Christian theology of the steward.

Faith and Knowledge

This discussion of Christian epistemology has led us to the conclusion that the God we know in Jesus Christ is a God in relationship, and that should tell us a great deal about what it means to have been created in the image of this God. We have said that *steward* is a relational term, and only as we see ourselves as creatures in the image of the *trinitarian* God can the full implications of that term be understood. God by nature is unity in diversity. In the work of Jesus we are called into relationship with God in and through Jesus Christ. We are called into a life of participation of the Son's knowledge of the Father. This is the necessary prerequisite for Christian ethics. Brunner reminds us that ethics are not detached principles. Of the ethic of love he concludes,

> Every attempt to conceive of love as a principle leads to this result: it becomes distorted, either in the rigoristic, legal sense, or in the hedonistic

---

[8]F. F. Bruce, *The Gospel of John* (Grand Rapids, Mich.: Eerdmans, 1983), pp. 335-36.
[9]Douglas John Hall, *The Steward* (Grand Rapids, Mich.: Eerdmans, 1990), p. 44.

sense. Man only knows what the love of God is when he sees the way in which God acts, and he only knows how he himself ought to love by allowing himself to be drawn by faith into this activity of God. "To know God in His action" is only possible in faith.[10]

We have seen earlier how this participation with God in order to "do" theology is a departure from the "scientific" approach that seeks objectivity, noninvolvement and distance, and the maintenance of the strict object-subject relationship.[11] Here now we must go a step further. We must describe what it means to *participate* in the Son's knowledge of the Father, and that will lead us to the inevitable discussion of the distinction between faith and knowledge. In this discussion of our way of knowing we have held back from the proclamation that must now be made. We are the object and not subject vis-à-vis God in our doing of theology. The knowledge we seek is not accessible to us through our own efforts, senses or innate abilities. Instead true knowledge of God is given through a special revelation that not only reveals the sender but radically transforms the receiver and calls the receiver into a new reality defined by a new relationship with the one who is self-revealing. Therefore, the task of "doing theology" is possible only for those who have been transformed, who have entered into this new reality, who are in this new relationship with the God who is the self-revealer. In short, only the Christian and only the Christian community can be involved in the discipline of seeking to do the impossible, to speak about God. Only as Christians can we know the God who has called us to be stewards in his kingdom. For this reason, we must enter into the discussion of the relationship between knowledge and faith.

A Brief Historical Sketch
Before starting this brief sketch one might rightly ask, "Why spend time

---

[10]Emil Brunner, *The Divine Imperative* (London: Lutterworth Press, 1942), p. 84.

[11]Thomas Oden provides us one sense in which the task of theology can adopt the subject-object context of the sciences. He posits that the "object" of theological investigation is "the understanding of God as known in the Christian community." He goes on to state, "There is no reason one cannot take as a subject of scientific investigation the modes of awareness of God that recur in Christian communities: the belief in God, that God exists, that God is triune, and that God pardons sin" (Thomas C. Oden, *The Living God* [New York: Harper Collins, 1970], p. 352). While this is a helpful distinction, we must raise a warning flag, for it is a short step from seeing "the understanding of God" as the object of our inquiry, to making *God himself* the object. Because this line has been crossed so often in Christian theology and ethics, we must proceed even here with the utmost caution.

looking at this history?" This section will be challenging reading and you may ask just what all this has to do with our topic. Let me explain. If we are called to be a people who proclaim the gospel to a lost world, then we better have at least a basic understanding of the philosophy and world-view that is held by those around us. Like the apostle Paul on Mars Hill, we can best communicate our faith when we know the mindset of those to whom we are called to witness. If we are to be tue stewards in God's kingdom, I am positing that we must first know *with certainty* who our God is. That immediately throws us into sharp conflict with a host of per-vading themes in our society. Those themes are the result of a history of thought on the whole subject of faith and knowledge. To know a little about this history, and therefore to understand from where these current themes have come, is critical to our work as stewards of the message of grace. For that reason, I offer this brief historical sketch, and I encourage you to work through this short section for what it will mean to the theo-logical foundation we are creating for a theology of the steward and the Christian life lived in all of its fullness.

Certainty of our knowledge of ourselves and our world has been the subject of debate among philosophers from Socrates to the challenges of postmodernity today. How we know things, how certain we can be of what we know and how faith is related to our knowing has been at the center throughout the history of philosophical and theological debate. For our purposes we must understand the place of special, revealed knowl-edge and faith in the greater discussion of faith and reason. If we are con-cerned about knowing the God to whom we are called to be stewards, then we must be sure we can rightly define the term *know*.

As thinking creatures we naturally seek to apply reason, logic and our senses to the acquisition of knowledge about ourselves and the world around us. In early periods in the history of the church, faith steered the direction of logic, subsuming it under the lordship of the supernatural, specially revealed knowledge and language of the church. The early church established the quadrilateral sources of knowledge: Scripture, tradition, experience and reason. In doing so it sought both to acknowledge the importance of tradition, experience and reason as sources of God-knowledge and also to set these three firmly in subjec-tion to Scripture as the primary source of divine revelation. Thomas Oden remarks, "When the word becomes written, we appropriate it amid changing cultural experiences, reflect upon it by reason, and per-

sonally rediscover it in our own experiences. The study of God best proceeds with the fitting equilibrium of these four sources, one primary
and three secondary."[12]

From Athanasius and Augustine through the Reformers this understanding of the four sources was employed in some form. It served to
keep theological inquiry grounded in Scripture—and therefore an activity
of faith—undertaken in a community of faith that interpreted Scripture in
forming its traditions, all while also allowing for the fullest use of the
God-given gift of reason and recognizing the role of faith in our individual experiences. The key then and now is balance within the hierarchy
that places Scripture at the head of the table.

Anselm and *Fides Quaerens Intellectum*
In the eleventh century, Anselm of Canterbury sought to prove the existence of God through his famous "ontological argument." While this may
seem to be an example of medieval scholasticism,[13] the motivation of
Anselm is of great importance to Christian theology. Anselm believed
that faith in God compelled one to seek greater knowledge and understanding of this God who has come to us in Jesus Christ. There is a sincere
seeking after understanding that is not prior to faith, but which is neces-
sarily the product of true belief. Anselm used the phrase *fides quaerens
intellectum* (faith seeking understanding) to indicate that our faith sets us
on a mission to know better and understand more fully the God in whom
we believe. This quest for understanding brought the task of proving
God's existence squarely into the realm of Christian theology proper.
Therefore, unapologetically, Anselm constructed his theories on how
God's existence can be "proven," yet he did so all the while reminding us
that we are proving God's existence not in order to have faith but because
we already believe. Our epistemology is not an excuse to lay aside reason
and logic but just the opposite. It creates the context in which we can fully
employ the God-given skills of clear thinking and reasoning.

It is important here to point out that reason is not to be abandoned in

---

[12]Ibid., p. 341.

[13]A simple definition of medieval scholasticism is a system that was devised to subject theological beliefs to mathematical and logical proofs. The purpose was not to refute the beliefs
but just the opposite. In a world that had rediscovered the logical teachings of Aristotle,
the church felt it necessary to use these methods to give a logical basis to their creeds and
confessions. Therefore, much effort was spent on developing long, convoluted, logical con-
structions to "prove" the basic tenets of the faith.

the faith commitments of special revelation. Reason as a gift of God is to be employed in its fullest sense in pursuit of the truth. We are not seeking the unreasonable to prove our great faith, we are beginning with faith and applying our reason as one tool to speak about and better understand the revelation of God in Jesus Christ. To that end Donald Bloesch reminds us, "[Revelation] can bring reason into its service, but it strongly opposes autonomous or disobedient reason. Faithful reasoning is a sign that revelation has found its way into the inner recesses of our being."[14] This balance is critical if we are not to change our charge from "faith seeking understanding" to "faith seeking naiveté."

It is however the other side of this imbalance wherein lie many false starts in Christian theology and ethics. When *fides quaerens intellectum* becomes *credo quia intelligo* (I believe because I understand), then we have joined ranks with the world in seeking to interpret the *reality* of our existence in religious language. This shift was evident in the emergence of Middle Age scholasticism, where faith claims were pressed to fit within the rubric of Aristotelian syllogisms.[15] At the hands of scholasticism much Christian theology sank into a quicksand of argumentation over how many angels could dance on the head of a pin.

In response to scholasticism's attempt to subject every theological conclusion to the rigors of mathematical certainty and logical coherence, there emerged the wholesale rejection of reason through a return to mysticism. Part of this way of thinking was due to the captivity of the human mind to the darkness of Middle Age superstition and the power of the Church of Rome. Both demonstrated a theology out of balance. Together they helped set the stage for the modern era.

The Enlightenment and the Challenge to Faith

The Enlightenment saw the dawning of the age of reason. Copernicus began the undermining of the church's worldview by placing the sun, not the earth, at the center of our universe. The church's rejection of the idea on the grounds of Scripture and tradition unveiled a breach between faith and reason when mathematical formulae and Galileo's telescope proved the church wrong. In one of the pre-Enlightenment's first great clashes,

---

[14]Donald Bloesch, *Holy Scripture* (Downers Grove, Ill.: InterVarsity Press, 1994), p. 76.
[15]Aristotle had formulated the syllogism as a logic construct where "If 'A' is true and 'B' is true, then 'C' must be true." Middle Age scholasticism sought to make theological positions and doctrine conform to this logic.

the "faith" of the church came up wanting.

This was soon followed by the philosophy of René Descartes, who reasoned that the mind is the center of all that "is," and who went on to place all reality into categories that can be proven mathematically or through the new science of physics. Descartes found no foundation for a certain knowledge in the use of our senses that, as Copernicus had just demonstrated, could be deceived. In his search for reliable knowledge, Descartes reduced all that was "knowable" to that which could be known without any doubt. All reliable knowledge must stand up to a "method of doubt," which would apply the rubrics of mathematics, geometry and physics in the quest for certainty. Only those things that "are necessary, which must be the case, which cannot logically be otherwise, and which must be true in all circumstances and at all times" can be known for certain.

Descartes sought to unclutter the modern mind from uncertainties at a time when post-Reformation theology was filling the world with uncertainties. By placing human reason at the apex of certain knowledge, his philosophy served to sever the categories of faith and knowledge, leaving certain knowledge to the machinations of the philosophers and mathematicians, and resigning faith and the supernatural world to a morass of uncertainty and doubt.

Descartes had managed in his influential philosophy to place human reason at the center of our existence and had put all knowledge, and therefore all dynamic movements of the human mind and spirit, within its grasp. Trevor Hart notes,

> Galileo, by confirming Copernicus' hypothesis, had displaced humans from the center of the universe and thrown them into a crisis of confidence. Descartes' solution was effectively to put them back at the centre of things, if not cosmologically, then at least in terms of their power to step beyond the limits of their terrestrial vantage point and capture the universe by the power of reason.[16]

This optimism was furthered by the advent of Newtonian physics. Now the world had the scientific base from which it could solve its problems and usher in a utopian society. Here humanity finally stood triumphantly at the center of things and held the future in its hands. Here also the old teachings of the church that called people to simple faith, which

---

[16]Trevor Hart, *Faith Thinking* (London: SPCK, 1995), p. 32.

was clothed in mysteries such as Trinity and eternity, and which sought supernatural solutions to human problems, seemed even more a sad vestige of medieval superstition.

The legacy of Cartesian philosophy, however, was not the positive rise of human reason and the certainty of knowledge but indeed the exact opposite. Through the writings of David Hume and John Locke, the "human come of age" was exposed as a soul left mired in a swamp of subjectivity. Instead of making true knowledge possible, Cartesian philosophy had thrown certainty of anything into serious doubt. Left to reason alone, humanity could not arrive at anything that it could know for certain.

It was left to Immanuel Kant 130 years later to attempt an approach that could extricate humanity from its self-imposed captivity. Kant constructed a philosophical framework in which human reason could indeed know truth with certainty. Kant elevated the human mind to a higher plane where the world is created in the mind and through our like-mindedness we can accommodate constructs of truth and certain knowledge. We can know things for certain because we all have constructed a world in the same way, which therefore carries certain truths. Modernity was built in part on the notion of universal truths, where the "mind" created rules and norms that transcended cultures and contexts and prescribed for humanity its ethical imperatives. Kant's "categorical imperative" challenged humanity to act in accordance with the universal law of nature, a moral code written in us prior to the sensory inputs with which Descartes struggled so vigorously. Therefore, the idea of God is "known" through moral reasoning.

However, time and human sin would continue to witness to the problems in Kant's philosophy, and today we have vestiges of the fallout from that disillusionment. On the one hand we have *objectivism* where truth is rejected if it cannot be objectively proven. On the other, we have *relativism*, where truth is only valid in the context of those who hold it. In both, the universal moral truths espoused by modernity cannot be found. And what of faith? For Kant, faith in the supernatural was not wrong, it was simply useless to reason. And when morally transcendent ideas are introduced into religion, they yield negative consequences.[17] Therefore, Kant

---

[17]Kant reasoned that religion turns works of grace into fanaticism, miracles into superstition, mysteries into illumination and means of grace into thaumaturgy. See Immanuel Kant, *Religion Within the Limits of Reason Alone* (New York: Harper & Row, 1960), p. 48.

was left to label what he called "dogmatic faith" or revealed faith as "dis-
honest or presumptuous."[18]

Truth and Postmodernism

Today we live in the aftermath of the Enlightenment and its search for
certain knowledge and real truth. In our postmodern era we are experiencing a major shift in the worldview, the philosophical ethos and
the moral basis of our society. Postmodernism is characterized by a
pessimism that has supplanted the optimism of the Enlightenment
agenda of inevitable progress and self-actualization. For the first time
we are raising a generation that does not believe it is going to be better
off than its predecessors. Indeed, it believes that the world is fragile,
the environment is in crisis and our ability to "fix things" is in serious
doubt. As a result, postmoderns have rejected the idea of human reason as the arbiter of truth and of the sense of the possibility of a universal moral ethic altogether. Truth today is known through
nonrational sources such as intuition, emotions and the interpretation
of experience. Truth is therefore snatched from the domain of
detached individualistic reason and is found in the community of persons seeking wholeness. Truth is found in the corporate experience of
the community and is valid only for that community. In its rejection of
modernity's universal transcendent truth that underscored Kant's philosophy, postmodernity has relegated truth to the common experiences and norms of distinct communities that interpret for themselves
what constitutes their well-being. Postmoderns believe that the variety of truths that are held by the multitude of different communities
can exist side by side in peaceful coexistence. "Postmoderns live in
self-contained social groups, each of which has its own language,
beliefs and values. As a result, postmodern relativistic pluralism seeks
to give place to the 'local' nature of truth. Beliefs are held to be true
within the context of the communities which espouse them."[19]

In this way, truth has become relative and can only be understood from
the vantage point of a supreme pluralism, and "pluralism itself becomes a

---

[18]Ibid.

[19]Stanley Grenz, *A Primer on Postmodernism* (Grand Rapids, Mich.: Eerdmans, 1996), p. 15.
    Grenz goes on to conclude, "Beliefs are ultimately a matter of social context, and hence
    they are likely to conclude, 'What is right for us may not be right for you,' and 'What is
    wrong in our context might in your context be acceptable and even preferable.'"

new absolute that can tolerate no rival gods."[20]

A Return to Certainty

Postmodern philosophers have rejected the truth claims of both special revelation-based religions and modernity's sense of a morally transcendent truth ingrained in the goodness of the human spirit. Having set aside both views of the world and humanity, postmodern philosophy has left us with an understanding of truth that is bound up solely with our experiences together. As a result, they have created an even more difficult context for the church to speak about special, divine revelation that is universally authoritative for all humanity. The milieu in which we seek to live out the ethical imperatives of the indicatives of grace is ever more hostile to the message of God's gracious and graciously binding activity toward us. Therefore, the pressure on the church to soften its appeal, to couch its language in postmodern terms, to abandon its evangelical mission and to adapt its teachings on truth is overwhelming. This pressure has caused us to reexamine our ethics and the basis upon which they are established and maintained. The church today is seeking a credible basis for its ethical requirements and even for the ability to require anything at all of its followers. This ethical crisis is the product of the abandonment of the language of special revelation. It should not be surprising now to see that the loss of our common belief in how we know God is the forerunner of ethical collapse.

If truth is relative to the community in which it is held, and if knowledge is to be attained through reliance on nonrational sources and affirmed as true knowledge in the context of one's community, then the need for and the place of special revelation for certain knowledge of God is both *unnecessary* and *offensive*. It is *unnecessary* in that there is no one center, one reality of our existence. Therefore, God can reveal himself, herself or itself through all sorts of means to people in every context and for each community. The certainty of knowledge is established in the context of the community that appropriates it into their interpretation of "local" truth.

It is *offensive* in that it claims a universal reality and a binding truth of human existence. It goes even further in its offense—and this is its great

---

[20]Donald G. Bloesch, *A Theology of Word and Spirit* (Downers Grove, Ill.: InterVarsity Press, 1992), p. 31.

break with modernity's version of "universal truth"—by claiming that we as Christians know, and know uniquely, what this reality is; or more accurately, we know *who* this reality is. We claim to know the "metanarrative" or grand story that transcends and gives meaning to our human existence. And we know it with certainty!

Bloesch remarks of revelation, "Certainty of its truth becomes ours only in the act of decision and obedience by which the external truth becomes internalized in faith and life."[21] Tom Torrance sums up our epistemological certainty eloquently,

> It is, then, in Jesus Christ, through "union and communion" with him in love, and through sharing in the love of God incarnate in him, that we are enabled to know God in such a way that our knowledge of God is firm and sure, for it is anchored in the ultimate reality of God's own eternal being.[22]

If we indeed hold to a Christocentric epistemology (Christ-centered way of knowing), then the knowledge it conveys to us through faith will be certain and true, and the ethics that it produces will be borne of this certainty and truth. And they had better be, for they will also run in sharp conflict with the postmodern world in which we are living. The question the church faces today is one of faithfulness and sacrifice. Are we willing to be faithful to the gospel, and are we willing to pay the price?

These are the questions we must ask if we are to start right in our study of the call to be stewards in God's kingdom. We must avoid the pitfalls of relativism on the one hand and objectivism on the other and base our epistemological certainty on the gracious actions of God toward us. We must reject the postmodern agenda to relegate truth to community norms and shared beliefs, and we must return the quest for truth to a faith journey into which we participate in the one who came to us "full of grace and truth." We must begin with an understanding of who God is and how we can know that for certain. We must seek after true and certain knowledge of who we are, who we are called to be and how we are to respond to the gracious God who has reconciled us to himself in Jesus Christ.

This is where we must start in our discussion of the theology of the steward. We are stewards under the reign of this God who calls us into fellowship with him in Christ Jesus. This is the first step in understanding the relationship between steward and the owner of the resources that are

---

[21]Ibid., p. 21.
[22]Thomas F. Torrance, *The Trinitarian Faith* (Edinburgh, U.K.: T & T Clark, 1988), p. 32.

to be stewarded. This point is absolutely critical if we are to keep from straying away from the foundation we have built thus far. We are accountable to this God. We are serving this God and only this God. If we keep this epistemological point squarely in front of us, then we will be better equipped to deal with the complex issues that arise in the ethics of the steward.

The next step in our study is to understand how this God, revealed to us in Jesus Christ, is also God the creator. The purpose of God in creation is our key for self-understanding as stewards of that creation.

Chapter 3

Knowing God the Creator as the Triune God of Grace

TO KNOW OUR GOD IS TO KNOW WHAT CONSTITUTES REALITY. THE discussion of what is *real* is like the two sides of a coin. On the one side we must understand who our God *really* is, and on the other side we must understand who we *really* are. This process of discovery of what defines reality has a definite direction and methodology. This book on the theology of the steward is attempting to demonstrate how the ethical questions related to our call to be stewards should be approached if our practice of stewardship is to have theological integrity. This methodology is offered as an approach to all Christian ethics seeking to lay a firm foundation upon which to build the ethics of the church of Jesus Christ with confidence. Only upon such a foundation can we stand firm in a time in which the world is increasingly hostile to the claims of the gospel of Jesus Christ.

The previous chapter outlined the first side of this coin by offering a Christocentric epistemology—a Christ-centered way of knowing—as the only possible starting point for Christian ethics. From it we come to know, personally and sufficiently, our God as the Father of the Son revealed to us in the Spirit. Therefore, our God is triune by nature. We know this through God's self-giving in the Son's work of incarnation and redemption, and we are able to believe this through the Spirit's work of regeneration and sanctification. What we know in Jesus Christ and what we believe in the power of the Holy Spirit is that this God is a God of grace, a God who is *for us!* We know and believe that Christ came to establish his kingdom and that through the Spirit we have been called as people of that kingdom. Therefore, we also know and believe that our God has a purpose for us and a future for us. All this we know for certain because the Word was made flesh and dwelt among us. All this we believe with confidence because the Son has revealed the heart of God to us, and that revelation is revealed and confirmed to us by the Spirit. That is who God is: Father, Son and Spirit, one God, for us, gracious and merciful, calling us into his kingdom through repentance, redemption and justification. We know God from the vantage point of the manger, the foot of the cross, the empty tomb and the presence and power of the Spirit in the church. It is *this* God who calls us to be stewards. It is *this* God's resources that we are called to steward. It is *this* God's creation that we are to care for and use. It is *this* God who defines for us who is our neighbor and how we are to respond to our neighbor's needs. And ultimately, it is to *this* God and none other to whom we are accountable. That is the first side of the coin in our understanding of the *reality* of our existence.

The flip side of this coin addresses the question, "Then who are we?" How do we define ourselves, our purpose for being here, our vocation and our future? The process of understanding who our God is, and therefore of understanding what is *real*, leads us to the realization that knowing who our God is determines our self-knowledge. We were created by *this* God, and we were loved, saved, called and empowered by *this* God to be the people of the kingdom of *this* God. If we are created beings, we can only "find ourselves" in an understanding of the heart of our Creator. Apart from that certain knowledge, our entire existence is called into question.

Without knowing the one who created us, we are left to ourselves to define what is noble, what is worthwhile, what is meaningful, what constitutes success, what defines fulfillment and what can bestow genuine purpose on our existence. Just as in a human-centered knowledge of God (anthropocentric epistemology), here too we are thrown back upon ourselves to define these experiences. And we can only do so according to our fallenness, which inevitably results in a distorted way of measuring success, defining meaning and purpose, and experiencing happiness. Our ethics once again become captive to our social norms, with no more of a basis for understanding the purpose and meaning of *real* human existence and worth than the religions and spiritual movements of our world.

Within the church this lack of anchoring of our ethics to our self-understanding found in Jesus Christ leads too often to a detached biblicism where the Bible is read as a spiritual first-aid book, leaving us to pick and choose remedies that seem applicable to the ills of our day. The mission of the church and its success are articulated in terms of social outreach, member services and numerical growth, instead of raising up the people of God for the work of the kingdom. Consequently, in this lack of grounding and certainty, stewardship studies have to define their purpose according to secular values such as a sense of altruism ("just because I'm a good person") or a general philanthropy ("love of humanity" in general), or in the less enviable motivations such as guilt ("all those starving children"), fear (you too may one day have cancer), personal gain (it's deductible, after all), recognition (brass plaques galore!) or a misplaced loyalty (the church says, "Do it!"). When these are the driving forces for our ethics of stewardship, they always lead us to a dead end. This is the quagmire of a stewardship ethic detached from a self-understanding that comes from the heart of our Creator.

What joy it is to know that the heart of our Creator has been revealed to us in Jesus Christ. What joy it is to know that our lives are of inestimable value, that we were created for a high and noble purpose, that we are called to a dynamic and meaningful existence, that our future is certain and full of promise. This is what defines us. This is the good news that we are called to spread to the world. We cannot be the people of God apart from this self-definition, and we cannot understand God's call on our life as obedient disciples apart from this self-definition. We certainly cannot talk about the call to be stewards in the kingdom of the triune God of grace apart from this self-definition.

In this chapter we will develop this self-definition and how it informs our ethics of the call to be a steward. If the revelation of "who our God is" is found first in the revelatory work of Jesus Christ, then the revelation of "who we are" is found first in the work of God in creation, which, as we will see, brings us back again to Jesus Christ.

When we look at the world around us and see its pain, its suffering and its brokenness, we may well wonder why God created us in the first place. If there is meaning and purpose in this life, it is often very hard to find and harder to experience for any length of time. For that reason every one of us seeks the answer supposedly found in the guru on the Tibetan mountain, "What is the meaning of life?" From this reply will come the equally important answer, "How then should we live?" Ethical imperatives follow the indicatives of our existence.

To answer this question as Christians, we must look to one place and one place only—to the heart of our Creator. We have seen why it is so important to seek all knowledge of God in God's self-revelation in Jesus Christ. That can be seen in no better place than here. What do we learn if we see the God revealed to us in Jesus Christ as the Creator of the world?

God's Nature: Freedom and Love

First, we see that there was a gracious and loving intent in our creation. Our understanding of God tells us that God chose freely to create another outside of himself. God was not bound by any need nor coerced by any power that made creation "necessary."[1] God created us freely and out of love for us. Freedom and love are the marks of our creator God. In his love he commits himself to be our God, to be for us, to become subject to limitation, to suffer and to bear our sin. Yet he chose this freely in accordance with his divine nature. He is the God who loves in freedom and who is free to love. His freedom is not arbitrary but subject to and defined by his love. His love is not obligatory but is given out of his freedom. If in creating us God was either under coercion or if he had ulterior motives other than love, then God's self-revelation to us in Jesus Christ is a forgery, and our entire Christian faith is called into question. This is the first thing we can and must say.

---

[1]This statement aligns us with Reformed thinking and in opposition to a host of modern theologians. Among them is Jürgen Moltmann. Moltmann argues that "God is only entirely free when he is entirely himself" (*God in Creation* [London: SCM Press, 1985], pp. 82-83). That, for Moltmann, is when God is acting as Creator. Therefore, there is an inner necessity that obligates God to create, since God is by nature the Creator. While this may seem logical, it leads us in a disastrous direction. For once we concede that creation is in any way necessary to God, then the future of the world becomes in some sense the future of God. The distinction between God and creation becomes blurred and a latent panentheism seeps in. We will see this when Moltmann and others are left to concede that there is no distinction between the immanent and economic Trinity and that God's future is bound up with his creation. This is a path we must be careful to avoid.

Understanding God's nature as freedom and love provides for us a powerful corrective for another error that is devastating for the ethics of stewardship. The debate concerning the nature of God's immanence and his transcendence continues to offer viewpoints on either extreme. These polar views are unacceptable and wholly unnecessary.

On the one hand, theologians have argued that God is basically transcendent. From deism, agnosticism and an over-stressed monotheism we have produced a God who is so far above that he is untouched by human life, inaccessible to human pleas and unconcerned with human need. This God created the world and left it to us to sort things out. He gave us reason, logic and intelligence, and the command to subdue the earth. The rest is up to us. With God having basically left the scene, the void in "leadership" is quickly filled by an all too willing human nature which, as we remember from Genesis 3, seems always ready to jump at the chance to be "like God." If God is only known in transcendence, then he/she/it will quickly be deemed ultimately unknowable, and we will step in to fill the void.

Left to us, the creation, including our fellow men and women, becomes a "resource" to be employed efficiently in our pursuit for self-betterment. It is easy to see how quickly the role of the steward here regresses back into the categories of secular values we outlined above. Simply put, if we do not know who our God is, then we do not know who we are. Our loss of self-identity is exemplified in our grasp for counterfeit power to provide some sort of self-definition. Since our identity cannot come from within us, it must be bound up with the externalities of life. And so position, possessions and power are the determinants of meaning and purpose in a world where God is unknowable. If our stewardship studies allow even a hint of this worldview, we have again started falsely, and our resultant theology of stewardship will do nothing more than support the status quo and lend credence to the sinful imbalance in the distribution of God's creation. This is what is at stake if the freedom of God is upheld at the cost of his love that binds him to his creation as Creator *and redeemer*.

The other extreme is more subtle and widespread—and just as damaging. The postmodern mindset has no trouble with an immanent God who inhabits his creation in specific, loving and communal ways. God's act of creation is understood as an emanation out of himself in which God creates, indwells and brings all things back into himself. God's love and care for creation involves him in the most intimate relations with his creatures to the extent that the distinction between Creator and creation is blurred or obliterated altogether.[2] What must not be missed here is that the temptation of human nature to take the place of God is no less real in this polar extreme than in the other. Here God is so immanent that he/she/it again ceases to be knowable. With the distinction between creature and Creator eliminated, God ceases to have any distinct identity, and humanity is again obliged to stand in for a God it does not know and control its own destiny.

Stewardship is no less damaged at this extreme. While the case can be made for a deeper sense of care for creation by those who hold such a panentheistic worldview, the loss of self-identity through the denial of a normative epistemology destines us to a relativism that simply cannot embrace the category of steward. If the true owner is unknowable, unavailable for any real relationship and perhaps even indistinguishable from ourselves or creation, then the notion of steward is nonsensical. Where the overemphasis on God's transcendence makes stewardship unnecessary, the overemphasis on God's immanence renders it impossible. Both errors have at their root a denial of the one nature of God expressed in freedom and love. Both leave us with a badly flawed epistemology. Both make knowledge of God impossible, and so both make knowledge of ourselves impossible. If we are to understand what it means to be stewards in the kingdom of the triune God of grace, we must reject both extremes and hold to the view revealed to us in Jesus Christ, that of a God who loves us in freedom and who is free to love.

God's Purpose: Covenant and Glory

Second, God's purpose in creation has a *telos*, an end. If we are to be true to a trinitarian understanding of creation, then God's covenant with his creation must be seen as the basis that provides for creation its internal consistency. If Paul's letter to the Colossians is trustworthy, then we must seek to understand what it means that everything was created "by and for" Jesus Christ. God's covenant with his creatures predated creation itself, which means we must take care never to separate creation from

---

[2]Two recent examples of this error, in addition to Moltmann cited above, are Ted Peters, *God as Trinity: Rationality and Temporality in Divine Life* (Louisville, Ky.: Westminster John Knox, 1993); and Catherine Mowry LaCugna, *God for Us: The Trinity and Christian Life* (New York: Harper Collins; Edinburgh, U.K.: T & T Clark, 1991).

covenant. Our redemption was prefigured in our creation. God the Father chose us in Christ "before the creation of the world" (Eph 1:4). Our names are written in the book of life "belonging to the Lamb that was slain from the creation of the world" (Rev 13:8). Covenant theology recognizes that there is an unbreakable link between creation, covenant, redemption, reconciliation and final glorification. God's plan for creation assumed the Fall, anticipated the incarnation, cross and resurrection, and moved creation toward the second coming.

Our self-identity as children in the kingdom of *this* God emerges from this one great idea that we were God's children from the very foundation of the world. Before God created, he saw us as his children, as saved in Christ, as raised in Christ and as now "seated us with him in the heavenly realms in Christ Jesus" (Eph 2:6). If God's purpose for creating the world is to have fellowship with us in Jesus Christ, then our purpose as God's creatures is to participate in this fellowship with joy and gratitude. We are the covenant partners of God. We do not stand as equals, as cosigners of a contract in which each party is obligated to uphold his or her terms of the agreement. We are saved by grace through the love of the one who created us for himself. We did not enter into an agreement as equals, but "while we were still sinners, Christ died for us" (Rom 5:8). It was God's grace that "made us alive with Christ even when we were dead in transgressions" (Eph 2:5). That is the core of our identity; we are saved sinners by the grace of God who covenanted with us before the world was called into being.

This covenant of grace sets up for us the context for the role of the steward. All that is given is given freely and out of love in one direction—from God to us. All that is owned, all that is created, all that is provided is from God to us. The freedom and therefore the eternal omnipotent splendor and transcendence of God is never compromised. Out of his freedom he responds lovingly, graciously, mercifully toward us. We stand as ones who have received.

Our part of the covenant is to receive from God freely and with gratitude, and to respond in joy through our work as stewards in his kingdom. In no part and at no time in the covenant relationship do we ever assume the role of owner, creator or provider. We stand in the total need of God for all we have and all we are. We can never switch places with God unless we can somehow render God either unknowable or unnecessary, or if we can turn his gracious covenant into a contract between equals. If understanding God's nature as freedom and love keeps us from the former error, understanding God's covenant keeps us from the latter.

To be a steward in *this* God's kingdom is to come to the job in a full understanding of what it means to be his covenant partner. Not cowering or crowing but confident in our place as God's beloved children upon whom he is pleased to lavish all the wonders of his creation and from whom he seeks fellowship through our worship, our obedience and our stewardship.

CROWING — ARROGANCE
COWERING — DESPAIR

God's Image: One in Three and Three in One

We can now see how vital it was that the church held steadfast to a proper trinitarian doctrine of God. Such an understanding is the key to everything we know about ourselves. There is an inner consistency to God's creation and an inner dependence. Our ability to see, understand and benefit from both is based on a balanced trinitarian theology of creation.

In the history of trinitarian thought there have been countless attempts to emphasize either the uniqueness, identity and work of the three persons over the oneness of God, or the absolute unity of the Godhead over any understanding of the distinction of persons. Both views have significant effects on the view of God and not surprisingly on the theology of the church that resulted. If we are to build our theology of the steward on our understanding of who God is as Creator, then we must not falter at this all important moment. To lose our balance here is to negate all that we have built so far. To make this point, let us look at the pitfalls of erring on either side.

One God . . . in Three Persons, I Guess

Assume that we have only general knowledge of God and that knowledge leads us to conceive of a God who is basically a monad: a singular, detached, transcendent, impersonal and all-powerful being. What can we know of ourselves as the creation of this God? And what of our purpose for existence, our vocation and our *telos* (end)? In this self-understanding we are predominantly individuals, independent from each other and called to "be all we can be." We exist for self-actualization. We are valued for our individual accomplishments, we are to find meaning in our self-advancement, and we move toward a future in which everyone is able to better themselves. We, like the God in whose image we are created, strive to be monarchs. We are people in quest of power—our power—power that is used on our behalf. It is not hard to see how a "rugged individualism" results from this view of God. It is not hard to see how relationships become means to the end of bettering ourselves. People are what we use to accomplish that which brings us meaning and purpose, self-accomplishment.

When this view of God becomes dominant in the church, we see the church as mainly a collection of individuals who come to church asking "What's in it for me?" The church acquiesces to these perceived values of its congregants by trying to help each person find reasons to become and remain a member. We establish programs that cater to individual needs, and we do not expect people to support programs in the church that do not reflect their "interests." The result is a tacit approval of the dominant individualistic worldview. Individuals wake in individual houses, drive to church in individual cars, sit in their same pews, greet the same small group of people they know and leave to return to their individual lives. The church has lost a sense of community because it has failed to help its members develop a self-understanding that reflects our creation in the image of a trinitarian God.

Now think how this effects our stewardship programs. Addressing a group of individuals whose self-understanding comes from this monistic God, the pastor and trustees are left to convince people that there is value for them in giving away the greatest single symbol of individual success—their possessions. The church alternatively will struggle to explain how the verses that command us to "have dominion," "subdue" and "rule over" do not condone dominance, exploitation and abuse, since the latter are all part of individual achievement, and therefore are a "reflection of the glory of God."

To help us, we turn to secular fundraising techniques and try to "Christianize" the use of guilt, fear, greed, altruism or pride. We use prodigious Bible verses to demonstrate God's command to give, our responsibility to give, the benefits of giving and the pitfalls of stinginess. In all of our haranguing, cajoling and pleading, we seek to remind our individual members that "God loves a cheerful giver." The results to date have been disastrous for the work of the kingdom and the breaking of bondage to possessions that is a true mark of transformation in our lives.

This continual bind we find ourselves in with regard to motivations for giving is based on a wrong-headed understanding of who God is (the first side of the coin) and consequently who we are (its flip side). This combination of misunderstandings is the basis for the prevailing concept that the reality of our existence lies in two distinct spheres, which is the topic of chapter six. Remember there that it has its basis here. For now, we must see again how the lack of understanding of who God is as the triune God leads inevitably to a distorted view of the purpose of our existence and consequently to a counterfeit ethic of the steward.

Three Persons . . . but Only One God, I Guess

There is a distortion on the other end of the scale that is equally heinous and has also found its way into the church and therefore into our stewardship work. The counter-assumption about the nature of God as transcendent monad is a latent tritheism where the three persons of God are held up to the extent that the unity of God is compromised. Here we have an overemphasis of the work of one person to the exclusion of the others. This is manifested in many ways.

Generally speaking, an overemphasis on the Father gives rise to a self-understanding that is akin to that of the detached monad, resulting in the patriarchal, domineering and all-powerful individual who seeks self-fulfillment in the expression of these characteristics at the expense of others. The work of Jesus and the Spirit are reread to fit this theology of dominance.

The overemphasis on Jesus has led throughout history to a Jesiology in which the nature of the Father is left in doubt and the work of the Holy Spirit is neglected. This is seen in theology that can only find love in Christian theology and has no place for wrath, justice or righteousness. It bespeaks of a modern-day Marcionism[3] that ignores the Old Testament except where it seems to speak about the coming Messiah. The self-understanding that proceeds from here is one who is created to "get along with everyone." There is perhaps no gathering of people who have more fear of conflict than the church. This may sound odd to those who seem to always be in conflicts in the church, but the point is that, even when we do have conflict, we always believe it to be wholly "un-Christian" and out of place in the church. We should be about loving everyone, accepting everyone and setting aside all that would divide us. Peace and harmony at all costs

---

[3]Marcionism comes from the teachings of Marcion, who was unable to reconcile the God of the Old Testament—the warrior God—with that of the New Testament—the God of love and grace. Therefore, Marcion posited two Gods, of which only the New Testament God was the true Father of the Son Jesus.

should prevail in all we do. After all, that is what Jesus was all about. The problem, of course, is that this is not what Jesus was all about! A trinitarian understanding of God helps us hold together grace and *holiness*, mercy and *righteousness*, the love of God and the *wrath of God*.

On the other hand, this overemphasis has led to a quest to historicize Jesus' ministry to find its moral core. This has given rise to finding in Jesus a moral leader, bereft of divinity but able to show us how we are to live to please a God we really never get to know. We seek to meet the needs of our neighbor, to emphasize the "social gospel," to live up to the call of the Great Commandment at the expense of the Great Commission. Our self-understanding throws us back on ourselves again to "work out our salvation," not in the rich and challenging way promoted by John Wesley but in the impotence of our own quest for purpose and meaning apart from our participation in the divine Christ who came to show us the heart of God.

When Jesus is the sole source of our self-identity, the problem for stewardship becomes more complex. The two scenarios above depict a lack of balance between the justice and love of God that is found in a truly trinitarian theology. Both will relegate the work of the steward to something "we do." To practice stewardship in these models means we either demonstrate our love for humanity by our giving, or we work out our salvation by our good works, including our stewardship. By ignoring the justice of God and finding in Jesus only the lover of the world, the call to be a steward lacks the dynamic of our salvation from a falleness that would find its way back into our motivations and practices whenever and wherever it could. The denial of the kind of sin that kindled the wrath of God and that should continue to kindle the wrath of God's people, seriously handicaps the work of a steward. This, too, will become more apparent in the following chapters.

Consequently, if our Christian identity is limited to following the examples of a moral teacher, the radical nature of the call to be a steward will have no basis. True stewardship involves sacrifice, self-denial (by the world's standards) and a wholesale commitment to God of everything we have and are. This fundamental level of discipleship can only be the result of the work of the Holy Spirit in the life of one who has been saved from sin by the work of Christ in life, death and resurrection. To think that such a high and noble calling can be achieved by trying to live a good life "like Jesus did" is a grand self-delusion.

Finally, the overemphasis on the Spirit is seen in some Pentecostal movements where Jesus' work is behind us and the Father barely gets a mention. Where the work of the Spirit dominates, "experience" becomes the rule by which authentic faith is measured. Self-understanding here can promote an isolationism from those who have not had the same "experience in the spirit," despite the call for unity in Christ. The role of the church today, and therefore of the members of the church today, can be read out of context with the tradition and history of the church throughout the ages. This is a further isolationism that breeds a sense of superiority and a cutting off of the commitment to community with all of those in the kingdom of God.

To steward God's creation requires a self-definition that includes the love and righteousness of the Father and the atoning work of the Son as well as the power of the Spirit. The overemphasis on the work of the Spirit threatens to cause a dichotomy of the physical and the spiritual. Can we be true stewards of God's creation if our self-understanding does not include the creator Father? Can we be true stewards if it does not include the Word made flesh? How do we talk about the care of creation, the care of our physical bodies and even the care of our neighbors' physical as well as spiritual needs? The lack of a self-understanding that includes the fullness of the Father and the Son will severely restrict the scope of our stewardship and therefore will keep us from being stewards in the kingdom of the *triune* God of grace.

Our Creation as Stewards on All Four Levels

If we are to understand our call to be stewards of this God, we must reject these overemphases and seek a truly trinitarian self-understanding. That requires a credible, trinitarian theology of creation. This is a weak spot in the rich history of the development of the church's theology. There has been far too little written and said on the church's understanding of creation, and especially of our creation as men and women in the image of our Creator. Clearly a study on the call to be a steward must not be weak at this crucial point.

We have laid the groundwork for what must be said here. We have spelled out the God we know in Jesus Christ. We have identified creation as the free act of God in love. And we have looked briefly at some of the problems resulting from a flawed understanding of the Trinity and consequently in our own self-understanding. We can now build a doctrine of creation that can properly inform our study on the call to be a steward.

We begin with the position that through and through creation is a trinitarian event. Genesis 1:26 rightly translated reads, "Let *us* make man in *our* image, in *our* likeness" (emphasis mine). John 1 places the Son at creation, "He was with God in the beginning" (v. 2) and he was there as cocreator, for "through him all things were made, without him nothing was made that has been made" (v. 3). Colossians goes further by claiming that the Son was the purpose of creation, "For by him all things were created: things in heaven and on earth, visible and invisible, whether thrones or powers or rulers or authorities—all things were created *by him and for him.* He is before all things, and in him all things hold together" (1:16-17, emphasis mine). Talk about Christocentric! We must also cite the writer of Hebrews who opens his letter by proclaiming, "In the past God spoke to our forefathers through the prophets at many times and in various ways, but in these last days he has spoken to us by his Son, whom he appointed the heir of all things, *through whom he made the universe*" (1:1-2, emphasis mine). These are but a few passages that depict the trinitarian nature of the work of creation.

As a trinitarian event, creation reflects the image of the Creator. As such, creation is endowed with the inherent traits of interrelationship. This creation is a system of mutually dependent parts that require fellowship, participation, cooperation and even sacrifice to survive and flourish. We have learned painful lessons of disturbing ecosystems, whether on the macro or micro level. We know that our bodies are comprised of a series of complex, interrelated systems that are dependent upon one another for health. Sociologists have helped us see how our family systems, relational systems, community systems and social systems are made up of individuals that are highly interdependent and that must both give and receive appropriately, freely and sacrificially if the individual and, consequently, the system is to survive.

A thoroughly trinitarian doctrine of creation informs our self-understanding as creatures of a wholly relational God. The God who by his very nature is fellowship in joy, created us for fellowship and joy on all four levels. This creative intent is depicted in the creation story in Genesis. Here Scripture provides us with a theological framework in which we are to understand the "image of God" and the intent of God for creation on all four levels. Consequently, the story of the Fall depicts the brokenness caused by sin on all four levels, and that will be taken up in chapter four.

1. GOD - HUMANWORD GOD'S INITIATIVE GOD IN HIS FREE ACT
2. HUMAN - GODWARD HUMAN RESPONSE HUMAN IN HIS FREE ACT OF GIVING LOVING RESPONSE

Knowing God the Creator as the Triune God of Grace   71

The Two-Way Movement in Creation

Before we look at God's original intent on each level, we must understand there is a movement that is found in creation that effects our relations at all four levels. That movement is a dual movement that can be described as "God-Humanward" and "Human-Godward." This is always the proper order for these two movements. These movements are also thoroughly trinitarian in nature. Therefore, the act of creation can be described as the work of the Father, through the Son, by the Spirit. God acts toward humanity in this trinitarian way. Conversely, we worship the Father through the Son and in the Spirit. This is our human response to God's work for us and in us. It too reflects the triune nature of God. All of our work as the people of God comes in this trinitarian form. We are moved by the Spirit in all of our ministry and work for the kingdom. We work in the name of and for the sake of Jesus Christ, whose body we are. And we offer our prayers, the work of our hands and lips, and our praises through our worship and adoration to the Father, our Creator. Yet we do this in one act of worship to the one God we worship. Therefore our worship, our work for the kingdom and our building of healthy relationships at all four levels are triune by their very nature, or they are not reflecting the glory of God.

The call to be a steward then is also a call that comes from the Father, through the Son and in the Spirit. God the Father creates us in grace and commands us in love to be his faithful stewards. God the Son redeems us by his precious blood and gathers us as the body of Christ to be stewards in the kingdom of God. And God the Holy Spirit empowers and equips us for our work as stewards and unites us with Christ in our worship of the Father.

Our response is motivated by the movement of the Spirit who we believe is at the heart of all we do as stewards. In the ministry of Christian fundraising we seek the guidance of the Spirit in our asking and our giving. We seek the movement of the Spirit in the hearts of the people of God in our fundraising efforts. We trust the witness of the Spirit in our storytelling. And we pray in the power of the Spirit in our decision making. Stewardship is Spirit-centered work. As we work in the power of the Spirit, we seek to be stewards and to train up stewards in gracious response to the love of God in Christ Jesus. Our work is our participation in the faithfulness of the Son to the will of the Father. We recognize that it has all been done for us. We recognize that we are recipients of grace by means of the covenant of God made complete in Jesus Christ. We respond with gratitude by participating in the ongoing work of the Son, in the name of the Son and for the sake of the Son. All this is done to the glory of God the Father, who created us for this work, saved us for fellowship with him, and called us to be his children in his kingdom now and forever. The work of the steward is a trinitarian event.

This special, privileged work as stewards is to be carried out on all four relational levels in which we were created: our relationship with God, with ourselves, with our neighbor and with our creation. Each level requires our stewarding, each was proclaimed as "very good" by God at creation, and each bears witness to our creation in the image of a trinitarian God. Before the Fall, Scripture tells us much about these relationships that round out our understanding of our Creator God and ourselves as his creation.

The Image of God: Humanity in Covenant

> So God created man in his own image, in the image of God he created him; male and female he created them. God blessed them and said to them, "Be fruitful and increase in number; fill the earth and subdue it." (Gen 1:27-28)

With these words the opening chapter of the Bible proclaims that we are created first for fellowship with our Creator. Therein lies the purpose and meaning of our existence. How else could a triune God create in his image than to create another for fellowship and joy? We are fulfilled, content and satisfied in our existence to the extent that we are in fellowship with our Creator. This is the first level that defines our existence and brings meaning to our life. *The Confessions of St. Augustine* open with the beautiful words, "Thou awakest us to delight in Thy praise; for Thou madest us for Thyself, and our heart is restless, until it repose in Thee."[4]

As we have said above, the image of God in which we are created is witnessed to in our status as covenant partners of God. That is, God has chosen us from creation to be his people. One crucial aspect of the revelation of God's covenantal love for us in creation is the clear understanding that God created us to be "with" us and not "over" us. God created us for fellowship. This is not as equals that we may be like God, but it is also not as underlings with no real worth or value apart from that bestowed upon

---

[4]*The Confessions of St. Augustine* (Oxford: John Henry Parker, 1838), p. 1.

us. To be created in God's image is to be created with supreme worth and value. God's relationship to us in creation is a life-giving relationship. God's dominion over us is an enriching, nurturing and wholly beneficial dominion. God's love for us bestows on us the status of covenant partner, friend, companion and one with whom God delights to fellowship and dwell. Our original created state was one in which we could stand to look into the face of God, walk with him in the stillness of the garden, talk with him about the affairs of our heart and dwell with him in perfect peace. We were created for nothing less. This is the heart of God both for his original creation and for his redeemed creation.

Once we chose separation through sin in the Fall, God moved to establish a formal covenant through Noah, Abraham, Moses, David, Benjamin and finally the new covenant in Jesus Christ. Van Dyke, Mahan, Sheldon and Brand provide a helpful perspective of the nature of the covenant:

> This covenant has five important features: (1) It is conceived and established by God. (2) Its scope is universal, embracing all creation under God's care and protection. (3) It is unconditional, without requiring merit on the part of Noah or any other living thing. (4) It shall last as long as the earth remains. (5) And its satisfaction hinges only on the Creator's benefice. In all these things the covenant is ordained and completed by God through grace.[5]

As the covenant partners of the God who loves in freedom and who is free to love, our responsibility is simply one of a free, loving response. Our whole life is a witness to the grace of God in our lives demonstrated by our response. For Adam and Eve that meant walking with God in the Garden, listening to his Word, tending his garden with joy and following his command to "be fruitful and multiply and replenish the earth." It was to trust that God has chosen the best for his creation, to rest in his loving care, to listen only to him for their direction, and to live peacefully within the bounds set up for them by their loving Creator.

For us, we witness God's grace in our lives when we live out our call to be stewards. Richard Niebuhr commented rightly when he said that stewardship is everything we do after we accept Christ. Stewardship, like discipleship, must be understood as the free and loving response to the

---

[5]Fred Van Dyke, David Mahan, Joseph Sheldon and Raymond Brand, *Redeeming Creation: The Biblical Basis for Environmental Stewardship* (Downers Grove, Ill.: InterVarsity Press, 1996), p. 73.

grace of God in our lives. Its various forms—worship, Bible study, prayer, service, evangelism and the like—are the joyous acts of a people who can do nothing less. If our relationship to God does not engender joy and celebration, then we have missed the good news.

The relationship into which we are called as children of God in Christ Jesus is both freely given and one that requires our stewardship. We are to be caretakers of this precious gift, even though it is a gift of grace. Perhaps we should say *especially* because it is a gift of grace. Our part of the covenant does not condone nominalism. Again, if we respond in such a laissez faire fashion, we have missed the good news. The proclamation of the divine intent in the *imago Dei* is both gift and command. We are both to receive freely and respond freely. Our response is our commitment to steward this relationship.

To do this we must first understand that our relationship to God through Jesus Christ and in the Spirit requires the work of the steward. This relationship is not "ours." We did not initiate it (or even want it!); we did not sustain it, empower it or bring it to fruition. We simply accepted it and thanked God for it. As it continues today, we do not provide the means for it to grow stronger, nor do we control its hold over us. This is all a continued outpouring of the grace of God. Yet we do have a responsibility to steward this relationship. We are called to pray, study the Scriptures, be in fellowship with our brothers and sisters in Christ, partake of the sacraments and so forth. These are acts of stewardship, and their mission and purpose is to bring God glory. That is the vocation for which we were created, that our relationship in and with God in Christ may bring us fulfillment, meaning and purpose, and may bring God glory. We participate in that calling by being stewards of this relationship.

The Image of God: Body and Soul

Second, we were created for personal wholeness. Without recounting the history of the debate over the relations and division of mind, body and soul, it must be held that there is a physical, mental and spiritual aspect to our humanity. These form a system that is mutually dependent. The growing openness of the medical profession to the role of prayer, laughter, positive thinking and Eastern medicine is evidence of this systemic wholeness. Clearly an assessment of our overall health must include all three areas, and every disruption to any of these three aspects will affect the other two. God created us to be whole persons, to live with strong bodies and sound minds, and to be filled with the Holy Spirit. We are commanded to love God with all of these: heart, soul, strength and mind. This personal wholeness is a reflection of our creation in the image of a triune God.

Perhaps the hardest and least talked about level of our steward responsibilities is the personal level. To think of our mind, body and spirit as not really ours but a gift to be stewarded is probably new to most of us. However, as we will see when we look at the effect of the Fall, whenever anything at any of these four levels becomes "mine," it is ripe for distortion and destruction. This is nowhere more evident than in the health of our body, mind and spirit.

A major reason for this difficulty is the centuries old distortion in our understanding of the relationship between body and soul as God created us. Many recent theologians are beginning to point this out and provide a corrective that rejects the classic Platonic dualism splitting body and soul and naming the former "evil" and the latter "good." Samuele Bacchiocchi argues correctly that the Hebrew word *nephesh* is used in the creation story to depict a wholeness of body and spirit and not a detached soul.

> The expression "man became a living soul—*nephesh hayyah*" does not mean that at creation his body was endowed with an immortal soul, a separate entity, distinct from the body. Rather it means that as a result of the divine inbreathing of the "breath of life" into the lifeless body, man became a living, breathing being, no more, no less" Simply stated, "a living soul" means "a living being."[6]

God's creation of humanity as body and soul as one complete entity was pronounced "very good." The tendency to attribute sin, uncleanness and evil to the "flesh" while elevating the soul to a higher state has had devastating effects on Christian ethics and stewardship.

First, it continues the gnostic heresy that spiritual maturity requires a mortification of the physical and a glorification of the numinous or spiritual. Growth is defined by our ability to get outside our bodies and more fully discover our inner selves, for it is in our souls that God is to be

---

[6]Samuele Bacchiocchi, *Immortality or Resurrection?* (Berrien Springs, Mich.: Biblical Perspectives, 1997), p. 46. This understanding of *nephesh* is very helpful to our study, and Bacchiocchi's book is helpful in this area. However, this notation does not indicate my agreement with the preponderance of the book.

found and experienced. This bifurcation of our beings is further enhanced when salvation is seen as effecting only our souls and not our bodies. The logical end that many reach is that there is no need to care for our bodies—or the bodies of the poor, for instance. The total concentration should be on the saving of the soul. The call to discipleship is, once saved, to nourish the soul while tolerating the body until death finally separates the two.

This self-dissection carries over secondly to our view of the world around us. We read that the world is "passing away," and we understand that in the same dualistic way. Therefore, our care for creation is a waste of time, the futile attempt to preserve a sinful creation designated for destruction anyway. If creation can be used (read "exploited") for some good before its inevitable demise, then use it all you can. So Christians adopt a utilitarian approach to the stewardship of creation, bolstered by a flawed dualistic understanding of creation. Here Moltmann's comments are helpful, "If human society is to find a home in the natural environment, the human soul must correspondingly find a home in the bodily existence of the human person."[7]

This point is too important to pass by without further comment. The link between self-image and worldview is dramatic. Our perception of the world is colored by our perception of who we think we are. Therefore, how we see the world will depend on how we see ourselves. Philip Sherrard comments, "Our model of the universe, our world-image, is based upon our self-image. When we look at the world, what we see is a reflection of our own mind. Our perception of a tree, a mountain, a face, or a bird is a reflection of who we think we are."[8]

It is easy to see that if our self-image allows for this bifurcation between body and soul, the denigration of the material in our personal self-image will carry over into our worldview. The exploitation of our world is the sad reflection of a lack of our self-esteem as a species; a telling characteristic of the work of the enemy of the good creation of God. Whenever God becomes unknowable, our self-image will suffer, and consequently so will the creation in which we live. Sherrard continues, "We do not have any respect, let alone reverence, for the world of nature because we do not have any respect, let alone reverence, for ourselves . . .

---

[7]Moltmann, *God in Creation*, p. 49.
[8]Philip Sherrard, "Sacred Cosmology and the Ecological Crisis," *Green Cross* 2, no. 4 (1996): 8.

our contemporary crisis is really our own depravity writ large."[9]

This simple truth demonstrates the radical nature of a Christian ethic that commits itself to knowing ourselves only in light of who God is. Only when our God is seen in his self-revelation in Jesus Christ can we fully appreciate who we are as his beloved covenant partners, created for fellowship and redeemed by the blood of his Son. Only understanding ourselves as such can we develop the balanced self-esteem that will allow us to raise up our created world to the level of dignity with which we were fashioned. Only as stewards in the kingdom of the triune God of grace can we deny this dualistic heresy and understand ourselves as whole persons created body and soul for the work God has called us to do. Until then this dualism will continue to manifest itself in ways that are demeaning to us as God's creatures and detrimental to the creation that we have been called to tend.

We even see this dualism crop up in our understanding of people in relationship. We can easily split the essence of a person from their existence. This is seen in no more powerful place than in human sexuality. It should be interesting here to note that in Genesis 2:24 God did not say that the result of the union of male and female will be "one spirit" but "one flesh." If we read Genesis correctly, we will see that the unity spoken of involved a physical, sexual union but not at the expense or in the absence of the union of spirit. The two were never meant to be separated and treated differently.

There is a spiritual dimension to sexual union that cannot be denied. Therefore, Paul warns the church, "Do you not know that your bodies are members of Christ himself? Shall I then take the members of Christ and unite them with a prostitute? Never! Do you not know that he who unites himself with a prostitute is one with her in body?" (1 Cor 6:15-16). The oneness of sexual union speaks of a dimension beyond the mere physical act of intercourse. There is no room to drive a wedge between who we are in spirit and who we are in our physical form. We were created body and spirit in the image of God and declared to be very good. We will be raised with a glorified body and spirit to spend eternity with God. In this picture there is no place for a hatred of the physical or the elevation of the spirit. Both together comprise who we are as children of God. Both together equip us for fellowship in God's created world. Both together require our stewarding as God's gracious gifts.

---

[9]Ibid., p. 14.

To illustrate this we need to return to the creation story. We are told that Adam and Eve were "naked and not ashamed." I recently led our eighth-grade confirmation class in a discussion of stewardship, and I began by laying out the original creative intent of God. We spent over an hour on a variety of topics, but the one point that nobody could understand was how Adam and Eve could be naked and not ashamed! Notwithstanding the hormonal tension of a room full of eighth-grade boys and girls when the term *naked* is mentioned, it pointed to our general inability to understand the original, perfect equilibrium between our essence and our existence. Sexuality was a natural gift of God that was consummated by a physical and spiritual act. Since both physical and spiritual characteristics of humanity were part of God's good creation, there was no shame in nakedness. We will see how the entrance of sin brought about an immediate recognition that a rift had occurred between existence and essence, causing Adam and Eve to hide in their shame. Even as God's redeemed children we have a difficult time rectifying our physical, sexual, created body with the goodness of God. Until we do, we cannot be stewards in the kingdom of the triune God of grace.

If we seek to be true to the holistic nature of our beings, we are led to ask what it means to be a steward of our bodies and our spirits? What does it say about what we eat, how we exercise, our use of the medical expertise available to us? And what of our minds? Can the church continue to foster an anti-intellectualism if it takes seriously our call to be stewards of our minds? Can we let that which we are to steward grow moldy, become stratified or harden? What does it mean to "love God with all your mind"? We must begin to talk about the stewardship of our bodies and minds if we are to be stewards of the God who created us in his image for his glory.

The Image of God: Being "Relationally Wired"
Third, we are created for fellowship one with another. This need for fellowship began in Eden when God created the woman out of the need of the man for another like him. The scenario in Eden is a theological statement about our creation as male and female. God surely knew that Adam would not find a partner among the beasts of the earth. It was not for God's sake but for Adam's that the parade of animals was assembled in search of a mate for the man. Adam's discovery is one that we need to revisit in our sexual ethics over and over again. Adam found that his cre-

ation in God's image made him and his needs unique among his fellow creatures. There was no beast that could provide for Adam the fellowship that would allow him to live as truly one created in the image of a God in relationship. Neither by himself nor even amid the great varieties of creation could man truly be God's image. Man needed one enough like himself to be equal in every way, yet different enough to engender a relationship on a supernatural, godlike level. When Adam understood this, God created that perfect partner. Now neither man nor woman is to look elsewhere—neither to themselves, nor to creation, nor to one just like them. There is a place for relationships between human and creatures (a place and a responsibility) and between men and women separately. However, these can never be more than vestiges of the greater communion God created for male and female together. The creation story teaches us that men and women were created to be together, to live and work and play and worship together in the kind of fellowship that reflects the character of God and therefore brings him glory.

Within this fellowship one with another there is reserved the very special fellowship of male and female. Each were created physically, psychologically and spiritually to come together to form a unique union that, when blessed by God, forms "one flesh," which is perhaps the greatest single example we have on earth of the *perichoretic* unity of the Godhead. The marriage of one man with one woman with Christ at the center reflects the glory of a triune Creator in a magnificent way. In marriage, in the family, in the church and in society we bear witness to our creation in the image of a triune God.

We can begin to see how the second level of relationship, as well as the third and fourth, are dependent upon the first. When we are in a right relationship to God, we are able to steward relationships with one another. Again the term steward is appropriate here because these relationships are not "ours." The people we live with are God's creations, the circumstances that bring us together are not dictated by us, the gifts of fellowship, even the very possibility for fellowship is part of God's created order. Therefore our marriages, our friendships, our families and our church communities are gifts, precious gifts of God. Our call is to steward these relationships as precious gifts. That may require our time, our money, our talents, and it will always demand our commitment, sacrifice and love. It all begins by understanding all of our relationships as gifts given to us and of our consequent responsibility to be stewards of each.

The Image of God: Dominion and Rule

Finally, we are reminded in Scripture that while we are the "crown of creation," we are also counted among the creatures in God's creation. We are part of the animal kingdom that has a place in the created world and a role with responsibilities. While it cannot be said that the animals were created in the image of God in the same way as humans were, it must be said that all creation bears his image in the sense that its interdependence and its robust vitality all glorify God as the Creator of all things. Therefore, there is obligation to glorify God in our relation to and responsibility for his creation. A well-cared for, healthy, balanced and productive creation is the purpose for which God created this world and us in it.

There is an unmistakable responsibility we have to the creation of which we are a part. Sin here has done its best to distort this responsibility, but here we need to be clear that we are called to be stewards of God's creation. Again, this creation is not "ours." Despite the ability to own land, buy natural resources, purchase mineral rights and so forth, we at no time are ever the ultimate owners of any part of this creation. We did not create it; we do not cause the rain to fall, the sun to shine, the seeds to grow, or any of the natural forces that characterize this splendid creation. For all that science and technology have done for us, they deceive us when they lead us to believe that whatever control we may be able to harness carries with it the right to absolute ownership.

Care for creation is akin to our care for ourselves, and perhaps the most remarkable blot on our generation will be our inability to see the destruction of our environment as our own self-destruction. This stewarding of ours is also a triune event. We are called to care for the Father's world, which is redeemed by the Son and sustained by the power of the Spirit. We know that, "The creation waits in eager expectation for the sons of God to be revealed. For the creation was subjected to frustration, not by its own choice, but by the hope of the one who subjected it, in hope that the creation itself will be liberated from its bondage to decay and brought into the glorious freedom of the children of God" (Rom 8:19-21). And because of that subjection, "We know that the whole creation has been groaning as in the pains of childbirth right up to the present time" (v. 22). While it awaits with us the end of all things and the ultimate glorification of God in heaven *and on earth,* we are called to steward this creation with love, care and compassion as a fellow sufferer under the continued effects of sin.

Here we must shed some light on the problems and mistreatments of the command of God to "have dominion," "subdue" and "rule over." Here is where our "theological" approach to the topic will take a different tack from the great number of exegetical treatments of this issue. It is important that many studies have looked into the root meanings of *dominion, subdue* and *rule over*. Careful exegetical work is important in understanding our role as stewards. However, it is also of paramount importance that we stay true to our commitment to understand the ethic of the steward in light of who our God is and therefore who we are as created in God's image. We must also keep to the dual direction we laid out for the relationship between God and us in his free and loving act of giving, and between us and God in our free and loving response. Being true to both means we must be clear that whatever the biblical roots and contextual interpretations offered by skilled biblical scholars concerning these words, we are committed to seek our understanding of these words in the context of God's original intent in saying them to his creatures who he created for fellowship. Therefore, the definition of these words lies in the one who proclaimed them and nowhere else.

How were Adam and Eve to know what God meant by these words? Very simply, they understood "dominion" and "subdue" in light of their Creator. Adam and Eve were commanded to have dominion over the created world *just as God had demonstrated his dominion over them*. They knew God as the God who sought to be *with* them rather than *over* them. They knew in God one who lovingly provided for them, who sought only their good and who they trusted intimately for their very existence. They saw a God who was for them in every way, who sought their best and with whom they were at peace. And they saw a God who created for them an environment in which they could grow and flourish, one that worked together in harmony and one that provided abundantly for their welfare and future.

It was *this* God and no other that gave to the first humans the precious responsibility to have like dominion over creation. To subdue it like God had subdued them. To rule over it like God ruled. And this meant a call to loving service and godly care for God's creation. This is the only proper way in which we can understand the command to have "dominion," "subdue" and "rule over." The biblical interpreters provide exegetical support for this understanding, and the integrity of the entire theological methodology of this book can lead us to no other conclusion. We must therefore avoid taking post-Fall, sin-filled definitions of *dominion* and *rule* and foist them back upon God's original proclamation in a way to lend credibility to the exploitation of the planet. Only after the Fall does *dominion* become *dominance, subdue* become *exploit,* and *rule over* become *abuse.* We must not read these back into God's original divine intent.

Our methodology has committed us to seek truth only in God's self-revelation to us in Jesus Christ. There and only there do we have certain knowledge of who God is and consequently who we are. There we hear the God who created freely out of love command that his covenant partners live as precious children created in his very image, that their care for creation might reflect the nature of his care for them.

At no time prior to the Fall did it endow them with the right or power or authority to claim some kind of alien dominance or counterfeit rule. They simply knew nothing else but godly, grace-filled rule and dominion. Vera Shaw puts it beautifully:

> The story of Eden is the story of humankind's relationship with an ideal environment and with the Creator of that environment. In the perfectly balanced ecology of Eden, during the days when humans walked there with God, the Creator shared his dominion over the garden with his human creation. God gave them the wonderful responsibility to till and keep the garden. Human responsibility to preserve the environment was an important part of the harmony of Eden. It is a beautiful image—the sovereign Lord created His masterpiece and then created one made in His image to preserve and care for the garden. How much He loved humankind to want to share His handiwork! What a joy for Adam to be given the high honor of keeping God's own creation.[10]

This then is the state of humanity in God's created order before the Fall. It is a picture of Adam and Eve as stewards in God's kingdom, living as his children, loving creation as God loved them. Their acts of stewardship were nothing less than their acts of worship. God's creatures praise and glorify God by caring for his creation as he cares for them. What more could bring God glory than honoring his creation and living according to his will? If God in his very nature creates us out of love and freedom and then commands us to be "life-givers" to his creation through our role as stewards, how can our obedience to that high calling be anything less than doxology?

These four levels all bear witness to a triune, loving and free Creator.

---

[10]Vera Shaw, "The Ecology of Eden," *Green Cross,* winter 1995, p. 4.

All four have striking similarities, and all four require maintenance, care, love, investment and time if they are to continue to be reflective of our God.

This is the role of the steward who understands that the one who is the owner is the triune God of grace. This God is by nature both loving and free, both transcendent and immanent, both three persons in oneness and one God in threeness. The nature of our call to be stewards on all four levels is derived from our standing as children in the kingdom of the God who proclaimed the goodness of our relationships on all four levels in his creation.

The harsh reality of our existence is, of course, that the history of Eden brought a radical brokenness into this idyllic picture, changing these relationships forever. We are not called to be stewards in Eden but east of Eden. Therefore, we must turn our careful attention to the results of sin in these relationships, their consequent impact upon our ability to be stewards and, most importantly, to the redeeming work of Christ, the faithful steward.

Chapter 4

The Sin
of the Steward

BEING A STEWARD IN EDEN WAS AS NATURAL AS BREATHING. RELA-
tionships on all four levels were sound, holy and God-pleasing.
We cannot relate easily to the Edenic state from our severely
limited vantage point on this side of Eden. For this reason we
must proceed here with great caution. The story that unfolds in the first
three chapters of Genesis is singularly theological. Its focus is the cross
and resurrection of Jesus Christ, and therefore its intent is *kerygmatic*. It
was not written to cause us to yearn for a return to Eden but to show us
our sin and our need for our Savior. It points us ahead to the coming of
the kingdom of God in its fullness, ushering in an eternity that will far
transcend even the idyllic Eden.

Because the opening three chapters of Genesis have this intent, we must
be careful how we read them and what we take from them for our lives on
this side of the Fall. Here we have the advantage of looking back through
the salvific work of Christ. We have seen the fulfillment of the promise
given to the exiled first couple. We have seen the blueprint for the consum-
mation of God's purpose in creation, namely the restoration of all things to
himself in Jesus Christ. For this reason we are people of hope.

However, we also have the disadvantage of the devastating effects of sin in our lives that twists our perceptions and distorts our understanding at every level. How do we properly understand the story of our fall into sin when we must seek such an understanding in a fallen, sinful state? How do we rise above the limitations of our fallenness to gain a vantage point that will give us a clearer view of that very sinfulness? In short, does the sin in our lives make it impossible to understand its full effect on our lives? Barth clearly saw this dilemma in concluding, "Access to the knowledge that he is a sinner is lacking to man because he is a sinner."[1] This is the challenge we face in talking about sin and the Fall from our location somewhere east of Eden.

For this reason we must return to our main epistemological point. Here more than anywhere in this study we need to grasp how critical it is that we seek understanding in a wholly Christ-centered way. That is, we must look back through the "who" of Jesus Christ if we are to understand the important lessons for us in the "what," "why" and "how" of the story of the Fall. "Only when we know Jesus Christ do we really know that man is the man of sin and what sin is, and what it means for man."[2] We have said that what we can know for certain of God and of ourselves comes solely through Jesus Christ. We must extend that here to say that all we know of the Fall, sin and redemption must come from the same epistemology. To cut our search for understanding of sin loose from our Christocentric anchor will only set us adrift to bob around from one theory to another, with no reliable criteria to help us choose among them. We must not let that happen at this critical point in our study.

What must be said instead is that the God we know in Jesus Christ, his nature as freedom and love, his purpose in creation, his covenant with his creation and his future for that creation are not somehow lost or diminished as a result of the Fall. We must read the account of the Fall and draw the important implications from it for our call to be stewards. We must do so without falling to the temptation to read back into the story a foreign concept of God, sin, our status as God's creatures or our future. The Fall did not change God's nature, his purpose, his covenant or his intended future for us. In all the radical changes the Fall *did* bring, we must never read these changes back into the nature or pur-

---

[1]Karl Barth, *Christian Dogmatics* IV/1, eds. Geoffrey W. Bromiley and Thomas F. Torrance, trans. Thomas F. Torrance (Edinburgh, U.K.: T & T Clark, 1956), pp. 360-61.
[2]Ibid., p. 389.

pose of God. That is what we can and must say for sure if we are to hold to a Christocentric epistemology as our anchor for all certain knowledge of reality.

The Root Cause of the Sin of Adam

Before we can understand the devastating effects the Fall had on our relationships on all four levels and thus our stewardship of these relationships, we must look closely at the cause of this first act of sin. This immediately launches us into perhaps the most challenging area of theology. It involves the questions of free will versus determinism, the problem of the origin of evil and its place in God's "good" creation, the doctrine of election, the true nature of God's intended future for his creation, and even the goodness and omnipotence of God himself.

We will seek here to discuss these important issues only in terms of what we must understand for our call to be stewards on these four levels. This does not avoid these difficult issues, but it will keep us focused so that we might negotiate our way through and come out with an understanding of sin that helps us build our theology of the steward.

Given our focus, we will move immediately beyond the first quagmire that concerns the origin of evil. What we must say here is simply that evil, or the possibility of evil "existed" in some form at the creation. We must also say that whatever evil's origin, it must "exist" within the tension that its very possibility for existence is both wholly controlled by God and yet completely separate from him. That is, God is both the Lord over evil and yet God is in no way its author. Perhaps the best way to think about evil is to see it as an empty "nothingness"[3] that has only a negative potentiality for any "existence" through something or someone that truly exists. Evil has no substance or form itself, but it has the potential for substance and form only as a parasite, latching onto and living out its evil intent through something that has a positive ontology, an existence.

If we can get a hold of this idea, we can see that to talk about evil prior to creation is nigh impossible, for if it existed, it did so only as pure noth-

---

[3]The definition of *evil* as "nothingness" received its greatest treatment by Karl Barth. Barth saw evil as the absolute absence of God, total godlessness and godforsakenness. In his section on *Das Nichtige,* Barth makes clear the two points we hold here as critical: the absolute defiance of God against all that is evil and his complete lordship over it. For a study on Barth's understanding of evil, see my book, *Evil and Theodicy in the Theology of Karl Barth* (New York: Peter Lang, 1997).

ingness—unrealized evil with no possible way to actualize its nature. The two points critical for us are first, God is not the author, originator or creator of evil, and second, as Karl Barth put it poignantly, "Whatever evil is, God is its Lord."[4]

The potentiality of evil arises in significant form when we consider God's decision to create a world outside himself and creatures in his own image. In deciding to create, the potentiality for evil to find a host in this creation was also created. What God eternally rejects as a natural part of his very nature would besiege his nondivine creation from its very first moment of existence. God's creation would immediately be ripe for corruption. The nonexistence of evil would immediately have possibility for "existence," albeit only a distorted and counterfeit existence. God's creature, even while being created in the divine image for fellowship, joy and stewardship, would be targeted as a vehicle for the expression of brokenness at every level where God pronounced this creation "good." In the end this good creation would be faced with a decision that would doom it to destruction. How does a God who we know as freedom and love decide to create in the face of this impending Fall?

God's Choice for Our Good

Two clear pictures emerge from Genesis 1—3 that help us understand God's intention for us as his children. The first is that in creating our world, God chose for us what was good and rejected what was evil. The whole creation story is one of God choosing *for us* that which is good for our well-being. He chose light for us over darkness. He chose solid ground for us to live on, separating it from the water of the sea and the air of our atmosphere. He chose the warmth of the sun by day as our time of work and play separating it from the cold and darkness of night. God chose an environment full of life, in harmony and able to re-create itself through procreation. He chose food that nourished us and an earth that produces new crops each year. And finally he chose to make us male and female, like himself in his distinction yet his complete oneness. God chose fellowship for us over self-dependence, intimacy over isolation and a completion of ourselves in one another over self-actualization. Everything that was for our good, God chose for us. Likewise, everything that threatened our existence, our vitality and joy, God separated from us and

---

[4]Barth, *Church Dogmatics* IV/1, p. 408.

in some instances rejected for us. This is the state in which we find the first man and woman: whole before God with one another, in themselves and with all creation. There was nothing they needed for perfect happiness and wholeness that God had not chosen for them and placed before them.

Over the centuries voluminous ideas and opinions have been set forth on the topic of "why" Adam and Eve fell. The question, however, still perplexes us today. What motivated them to take this drastic and ultimately fatal step? Was there something in the serpent's words that opened up to Adam and Eve this possibility? Was it an appeal to pride, a thirst for power, a natural progression in their development, a crisis of faith? Perhaps more vexing is why God chose to place the tree of the knowledge of good and evil in the Garden in the first place. Why give such a choice to the creature and thereby give such an opening to the serpent?

If we hold to the understanding above that God's acts of creation were decisions in which God chose the good for us at every turn and rejected the evil that we could not reject, then the placing of the tree of the knowledge of good and evil in the Garden can be seen as God's way of providing for Adam and Eve an opportunity to affirm their trust in his creative work. By placing the tree and giving it this name, God said to his creatures, "Trust me that I, who know good and evil, have chosen for you only good and rejected all that is evil. Trust me by refusing to grasp for yourself that same knowledge." God gave to his creature the gracious opportunity for loving response. God gave to humankind a nature that was free to choose for God in love and that could demonstrate its freedom and love—for it was created in the image of the God who is freedom and love—in its free and loving choice of obedience. It was the nature of the response of the man and woman, not the God-given freedom for that choice, that became the target for the serpent.

The serpent's words questioned the goodness of God. They challenged the idea that Adam and Eve should trust that God had indeed chosen the good and rejected the evil. How were they to know that perhaps God did not choose all the good or reject all the evil? How were they to know unless they could choose for themselves? And how could they choose unless they had the same knowledge of good and evil as God? Could they allow God alone to judge for them? Or must they not become a judge themselves of what is good and evil? In short, aside from faith, equality with God was the only way that Adam and Eve could know for sure. And a decision was put before them: trust God and live in peace, or question God and grab power for themselves.

If this scenario is correct, the decision by this first human couple to eat of the forbidden fruit was an act of distrust and therefore the ultimate act of disbelief in the goodness of God's choices and decisions on their behalf. And Adam and Eve received exactly what they sought. In an instant they knew good *and evil*. In a flash of illumination they understood that God had indeed rejected evil for them. They also realized that by their action they now stood in place of God, choosing right and wrong for themselves. And in this instantaneous moment of enlightenment they understood that as creatures of God and therefore as nondivine, they could only choose the evil that was now already upon them. It is impossible for anyone to stand in the place of God. The evil that God had separated and kept far from the first couple in his loving and gracious creative choice for them now rushed onto the stage of creation, invited in by an act of distrust and faithlessness. Evil had found its host in the unwillingness of this pair to trust in the goodness of God.

God's Covenant Faithfulness

The second picture that emerges for us is the role of the covenant faithfulness of God in spite of, and we might rightfully say, in anticipation of this fatal act of mistrust. Without steering us into the heady debates over the supralapsarian and infralapsarian views of election, we can say that God's plan for his creation anticipates the Fall and already moves to undo its devastating effects on his creation. We have already cited some of the verses in Scripture that point clearly to the central role of the Son in creation and the choice by God prior to the Fall to elect his people to be his own in and though the work of Jesus Christ. In creation, God had a covenantal intent. If in his omniscience he knew that his creation would make this devastating choice, in his heart he determined to be for his creature even at the cost of his own Son.

Equally so, if everything that was created was created through the Son and for the Son, and if we were chosen in Jesus Christ before the foundation of the world, was there not an equal and complete commitment of the Son to the restoration of all things through his own sacrificial death on the cross? We are led to conclude that the trinitarian decision to create was *at exactly the same time* a trinitarian commitment to the cross, the empty tomb, the formation and work of the church and the completion of creation at the second coming of Christ, the victorious Lamb of God. God's covenantal faithfulness to us was commensurate with his loving and free act of creation. This connection must not be lost.

This is to some extent the justification of God in the face of the evil of the world. If we dare to seek such justification (which we always do, even though we should not!), we can find a part of the answer in God's covenantal faithfulness. If God's choice to create provided for evil the possibility that it may find a host and gain a sense of existence to the detriment of God's creation, then his covenant faithfulness is God's response to the effects of that decision that he took on himself before the first commands of Genesis 1.

This also speaks to the extent of this covenantal faithfulness to undo what was done at the Fall. There are two key points here for our study of the call to be stewards in God's kingdom.

The "Goodness" of Creation

The first implication of this understanding of God's covenantal faithfulness is that we need to revisit our understanding of what God meant when he decreed that the creation was "good." Traditional interpretations have tied the goodness decree to the state of creation prior to the Fall. That is, creation had a goodness in its original state that in some way was either significantly diminished or lost altogether in the Fall. What results is an understanding that God's once good creation is now much less than good—and perhaps downright evil. If the goodness decree is tied only to the original state of creation, then its fallen state leaves us with a question as to how God views creation now. Is it perhaps really passing away and therefore to be used by us without regard for its well-being and preservation? Remember here that we are talking about ourselves, our neighbors and our created world. If nothing we know today as "creation" can be considered good, what does that mean for our stewardship? I see two equally misguided answers.

One is that indeed if creation is no longer "good," it should be treated as such, and therefore it is ripe for abuse in the quest for a more lofty, spiritual, soul-related experience. In pursuit of a social good (better housing, services, fuel, food), we rape the creation. In our quest for actualization of our individual soul, our inner self, our true essence or being, we use others, manipulate relationships and deceive ourselves. If creation is fallen to the point that it has no inherent goodness, then it is ours to dominate and exploit without guilt or shame. Indeed, for some it is our God-given right to abuse the material in the search for the spiritual. This is one direction to which we are led in this misunderstanding of the goodness of creation.

The other direction leads us to believe that it is our job, our calling, to restore the goodness to creation. We are responsible to restore creation's goodness by loving it and caring for it. Many facets of liberation theology have placed the restoration of creation into the formula as part of the church's work to usher in the kingdom through the reestablishment of justice on earth. Likewise, there is a latent "Christian deism" that is rampant in our churches that sees God at an epistemological distance to our everyday lives. We are endowed by God to be good people, to live peaceably together and to be caretakers of the earth to which God has entrusted us. Ours then is the work of restoration, of bringing to fruition and perfecting nature, environment and our human race. This utopianism is on the decline, but there is a strong segment of our church population that sees the restoration of a goodness to creation as our work.

We must be clear to guard against both of these misdirections in our understanding of God's decree of the goodness of creation. What both views lack is a Christocentric doctrine of creation through which we see and understand God's intent. If we have understood God's covenantal faithfulness as it has been revealed to us in Jesus Christ, then we must seek to find in what way the decree of the goodness of creation is bound up with the salvific work of Christ through whom and for whom creation was made.

What we find is that the goodness of creation as decreed in Genesis 1—2 was not a pronouncement upon its prefallen state only, but it was a judgment of its fitness to be the place in which God's covenantal faithfulness would be demonstrated. That is, creation was "good" in that it was properly prepared to be the place where the Son would triumph over sin and death, the place where his kingdom would be established, and the place to which he would return to restore all things to himself. It was "good" because it was created through him *and for him*. The goodness of creation has its basis in Jesus Christ and nowhere else. It is not inherent in its pre-fallen state; it is not in a potentiality that we must somehow unleash; and it is not a goodness that has been lost, relegating creation to a defiled resource to be used up at our good pleasure and discarded. Creation is good because it is fitted for the service for which it was created, as "the theater of the glory of God."[5]

The Restoration of All Things in Jesus Christ

The second implication for our study of the work of the steward is the extent of the restoration of all things in Christ. If the goodness of creation is a reflection of its preparedness to host the work of salvation, then to what extent did that work truly restore all things? This is a key question, for as we will see shortly, sin had a devastating effect on all four levels of the relationships in which we were created. Again the temptation is to see the effects of the Fall in one of two equally erroneous ways. Either it was so devastating that restoration, even in Christ, is not possible—and therefore we have cause to devalue these relationships—or it was primarily our work to restore these relationships, leading us to succumb to a works righteousness that will be both unsuccessful and unsatisfying.

Scripture instead points us to one clear conclusion on this matter, and that is the whole and complete restoration of all things in Christ. Paul's strong words to the church in Rome leave no room for misunderstanding,

> But the free gift is not like the trespass. For if many died through one man's trespass, *much more* have the grace of God and the free gift in the grace of that one man Jesus Christ abounded to the many. And the free gift is not like the effect of that one man's sin. For the judgment following one trespass brought condemnation, but the free gift following many trespasses brings justification. If, because of one man's trespass, death reigned through that one man, *much more will those who receive the abundance of grace and the free gift of righteousness reign in life through the one man Jesus Christ.* (Rom 5:15-17, emphasis mine)

In Christ we have not only the complete restoration of what was lost in the sin of Adam, but we are assured that this restoration offers us *much more*. The life we live as children of God gives us a glimpse of an eternity in which we will realize the *much more* of God's redemptive acts for us. The future to which we move is a greater one than the lost Edenic state that lies in our past.

This complete restoration must be accepted by faith, and we must live

---

[5]John Calvin gave creation this label, and for all of the possible misuses of the term, it still stands as an excellent reminder of the need to read all of our theology through the lenses of the work of Jesus Christ for us.

according to that faith in hope. As such, we must view our relationships on all four levels as having been redeemed, restored and destined for an even greater form. The restoration of relationship with God, with each other, with ourselves and with our creation is not something we can either claim as our own work or that we can disregard as our own work. It is God's work, it is completed work and it is gifted to us as such. Therefore, we can and must receive it in grace, embrace it in faith and make it our own work in gratitude and hope.

This is the proper attitude of the steward. This is the balance we must maintain if we are to be stewards on this side of the Fall, and in anticipation of the final parousia. Both the choice of idealism, where this restoration becomes *our* cause, and nominalism, where it ceases to move us to act, must be denounced as wholly un-Christian. As with our understanding of God and of ourselves, all we can know for certain of our sinfulness, our salvation and our future hope is found in Jesus Christ. If we will stay true to this focus, we will avoid the pitfalls that lay in the path of every Christian ethic, especially that of the call to be stewards in God's kingdom.

The Consequences of the Fall

It is only in understanding the glory of our created state that we can begin to discern the depths to which we sank in the fall of humanity. As the parasitic nature of evil was able to find its host in the untrusting creature of God, the very relatedness that defined the creature was rent asunder. Evil had its "three moments" in the history of humankind: rebellion against God, enmity toward neighbor (and creation), and sin against self. Both that which defined our essence and that gave meaning to our existence were destroyed in our great act of unfaithfulness, an act we repeat every day in our sordid solidarity with Adam. We will look briefly at the loss on all four levels in preparation for the truly good news of their restoration in Christ.

The Loss of the Vertical

Perhaps the saddest words ever uttered in all of Scripture are God's call to his beloved creature, "Adam, where are you?" In one moment, Adam and Eve had their confident status before their Creator snatched from them. They lost their precious fellowship with the one who created them for fellowship. They lost their place at the side of the God who created them solely to be *with* them. In short, they lost the very reason for their existence.

It must have been terrifying suddenly to fear this God! Adam and Eve must have sensed immediately that they were somehow now distinct from God in a way that was alien, in a way that disqualified them from assuming fellowship with God. They suddenly saw themselves as being *apart from God*, and in that distinction, they saw how terrifying it was for them, as sinners, to stand in the presence of the holy God. Sin brings separation, brokenness and a sense of one "over and against" another.

Their response to God also shows that for the first time they began to consider themselves in a distinct way. That is, where in the past their self-identity was indistinguishable from their being as the creatures of their creator, now they were suddenly identified by themselves *alone*. With their self-defining relationship broken, they were forced to reckon with themselves as they were, separate, defined not by fellowship but by isolation. They also must have been devastated at the loss of purpose that this realization brought to bear. Their existence was wholly wrapped up in their relationship with God and their care for his creation. In the first instance, sin brought this primary relationship to an end, and with it went their purpose for living. Perhaps it was into that momentary void that the thought of carving out a place for oneself began to take hold. In losing their fellowship with God as the core of the meaning of their life, Adam and Eve may have moved immediately to replace that loss with what would only be natural given their isolated state, namely, with the desire to create, acquire or take by force those things that would re-create purpose and meaning in life. By doing so they accepted a new paradigm in which life-taking replaced life-giving, where self competed with God for sovereignty, where words like *dominion, rule* and *subdue*, which were once imbued with grace, were now redefined for use and abuse in a more *realistic* world. This new state of sin would create the need to put self-interest at the center of existence, and it would raise up distortion as its one defining characteristic.

From the very first moment of sin's entrance into the world, its ability to distort God's truth is evident. Distortion entered into all four levels of relationship, beginning with its most devastating impact, our deception of who God is and who we are as his creation. Today there is no greater challenge for the church than to help people develop a better understanding of who God is. From the moment in the garden when Adam and Eve hid from a God they now realized they did not know, we have been searching for certainty in our knowledge of God. Our greatest challenge comes not from the availability of that knowledge—for that is exactly why the Word became flesh and dwelt among us—but from our seemingly unbounded ability to distort the word and works of our Creator. From the side of the creature, sin changed life at the most profound and fundamental level.

And so God finds his beloved creatures cowering in the shadows, covering themselves in shame and trembling at the very sound of the voice of the one who called them into existence. The exchange in Genesis 3 between the two creatures and the Creator is heart-wrenching. Blame, accusation, anger and despair mark the beginning of the history of fallen humanity and a grieving, yet just God. For God, the effects of the act of mistrust were absolute and final. According to God's love, he announces the covenant. And according to his freedom, he banishes them forever from the garden. In love he leads them into the world to fulfill the call to be fruitful and multiply and replenish the earth. In freedom he informs them that the creation is no longer friend, that childbirth will bring as much pain as joy, and that the very ground from which they were formed would yield only grudgingly their daily sustenance until they return to it. Finally, in love he sets in motion "covenant history" and the promise of ultimate redemption and a return to the side of God. And in freedom he pronounces the death sentence upon them. God and his creature will never be the same again. But God promises that by his mercy, it someday will be even better.

For God, the evil that he eternally hated, banished and totally rejected had now become the characteristic mark of his beloved creation. His man and his woman had chosen what he hated in favor of freely choosing for him. They had cut themselves off from everything that gave meaning and purpose to their life. They had clothed themselves with all that God, in his holiness and righteousness, moves against with wrath and utterly destroys. They had aligned themselves with nothingness, with absolute godlessness. And God's reaction was both loving and just. This godlessness would once again need to be separated from creation, or creation itself would be destroyed. God's justice would be meted out not by an act of his wrath against us as sinners but in an act of his almighty love. His wrath against sin itself would be unleashed in the ultimate act of love, the act of giving *himself* over to the sentence of death. That is the power of the covenant and the importance of holding creation and covenant together.

The Loss of the Horizontal

Equally devastating to humankind was the radical change in our relationships to one another. We have seen how our creation in the image of God marked us as creatures who would find fulfillment, joy and meaning in relationship with God and with others. In Eden we were properly "lords and servants." In Eden the first couple understood *lordship* not in terms of power and manipulation but in terms of servanthood. God was the Lord over creation. His love and care for the first human was the model of what lordship looks like. The definition was filled out with acts of selflessness, service, provision and compassion. *Lordship* in Eden meant the cherished opportunity to care for another as God cares for all creation.

In relationships this lordship was demonstrated in a constant concern for the other. It was a call to be caretaker, nurturer, provider, enabler and empowerer. That is how Adam and Eve knew God, and that was all they knew of lordship in the innocence of holiness. To be "Lord in Eden" was to act for others and all creation like God acted toward his creature and creation. To be "lord and servant" was to be "steward"!

There is another striking feature to the prefallen state of relationships in Eden. The individual creature was not able to think of himself or herself *in abstacto*. That is, there was no awareness of self that could be conceived of apart from that same self *in relation*. Adam was not Adam without Eve. That is the whole theology behind the second telling of the creation of humanity in Genesis 2. Male and female were complete together. Male and female were complete only in relationship to the God who created them and in the work of stewarding the creation that was created for them. As was said at the beginning of this chapter, being a steward in Eden was as natural as breathing. The key to this state was the lack of the independent self as a conceivable reality.

The shift that occurred in the act of rebellion and distrust can be measured in large part by the thunderous rise of the knowledge of the self, of humanity *in abstracto*. This is seen with devastating sharpness in the very first moment of our fallenness. The first sign of the effects of our fallenness was not an act of defiance of God, nor an act of dominance over creation, nor even an act of enmity against another. The first realization that evil had found its host was in the recognition that male and female were different in a way that devalued the difference, brought immediate shame and soon led to distrust, accusation and blame. Suddenly the creature whose very existence was defined relationally was faced with the shocking revelation that in sin, the creature was now defined *as an individual!* Relationships that once were the creature's natural state of being would forevermore be the product of hard work and sacrifice. They would be ripe for distortion, filled with suspicion and would become the domain of manipulation, blackmail, power games, envy, hatred, abuse, deception and death. Every form of evil that the created world now hosted would be born out in this one area that, more than any other, defined the creature as being made in the image of the Creator. This is the significance of the loss of our natural relatedness at the Fall.

In this rise of the individual self the fall brought about another movement within the creature. We have said that in the created state lordship was akin to servanthood. The effect of the Fall was to refocus the creature's attention away from servant and onto a counterfeit form of lordship. By grasping at the chance to be like God, the creature changed from being the "servant of the Lord" to being the "Lord over servants." Barth comments, "Wanting to act the Lord in relation to God, man will desire and grasp at lordship over other men, and on the same presupposition, other men will meet him with the same desiring and grasping."[6]

And so it begins, the history of "man's inhumanity to man"! We have changed from seeking servanthood to seeking power, from being life-givers (a beautiful definition of the steward!) to life-takers,[7] from finding meaning in relationships to finding meaning in position that places one over and against another in relationships. At the core of this brokenness we find the rise of enmity between male and female. Their created state of perfect oneness in intimate relation to one another was now grotesquely disfigured. The glory of their manhood and womanhood became their shame. The subtlety of the strengths and weaknesses of each, which would have enhanced the unity of the two as "one flesh," now became the ammunition for the "battle of the sexes." Instead of celebrating maleness as complete only in and with the female, and femaleness as complete only in and with the male, the history of God's creatures would instead be one of a detached, abstract masculinity that leads to an arrogant domination and patriarchy, and an equally detached and abstract femininity

---

[6]Barth, *Church Dogmatics* IV/1, p. 436.
[7]This concept of our being "life-givers" in our creation in the image of God was developed by John Kinney, dean of the Samuel DeWitt Proctor School of Theology (Virginia Union University), who was the Frank B. Mitchell Lecturer at Eastern Baptist Theological Seminary in February 1998.

that reacts through a jealous movement for feminist emancipation and a desire for a mechanically produced "equality." Both errors fail to see and understand first who God is and then who we are as created in his image. Both fail where they are most vulnerable, at the point of allowing self-definition to be wrapped up in another. As such, both reenact the Fall over and over again.

We are led inextricably to a sweeping conclusion. *Every* ethical, moral problem we face in our fallenness has at its very roots a misunderstanding of who God is and consequently a deceptive or deficient understanding of who we are as God's creation. Take racism for example. For racism to exist there must be either ignorance or a direct rejection of the Father revealed to us in the Son in the power of the Spirit. To be racist we must believe that we are someone other than the child and creation of the triune God of grace. We must believe that God is some other God than the Father of our Lord Jesus Christ. Or we must believe in no God at all! When we come to know God through Christ, we can see only our need for mercy and redemption. We can see only the love of God for all humanity evidenced both in the creation and the incarnation. When we see God in Christ, we can only see the common cause of all humanity before God. We as his redeemed can only see our brothers and sisters of every race and kind as one like us and with us, rescued together from our sinfulness by the mercy of God. The root cause of racism is the sin of ignorance, ignorance of who our God is—the triune God of grace—which leads to an ignorance of who we are—children in the kingdom of the triune God of grace.

That is again why this study is focusing so intently on a proper methodology for the call to be a steward. If we get this wrong, all other good and right and helpful things we may say about steward*ship* are founded on sinking sand. They simply will not hold up under the pressure of any Christian ethic in our postmodern world. The reason why this is so critical to the church is that the care for our relationship to God, our relationship to one another, our relationship to our self and our relationship to our creation *is a stewardship issue!* To be a steward in the kingdom of the triune God of grace is to understand our fallenness and its effect on all four levels, and to understand the grace of God and the work of Christ that brings redemption and wholeness to all four levels. Our work is the compassionate, obedient and ultimately thrilling task of stewarding each relationship for the building of the kingdom and the glory of God.

The Loss of the Self

To all that has been said, we must add some additional comments about the loss of the relationship we have to ourselves as a result of the Fall. Every act of sin, no matter to whom or what it is directed, is ultimately a sin against oneself. To sin is to perpetuate the lie that we are still slaves to sin, that evil still holds sway over us, that we have not been "bought with a price," that we are still under the penalty of sin and death. When we sin we become someone other than who we truly are in Christ. We become as stranger to ourselves. This is the root of the problem of the loss of our self in our sinfulness and fall.

To understand the root of the loss we must return for a moment to the first couple standing naked and unashamed in the Garden. We said above that there was no possibility of a self-definition that did not include the other in relation. To know oneself was to know oneself in relation to God, to the other and to creation. There was no act in which the abstract self was considered. To be human meant to be male and female together. It meant to be creatures of God in fellowship with God. It meant to be caretaker and partaker of creation. Humanity had no basis for reality apart from these relationships. Therefore the "self" was confident, at peace and whole as it participated in that which gave it its definition, meaning, purpose and function.

We can say too that to be human was to be steward, for the work of stewardship was the natural result of these relationships. The self-understanding of the first couple was realized not only by who they were but by what they did. They were stewards. Their command was to be fruitful, multiply and replenish the earth. Their command was to have dominion and care for the earth just as God has modeled dominion and care for them and all creation. Being stewards and following these commands were part of their self-understanding. "Being" and "doing" were enmeshed in our original created state.

The most significant thing we can say about the effect of the Fall was that it caused the creature to lose self-identity. It became lost in that he or she was forced to consider it in abstraction. Instead of asking, "Who am I in relation to God?" he or she was forced to ask, "Who am I over and against God?" In other words, "Who am I alone?" Who is man without woman, woman without man, and woman and man over and against creation? If we can no longer define ourselves by our relationships because those relationships are broken, then we must define ourselves according to other criteria—inevitably foreign and counterfeit criteria. The rise of the self and the search for self-understanding and meaning have created a new standard for self-definition and understanding and therefore a new set of criteria to measure self-meaning and purpose. It should not be surprising that this new set of criteria is ensnarled in the deception that has come with our fallenness at all other relational levels. It is wrapped up in terms of power, dominance, personal happiness, self-actualization and gratification. It is the prize that we will sell our souls to gain. It is the end that will be able to justify any and all means, no matter how hurtful, exploitative, devious or perverse. We must have some purpose to our lives or we will lose either our will to live or our sanity. Barth comments,

> All human life is either the quiet and anxious striving or the noisy hunt for this thing, developing into bitter conflict for it, and finally ending in sad or cynical but always weary resignation when the earth has been ransacked for it in vain and it has not been found. It cannot be found, because the help in which man can be his own helper, the salvation which he can prepare and make for himself, is an illusion.[8]

By allowing sin into God's created world we have not only lost our relationship to God and each other, but we have lost our very self-definition. We have become deceivers to ourselves, and we now must seek to find purpose and meaning in some other form. In all of this we must never lose sight of the fact that in the eyes of God we never ceased being his beloved creation. The covenant of God with us, where he would be our God and we would be his people, was established for us before creation and in view to the work of Jesus Christ to restore to us what was lost in the Fall. Our loss of self-definition does not nullify the fact that we are still ontologically defined as the creatures of God. That ultimate self-definition will never be lost as long as God is the God of the covenant.

What we struggle with is sin's ability to keep us from seeing this as our true reality. We struggle to see in us what God sees in us through Christ Jesus. We are pulled into the world's mold and asked to give an account of our success, of our achievements and therefore of the purpose of our existence according to these measurements. We struggle with the world's definition of us. And we struggle with the person we see in the faces of those with whom we have less than perfect relationships. In the end we

---

[8]Barth, *Church Dogmatics* IV/1, p. 460.

struggle to see our worth, which is great in the eyes of God, when the bro-kenness that marks our relationships at every level feeds back to us our utter worthlessness. This is the state we find ourselves in: the loss of our self-definition in the sin of Eden.

The other side of this problem is the choice we make to replace that loss of self-definition with alien definitions. The enemy will always be more than glad to offer sumptuous substitutes for our self-definition as children in the kingdom of the triune God of grace. It began in Eden with "I am an individual man" and "I am an individual woman." These new definitions were twisted substitutes for "I am man with woman" and "I am woman with man." From individuality we have moved to a seem-ingly limitless array of self-definitions. Whether they are formed from natural traits, behaviors, social circumstances, achievements or patterns of reinforcement from others, they always stand on very shaky ground. In some cases they can be formed through self-deception or through the deception of the society. In every case, if they are formed and held prior to or in defiance of God's definition of us, they are wholly inaccurate and can only work for our destruction.

Christian ethics should force us to look again at our self-definitions in light of our creation in the image of God. Whatever attributes make up our self-perception, they must all come under the authority and lordship of the great definition given to us in the covenant established for us by God in Jesus Christ before the creation of the world. We are first God's child. We are first children in the kingdom of the triune God of grace. All other self-perceptions must come under that all-encompassing reality. To do this, we must become stewards of our self-perceptions. We must be caretakers of our self-definition that we do not allow alien perceptions to distort our self-understanding as children of God. We can only do that with the assistance of the Holy Spirit and in full knowledge of what was done for us in the work of Jesus Christ.

The Loss of Our Union with Creation

We have seen how the Fall affected our status on every level of relation-ship in which we were created. In sin we stand over against God. In a struggle for power, purpose and position we stand against our neighbor. And in search of meaning and self-definition we stand against ourselves. The effect of the Fall on our relationship to God's creation is none the less devastating or alienating. It also stems from the awareness of our self as abstract individuals and the development of our understanding of our needs and wants also *in abstracto.*

One defining mark of this fallenness is the shift in our self-understanding from steward to owner. This is a considerable shift! In defiance of the God who gives us all things freely, we become takers, usurpers actually of that which we can never ultimately own. This is a subtle distinction that we must speak of with great care. It is not ownership per se that is wrong. It is absolute ownership. That is, ownership may be necessary given our economic system and human needs. We may own a house, a car, furniture, clothing and the like. But this ownership can never be anything more than a pseudo-ownership, a "temporary use permit" allowing access to some resources in distinction to others. The problem here is twofold.

First, the sense of temporary ownership, which acknowledges that God remains always the ultimate and rightful owner of everything, is very hard to maintain. This goes back to Eden and the grasp at power to choose, to control, to stand on one's own over and against God. This sinful tendency makes it nigh impossible not to be swept up in the "right" of absolute ownership. It is our nature (our fallen nature) to take, to possess, to mark off our boundaries, to build our empires and to better our own lot in life with things that promise happiness, purpose and meaning.

Second, ownership carries with it both a positive and negative allure. Its positive side is in its ability to control something for our own use. Its negative but just as seductive side is that when we control an asset, we deny it to others. This quieter, more subtle side of ownership is seldom spoken of because I fear we really hate to admit it. However, when I own something in an absolute way, I control others simply by making that asset unavailable to them. It is really *mine!* It is part of what I have demarcated as my kingdom. It is mine in contradistinction to its being either "yours," or "anybody's" or even "mine unless you need it." Absolute ownership is a power we can exhibit over others. What we own not only defines us as successful, but it defines us as powerful. This is the darker and more subtle side of absolute ownership.

Alongside the move from steward to owner, there is a second shift that occurs when our relationship to creation ceases to be a part of our self-definition. Here we also begin to see creation in respect to its ability to supply us our needs and fulfill our desires. We value it for its contribution to our happiness, our success and our personal well-being; all of which are part of our new, alien definition of purpose and meaning in life. Creation ceases to have inherent value, and so stewardship ceases to make sense unless it is linked with some potential use for creation that serves our needs. We may be "stewards" of our community parks so that we can use them for our pleasure. We may be "stewards" of our money so that we can have plenty to spend on what we please. We may be "stewards" of our relationships so that people will be there when we need them. In whatever form, our attempt to be stewards in the midst of this fallenness inevitably means that we will find a way for it to be self-serving. If we are honest, it is very difficult to undertake a stewarding task without some ulterior motive. Such is the predominance of sin at this and at all four levels.

The end product of fallenness in this whole arena of creation is directly associated with the challenge to be stewards. It is most prevalent at this point because in this fourth area we are called not only to steward the relationship but to steward the resources themselves. This is why most all stewardship studies focus almost entirely in this fourth area. We are attempting a more balanced, theological approach, but we must say that there is a special understanding of the call to be a steward that is seen here more than at any other level.

This then is the effect of sin at all four levels. Left to ourselves we find the entire notion of stewardship meaningless. A theology of the steward must take seriously the brokenness of these relationships and the reality of sin. If we do not understand the depth of this brokenness, we will not respond with the gratitude and joy that distinguishes the life of the steward. That gratitude and joy flows from the truth of the gospel message that all four levels of relationship are assumed and redeemed in the incarnation, life, death and resurrection of Jesus Christ for us. Our theology of the steward must be built on both the seriousness of the sin that profoundly distorted our created relationships and the even greater restoration of those relationships in Christ. We will now turn to this great work of love and redemption for us.

Chapter 5

The Faithful Steward

WE CANNOT LEAVE HUMANITY IN THIS PRECARIOUS STATE: attempting but failing to be stewards at these four levels of broken relationships. We cannot leave humanity in this state because God did not leave humanity in this state. Indeed, if he had, there would be no need for stewardship studies; obedience and servanthood would be beyond definition and impossible to carry out. The entire theology of stewardship is based not only on the creation of these relationships but on their re-creation in the work of Jesus Christ. It is for this re-creation that the world was created, as we have seen. The goodness of creation lay in its ability to be the place where these relationships would be restored and raised to a higher level in Christ. The goodness in creation was preparation of the creation for the incarnation, through which would come salvation, reconciliation and hope. God's answer to our sinful desire "to be like God" was his eternal choice to become like us—the Word made flesh!

In speaking of the restoration of all things in Christ, we must avoid a misunderstanding that often creeps into atonement studies. The basis for all understandings of God's salvific work in Jesus Christ is the incarnation. If we miss the rich understanding of what happened there, we will stray down a path that leads to a distorted and less than truly biblical view of the atonement. To lead us down the right path, we will look at three aspects of the incarnation in which Jesus Christ assumed our humanity, reconciled these broken relationships and now calls us to participate in his great work of reconciliation as stewards in his kingdom.

Who Is This Jesus of Nazareth?

The temptation in the first place is to downplay the full significance of God assuming our humanity. This temptation can lead in a number of false directions, but let us look at a few that seem to gain the most popularity.

Throughout the history of the church there has been a recurring theme among some theologians to see in Jesus a supreme human example but nothing more. We are called to follow him that we may be good and moral and embrace servanthood as "Christians." If Jesus is our moral example, then the incarnation says nothing more than Jesus was truly a human being. Therefore, he felt what we felt, lived as we lived and died as we will die. Because he was "truly man" his example has efficacy. Because he was not above the pains and fears of this world, his life really can inspire us to "live as Jesus lived," to be better people and to love our neighbors as ourselves. An effort is made here to focus on the historicity of Jesus' time on earth in order to construct an accurate portrayal of the human Jesus devoid of the "mythology" and supernaturalism of sympathetic interpreters. This is referred to as a theology *from below*. Often the divinity of Christ is either questioned here or pushed to the back as either not important or at best not verifiable.

The challenge in this understanding of the work of Jesus Christ is that we are simply thrown back upon ourselves to work for reconciliation when nothing ultimately has changed. "In that case the covenant would still have not received a permanent basis."[1] This Christ showed us how to live, but he left us the same. Our hope lies only in our ability to imitate Christ, which we can do no more successfully than the children of Israel who were repeatedly called to be obedient followers of Yahweh. Relationships remain broken, and while we may have a blueprint for how they were once healed in one day and time by one person, this example will fall woefully short of providing us the means for doing the same our-

[1]Hendrikus Berkhof, *Christian Faith* (Grand Rapids, Mich.: Eerdmans, 1979), p. 287.

selves. We are left here with the same sinful nature, operating in the same sinful world, with our hope resting on our good intentions and improved motivations.

It is interesting here that this view of the work of Christ is nothing more than a return to Genesis 3. Once again we are required to "know good and evil," and in that knowing to choose the good and reject the evil. The only difference is that now we try to do it "just as Jesus did." But it is still our work. That is why it so utterly and completely fails. If Jesus is only our moral example, our good teacher, one prophetic voice raising up one more world religion, then our ability to respond as stewards in this kingdom has no power, no hope and no sure foundation. This is a devastating dead end that must be rejected as we consider our call as stewards in the kingdom of the triune God of grace.

Another path we may take is to see Jesus Christ as a divine being that came to us to save our souls out from this sinful and fallen world. The incarnation was merely a way of saying that Jesus had a veil of flesh that allowed him to live among us, but he was always completely divine and separate from our sinful human nature. After all, how could the holy and divine Son bear human, sinful flesh? Here we see the resurrection of the old Platonic dualism where the material things of creation are treated as sinful and worthy only of destruction. The goal of salvation here is the saving of the immortal soul.

To effect this salvation, the incarnation only required of Jesus that he look like us and be able to live among us. It also required that he must never really be like us. He did not feel pain, know anger, fear, frustration, hunger, etc. After all, how could the almighty God feel such things? And even worse, this would place God in too close a contact with the sinfulness of the creature. In this approach, whatever the incarnation meant, the Son's divinity was never touched by the momentary, detached and utilitarian act of becoming flesh.

The work of Christ for us in this view becomes similar to the work of a doctor for us when we are ill. Jesus' life, death and resurrection purchased for us the remedy for our sin that will save our souls for eternity. What Jesus did *for* us he did *separate from* us, not as one of us or even one like us. His atoning work was as a divine spirit clothed in perfect flesh that he might offer us an antidote for this life-threatening illness we call sin. And so he comes to us to offer us salvation as a doctor offers a wonder drug. It is ours to accept and take and live, or to reject and die.

There is in this view a possible help for our relationship with God. This offer of salvation does carry with it a new relationship with God in which sin no longer yields the sentence of death. In this way there seems to be some reconciliation for us in this first level of relationship. However, this picture is fractured and far from complete. Again, nothing ultimately has changed. We are still sinners before God, we are still at enmity with one another, we are left devaluing the human side of our being and we have no basis to care for a creation that gets no mention in this brand of "salvation." We have a long-term assurance for our soul, but we are left with a muddled picture of who we are, who God is and how we are to live in the meantime. "If he were not a man, his way within humanity would be an isolated spectacle, of no concern to us."[2] This is referred to as a *theology from above.*

These two views have also historically been labeled "ebionism" (rejection of Jesus' divinity) and "docetism" (rejection of Jesus' true humanity). They both find new champions in each generation, often in more subtle forms. What we must recognize is that each is wholly inadequate to provide the basis upon which we can live with confidence as stewards in the kingdom of the triune God of grace. Whenever you hear people speak or read an "expert" in theology and come across descriptions of the work of Christ that seek in any way to lift up his divinity over and against his humanity, or his humanity over and against his divinity, your suspicions should be raised. Scripture tells us, and our church doctrine for nearly two thousand years has confirmed to us, that Jesus Christ was fully God and fully human and, as the Chalcedonian formula aptly put it, these two natures were "distinct but not separate."

Why is this so important to our study of stewardship? We have made the point that we are stewards of relationships at four levels and that our call to be stewards is a response to the grace of the God who created us for this service. It is only in a proper understanding of the incarnate Christ and his work that we can know the fullness of the restoration of these relationships. It is only here that we can understand our nature as we stand before God and our responsibility as we stand by our neighbor, with ourselves and in our created world. We have tried hard to understand the depth and radical nature of the brokenness of these relationships. It is critical here that we understand the extent of the restoration of

---

[2]Ibid.

all things in the incarnate Christ.

We also have said that the foundation for this study is our ability to know who our God is, if we are called to be stewards of this God in this God's kingdom as this God's children. It is only in the full appreciation of the work of the Son to bring us back into relationship with the Father that we have access to this sure and life-changing knowledge. "Salvation is possible not only because Jesus was fully divine, but precisely because Jesus was fully human. Jesus is not just the revealer of authentic humanity, he ontologically establishes it. His humanly divine life is not just the model for others' lives. His life is the basis for other's life."[3] This is the joyful and complete understanding of the great statement, "God was reconciling the world to himself in Christ" (2 Cor 5:19).

Finally, we must know how to act, to respond and to serve as stewards. We can only do so if we understand the way in which this great salvation was won for us. For these reasons this discussion is of the utmost importance to our study. We will proceed here looking at a third view of the incarnation that seeks to be true to the historic formulation of the Christian faith.

The Vicarious Humanity of Christ

Perhaps no place in all of Scripture gives us a better look at the two sides of the nature of Christ than the book of Hebrews. The author in Hebrews is seeking to maintain that Jesus of Nazareth was indeed the Messiah, the anointed one of God. It was crucial that the early church, made up of converted Jews, understood and accepted the full divinity of Christ. Therefore, the book opens with the memorable words,

> In the past God spoke to our forefathers through the prophets at many times and in various ways, but in these last days he has spoken to us by his Son, whom he appointed heir of all things, and through whom he made the universe. The Son is the radiance of God's glory and the exact representation of his being, sustaining all things by his powerful word. (Heb 1:1-3)

This is one of many places where the divinity of the Son is powerfully demonstrated. The full divinity of Jesus Christ as the second person of the Trinity is the foundation of the Christian faith. Salvation is only possible if God himself bore our sins on Calvary, defeated evil and conquered death for us. This is the core of our faith.

---

[3]Timothy Dearborn, "God, Grace and Salvation," in *Christ in Our Place,* ed. Trevor A. Hart and Daniel P. Thimell (Exeter, U.K.: Paternoster Press, 1989), p. 287.

Yet this core speaks also to the humanity of Christ as well as to his divinity. It was "our sins" he bore, it was "our humanity" that he saved and it was "our flesh" that was redeemed from death and destruction. The writer of Hebrews knew how critical it was that his readers understood this side of Christ's nature fully and without hesitation. Therefore, he went on to say,

> Since the children have flesh and blood, he too shared in their humanity so that by his death he might destroy him who holds the power of death—that is, the devil. . . . For this reason he had to be made like his brothers in every way, in order that he might become a merciful and faithful high priest in service to God and that he might make atonement for the sins of the people. Because he himself suffered when he was tempted, he is able to help those who are being tempted. (Heb 2:14-18)

Here the writer of Hebrews gives an uncompromising testimony of the full humanity of Christ and the salvific purpose for which such humanity was required. Only by sharing in the fullness of our sinful humanity could Jesus save that humanity in death and resurrection. Ray Anderson writes, "The humanity of Christ brings all humanity under the judgement in order to bring it under the gracious work of renewal and reconciliation through resurrection."[4] Here we must affirm and remember the great words of the Cappadocian divines, "the unassumed is the unredeemed!" If there was any part of our human nature that Christ did not assume fully in the incarnation, then it remains outside of his redemptive work for us. Praise be to God that Christ assumed it all! Therefore, Anderson can conclude, "The humanity of the church is thus grounded ontologically, not merely ethically, on the humanity and ministry of Jesus Christ."[5]

This does not mean that Christ was sinful, for Scripture tells us clearly the opposite. It does mean that his incarnation did not stop short of uniting him with us in a way that caused him to share in our sinful human nature and therefore to bear the penalty for that sinfulness. This is how we are to understand that he was "like us in every way yet without sin" and also that he "bore our sins on the tree."

Christ as the Faithful High Priest
The writer of Hebrews introduces us to the work of Christ as the "merci-

---

[4]Ray Anderson, "Christopraxis: Christ's Ministry for the World," in *Christ in Our Place,* ed. Trevor A. Hart and Daniel P. Thimell (Exeter, U.K.: Paternoster Press, 1989), p. 14.
[5]Ibid.

ful and faithful high priest" (1:17). This title is rich with meaning in the Jewish tradition, and we must understand it for our study of the steward. It defines *how* we are to be stewards because it defines our relationship to the God who called us to be stewards in his kingdom.

In the Old Testament, God established the Levitical priesthood for the children of Israel centered on the temple as the house of God and sacrifice for the atonement of sins. Throughout the year people would offer sacrifices for sins in the courtyard of the temple with the help of the Levitical priests. However, once a year, on the Day of Atonement *(Yom Kippur)* all of Israel would gather at the temple for the offering of the sins of the whole nation before God for his forgiveness. On this day the high priest would act *on behalf of the entire nation* in making atonement for sins. The ceremonial vestments of the high priest included the ephod (a tunic-like vest) and the "breastplate of judgement" upon which were the precious stones representing the twelve tribes of Israel. This symbolized the vicarious work of the high priest for all the nation. On *Yom Kippur,* however, the high priest was dressed only in plain linen, for this was a solemn day of repentance. In the ceremony the high priest offers a sacrifice of an unblemished lamb and carries the blood through the curtain that conceals the room called the holy of holies, where the ark of the covenant sat. In this room the high priest stood in the presence of the almighty God, and death was assured for anyone who entered it other than the high priest on this one day. The high priest would cover the mercy seat on the top of the ark with the blood of the lamb and pray for forgiveness for the sins of the people. If forgiveness was granted, the high priest would return back out to the front of the temple, raise his arms and declare God's favor for another year. This ceremony stood at the center of Jewish faith, and it defined Israel's relationship to God as mediated through sacrifice and intercession on behalf of the high priest.[6]

Think now what these words in Hebrews meant to the early Jewish converts to Christianity!

> When Christ came as high priest of the good things that are already here, he went through the greater and more perfect tabernacle that is not man-made. . . . He did not enter by the means of the blood of goats and calves; but he

---

[6]Two helpful resources on this subject are Alfred Edersheim, *The Temple: Its Ministry and Services* (Peabody, Mass.: Hendrickson, 1994); and Ervin N. Hershberger, *Seeing Christ in the Tabernacle* (Meyersdale: Choice Books, 1995).

entered the Most Holy Place once for all by his own blood, having obtained eternal redemption. . . . For this reason Christ is the mediator of a new covenant. . . . For Christ did not enter a man-made sanctuary that was only a copy of the true one; he entered heaven itself, now to appear for us in God's presence. . . . Now he has appeared once for all at the end of the ages to do away with sin by the sacrifice of himself. . . And by that will, we have been made holy through the sacrifice of the body of Jesus Christ once for all. (Heb 9:11, 12, 15, 24, 26; 10:10)

Here we can see the significance of the splitting of the curtain leading to the Most Holy Place when Christ died on Calvary. The split curtain is the sign that the eternal high priest now stands before God *for us* as our mediator. The work of Christ means that our understanding of the face of God has changed forever. He is no longer the feared God who hides behind the curtain in the temple demanding sacrifice and speaking through prophets. The writer of Hebrews spells out the full merit of the work of Christ in one of the most beautiful passages in all of Scripture (and my favorite!),

Therefore, since we have a great high priest who has gone through the heavens, Jesus the Son of God, let us hold firmly to the faith we profess. For we do not have a high priest who is unable to sympathize with our weaknesses, but we have one who has been tempted in every way, just as we are—yet without sin. Let us then approach the throne of grace with confidence, so that we may receive mercy and find grace to help us in our time of need. (Heb 4:14-16)

This is what it means that Jesus is our great High Priest. It holds together the richness of the full divinity and the full humanity of Christ. Only as fully human could he represent us in his atoning work, and only as fully divine could that work be efficacious for all humanity for all time.

The reconciliation of all things to God can be achieved only by him who is at once Christ the creator *and* a human being who restores the project of creation to its proper destiny by what he does. Because he is Christ the mediator of creation, he is of universal significance. But because he is Jesus of Nazareth, who lived, taught, acted as the agent of the eschatological kingdom, suffered, died and was raised, his universal significance is realized in this particular way.[7]

This understanding of the work of Christ also tells us that the reconcil-

---

[7]Colin Gunton, *The Promise of Trinitarian Theology* (Edinburgh, U.K.: T & T Clark, 1991), p. 186.

ing work of God for us in Jesus Christ has been fulfilled. The relationship between sinful humanity and our holy God has been redeemed in this priestly work of his Son for us. "Salvation is not simply *by* Christ, as if he died to purchase blessings for humanity that can be received upon fulfillment of the conditions of repentance, faith and obedience. Rather, salvation is *in* Christ, as one participates through the Spirit in his perfect life of repentance, faith and obedience lived vicariously on humanity's behalf."[8] There is nothing that is left to be done as in the docetic or ebionite views of the atonement. For us to add anything to this work is to strip Christ of his priesthood and proclaim that there is yet another act that must occur for atonement to be complete. This we must not do.

Legal Versus Evangelical Response

Even our repentance is a response to the grace already bestowed upon us. James Torrance speaks of two types of repentance: "legal" and "evangelical."[9] Evangelical repentance means we understand that we are not saved by our repentance, but we are driven to our knees by the proclamation of the gospel, which shows us our sin in the light of the gracious work of Jesus Christ to overcome that sin. Our response to the gospel of grace is repentance. Therefore, repentance follows grace, not the other way around.

Legal repentance means that we allow grace only to follow repentance where our act of repentance is a condition of grace. If we follow this path, we fall back into a works righteousness that the Protestant church has been fighting since the Reformation. We also undo the priestly work of Christ and find a place for ourselves in our own salvation. This distorted understanding of the nature of repentance and grace would also make us part owners of the relationship at this level instead of the thankful stewards we are called to be. When our salvation is partly our doing, our relationship with God comes under the realm of our control. We return to Eden to grasp some control for ourselves instead of trusting our gracious God who tells us that he has done it all. On the other hand, when we see repentance following the completed work of Christ for us, then we can truly be stewards of a relationship that is a gift from God from beginning to end. That is why it is so critical that we understand that our repentance

---

[8]Dearborn, "God, Grace and Salvation," p. 284.
[9]James B. Torrance, *Worship, Community and the Triune God of Grace* (Carlisle, U.K.: Paternoster Press, 1996), pp. 43-55.

is a response to grace and not a condition of grace.

There is an important place for our response in this relationship. It does not undermine the fact that our relationship to God has been fully restored in Christ. It does mean that while we cannot undo it, we can deny it, reject it and live in rebellion against it. We can act as children of the devil, we can side with evil, we can scorn our mediator, but we cannot resew the curtain back together. The blood of Christ has atoned for all humanity, and therefore our relationship with God is forever changed. We can choose against that grace, we can choose for hell and our own destruction, but that does not change the work of God for us in Christ. Our choice effects how we will respond to God's grace and gracious calling, whether we participate as children of God or rebel as children of the devil. However, it does not add or take away from the completed work of Christ for us or the redemption won for all humanity on the cross. That is why our life-long response is the work of the steward and not the owner. That is why grace is truly grace and not merit.

Even our response is an act of participation in the one great response made for all humanity in Christ Jesus. He lived the life we could not, he was the faithful one, the sinless one, the one who knew perfect union and communion with the Father. He prayed for us, was baptized for us, was obedient for us, died for us and rose for us. He has made the perfect confession for us, and now we are called to participate in that response with our own "amen." "Our response in faith and obedience is a response to the Response already made for us by Christ to the Father's holy love, a response we are summoned to make in union with Christ."[10]

We are called by the Holy Spirit to participate in the priestly work of Christ through our acceptance of this incredibly gracious act and our life-long commitment to steward this precious relationship established for us in Christ Jesus. As we do, we must never, not for one moment, allow this work of stewardship to become solely our work. We cannot act as the priest ourselves. We cannot take over the mediatorial work of Christ for us. We cannot stand on our own before the throne as if it was now our right apart from Christ. Everything that transpires between us and God in this new covenant does so solely through our participation in the already completed work of Christ. "A theology of participation integrates our faith and our works as a grateful response to the initiating faithfulness of God and makes

---

[10]Ibid., p. 43.

discipleship an ongoing and natural development of faith."[11]

This is why we pray to the Father in the name of and for the sake of the Son and in the power of the Spirit. That is why our worship is directed to the Father in the name of the Son and in the Spirit. Our relationship to God is trinitarian and Christocentric. It has direction, and it calls us to a life of service as servants of God in Christ. When we talk about stewardship of this first level of relationship, broken by our sin and reconciled and restored by the priestly work of Christ, this call to participation in Christ is the way in which we must speak. This is the biblical concept of stewardship as gracious response that runs throughout Scripture. It is not an autonomous act that is somehow glued onto our profession of faith but the one act of accepting what has been done for us in Christ and participating through prayer, worship, devotion and service, in the priestly work of the one we now call our Lord and Savior.

Here then is a critical moment for this study of the steward. Here we have said that our salvation and our understanding of our call to be stewards are based on our participation of an act already completed for us. This critical truth carries through the relationship between stewarding and owning at all four levels in which we were created. Once we shift our understanding of these reconciled relationships from our joyous response to a sense of our *required* work, then we move from steward to owner. We shift from being the gracious recipient of a gift to be treasured and stewarded to the owner and cocreator with legal rights and the ability to control and use these relationships to our own benefit. Whether it is the understanding of the grace of God for us in Christ, our place and vocation as the creatures of God in this world, our fellowship and communion with our neighbors or our standing and relationship with God's created world in which we live, our call to be stewards is based on our acceptance of each as a gracious gift and our rejection of the lure to play the owner. Each level was broken by sin and has been redeemed and given back to us in and through Christ Jesus. Each is a gift that needs nothing added to be "complete." Each calls to us to accept this redemption with humility, to participate at each level with joy and to enter into our call to steward each relationship with gratitude and passion. Each calls for an evangelical response and not a legal act. This is the foundation for a theology of the

---

[11]Roger Newell, "Participation and Atonement," in *Christ in Our Place*, ed. Trevor A. Hart and Daniel P. Thimell (Exeter, U.K.: Paternoster Press, 1989), p. 96.

steward. Everything we have said and will say stands or falls on this point.

Christ as the Faithful Servant

Once we have established "participation" as the means by which we fulfill our call as stewards, the restoration of all four levels of relationship in Christ becomes much easier to understand. We have dealt with the first level under the high priestly work of Christ. The restoration of the second and third levels of relationships can be seen in the servanthood of Christ. As priest, Jesus did once for all what the earthly high priest of Israel could only do provisionally, temporarily and in anticipation. As faithful servant, Jesus completed in his life, death and resurrection the work to which we were called but that we, as sinners, cannot do. Moltmann describes the "three-dimensional person of Jesus Christ" as being *eschatological, theological* and *social.* These refer to Jesus as the initiator of the kingdom of God *(Messiah);* as the revealer of God *(childlike human being)* and as brother of the poor and forsaken and of creation *(brotherly and sisterly human being).* This is a helpful way of understanding the four levels of the redemptive work of Christ. As he rightly points out, "Merely to take account of any single one of these dimensions in Jesus' person as the Christ leads to a one-sidedness that has fatal consequences."[12]

In Jesus' life we have demonstrated the right relationship we seek with ourselves and with our neighbor. Jesus lived the life we could not live. He was obedient where we were disobedient; he was faithful where we were faithless; he was a neighbor when we passed by on the other side. He knew who he was, why he was here, what his ministry was to accomplish. He knew his place before God, in the world and among his people. He did all of this while bearing our humanity. He completed in his life and confirmed in his death and resurrection the full requirements of the original relationship between God and his creature. By doing so, Jesus Christ redeemed our relationships at these two levels.

By redeeming our relationship to God, Jesus offers us back our own self-understanding. We can once again know who we are because we know *whose* we are. We can put aside the distortions that sin would inject into our self-awareness, and we can see ourselves, body, mind and spirit, as belonging to the God who created us for fellowship and redeemed us

---

[12]Jürgen Moltmann, *The Way of Jesus Christ* (London: SCM Press, 1990), p. 149.

in his Son. Jesus Christ bore our distorted self-image, our egocentricism, our self-hatred, our aimless quest for purpose and our self-disillusionment. We are now invited back into a right relationship with ourselves through our participation in the ministry of the one who redeemed us and through whom we have access to our Creator. The process of nurturing, strengthening and guarding that relationship we have with ourselves in the power of the Holy Spirit is the work of the steward. Again here we do not do it before Christ, after Christ or beside Christ, for in each we again are thrown back upon ourselves ultimately to fail. We are stewards here only as we participate *in* Christ in his work as the faithful servant of God. This participation is the work of the steward.

By redeeming our relationship to God, Jesus also calls us into a right relationship with our neighbor. The enmity and strife that was evidenced immediately in Eden, that was confirmed just as immediately by Cain, and that now characterizes our nation and our world was also assumed by Christ. His "becoming flesh" meant his assumption of this discord. His death for the sins of the world meant his overcoming this strife. His resurrection meant that we can now participate in his work of reconciliation. He has taken back our brokenness, assumed it, redeemed it and now calls us to himself to be children in his kingdom where we are empowered to live in right relationships with our neighbor.

The nature of this new kingdom that has come among us in the work of Christ is complete yet also transitional. It is complete in that it is the kingdom of the Son whose work to restore all things is complete. It is transitional in that it has come into this sinful world that does not know this restoration has been made for it at every level. Humanity still seeks to be God and thirsts for the control of Eden and therefore chooses evil over good. It rebels against grace and therefore chooses destruction over life. It still plays the owner in its legal understanding of relationships and therefore chooses exploitation and abuse over stewardship. Into this world the kingdom of God has come, and so we see it only in glimpses, only in the lives of those who have been called into that kingdom, who have repented in the face of grace and who have embraced the role of steward with joy. Hebrews 2 shows us this twofold nature of the kingdom of God in the work of Christ,

> You made him a little lower than the angels; you crowned him with glory
> and honor and put everything under his feet. In putting everything under

him, God left nothing that is not subject to him. Yet at present we do not see everything subject to him. But we see Jesus, who was made a little lower than the angels, now crowned with glory and honor because he suffered death, so that by the grace of God he might taste death for everyone. (Heb 2:7-9)

We see Jesus! That is the result of the work of the steward. In a world that sees everything but under Christ's control, people still see Jesus in the lives of the workers of his kingdom. The kingdom of God has come in the work of Christ. "God left nothing that is not subject to him." There is nothing that needs to be added to complete the kingdom or to usher it in from some heavenly waiting room. It is here in Christ, and we are the body of Christ!

The evidence of this new kingdom is found in the lives of the people of the kingdom who live as stewards in a world of owners. We proclaim the restoration of all things in Christ. That is the gospel that calls men and women to repentance and wholeness as children in the kingdom of the triune God of grace. We live as ones who have received an invaluable gift—restored relationships at all four levels in Christ. And so we respond by entering into our call to be stewards of these relationships, rejecting the temptation to take control, to add a legal requirement to a gracious gift, to abuse and exploit, to own and put into service for our own benefit or as an act of our own quest for self-actualization. By accepting this vocation and by rejecting these temptations, we live as children of Christ's kingdom. And as we do, the world around us is given a glimpse of the fact that all things are indeed in subjection to Christ. They are given a glimpse of the true reality of their creaturely existence. They are given a glimpse of what will be revealed in its fullness at the second coming of the Son, when what is now only seen in glimpses will be manifest in all creation. They are given a glimpse of Jesus.

In the kingdom of God the values that guide our lives are born out of our participation in the faithful servanthood of Christ. As we enter into these newly redeemed relationships as stewards, we begin to see with the mind of Christ and act in obedience to these kingdom values. We will spell these out in more detail in chapter seven, but here we must raise the point that restored relationships with our neighbor mean that we "see" our neighbor differently than before. Restored relationships on this horizontal level mean that we return to our creation in the image of a triune God for whom relationships form a self-definition. We realize that our relationship with our neighbor constitutes our own self-understanding.

We can no longer reckon with ourselves *in abstracto*. We have been redeemed from isolation and individuality into mutual dependence and community life. Our relationship with our neighbor is now a description of who we are, and our strife with our neighbor throws our self-definition into confusion. We are God's children in and through our stewardship of our relationship with our neighbor. With this understanding of the vital role of the restoration of our relationships to our lives as Christians, listen again to these powerful verses:

> Do not lie to each other, since you have taken off you old self with its practices and have put on the new self, which is being renewed in knowledge in the image of its Creator. Here there is no Greek or Jew, circumcised or uncircumcised, barbarian, Scythian, slave or free, but Christ is all, and is in all. (Col 3:9-11)

> You are all sons of God through faith in Christ Jesus, for all of you who were baptized into Christ have clothed yourselves with Christ. There is neither Jew nor Greek, slave nor free, male nor female, for you are all one in Christ Jesus. (Gal 3:26-28)

The unity of all in Christ is lived out in the life of the steward, in his and her participation in the life of the faithful servanthood of Christ.

Christ as the Faithful Steward

It may be dangerous for us to say even that our participation as stewards is "our work," for even here at this very final point our sinful nature seeks to rush in and secure a place of control for us back at the center of all things from which we have been redeemed and freed. It is too easy to say here that we have finally found a place where we can stand alone, on our own merit and in our own right to do our work alongside or in addition to the work of God for us in Christ. We must not falter at this last and crucial moment after all we have built to get us to this point.

Therefore, we must say that even our call to be stewards, even our joyous, evangelical response that we must make and even our work to be faithful stewards in the kingdom of God must be seen as our participation in the work of the one Faithful Steward and never separate from it. Douglas Hall has it exactly right, "The christological assumption of Christian stewardship is that as those who are (to use Paul's constant expression) 'in Christ' we are taken up into his stewardship."[13] If Jesus Christ

---

[13]Douglas John Hall, *The Steward* (Grand Rapids, Mich.: Eerdmans, 1990), p. 44.

assumed all of our fallen humanity, he assumed the sinfulness of the steward who gloats over the size of their gift in the donation plate next to the person whose change rattles at the bottom. It is the sin of the steward whose work for racial reconciliation must always be done in ways that are seen and admired and congratulated. It is the sin of the steward who wears his spiritual maturity like a blue ribbon, or her biblical acumen like a gaudy brooch. It is the sin of the Pharisee beside the publican, the mockers of the widow's mite, the disdain of the righteous at the extravagance of the costly perfume to anoint the feet of the Lord.

It is the sin of self-righteousness that finds a home at this last, final possible place in the life of the child of God. For this reason we must not lose sight of the fact that our work here is no different than our salvation; both are the result of God's work for us and in us, and to him alone be the honor and glory and praise. Here too, Jesus lived the life of the steward as we cannot. He stewarded his relationship with his Father, showing us what it means to be "sons of God." He stewarded his self-understanding, never letting the temptation of power, the lure of fame or the escape of suffering distract him from his calling. He stewarded his relationship to his neighbor and in a thousand ways showed us what that stewardship looked like. And he stewarded his relationship to the creation, using it in moderation, caring for it and teaching us our place in its midst.

At every level, that which the Son came to redeem, he stewarded for us. We are now called to participate as the body of Christ in that ongoing work of stewardship. It is not solely *our* work, but it is uniquely our *work*. If we can embrace the latter without falling victim to the former, we will truly be stewards in the kingdom of the triune God of grace.

Worship as the Life of the Steward

The invitation to participate in the life and work of the Faithful High Priest, the Faithful Servant and the Faithful Steward is an invitation to a life of worship. Worship is the center of the life of the steward. All of our life is and can only be a response to the grace of God for us, a participation in the work of Jesus Christ in and through his body, the church. Our work as stewards takes on the form of worship defined as a free and joyous response to the grace of God toward us in Jesus Christ.

This worship is the worship of our Creator, but it is not an escape from the world. Worship is that point at which we stand in the world, right in the center of it, receive it thankfully from God and offer it back with gratitude to God. In worship we recognize that the world is God's and that the death and resurrection of Jesus Christ will change not only our own lives but the very cosmos and creation in which we will live them, making not only a new heaven but a new earth.[14]

It is the life of discipleship in which obedience, sacrifice, taking up our cross and bearing each other's burdens are wholly redefined by the God who has redeemed us and called us to worship. At the same time joy, fulfillment, peace and contentment are redefined as well.

A theology of the steward is a theology of worship as a joyful response to the God who is for us in Jesus Christ. A steward is a new creation in Christ. A steward is a joyous servant in the kingdom of God. A steward is a child of the King. A steward has a mission and a purpose in life. A steward is one who knows God in real, personal and certain terms, and who knows that this God is for us. These are the foundations upon which a theology of the steward must be built.

A theology of the steward begins with the understanding that we have certain knowledge that our God is the triune God who created us for relationship, who is gracious toward us even in the face of sin and its devastation, who has redeemed us, and who in Jesus Christ calls us to himself for a fruitful life of fulfillment and joy. This God has established his kingdom on earth and has called us as his people to live in this kingdom, to exhibit its ethics, to be a light on a hill, an alternative to the lostness and brokenness of the world around us. We are, by definition, kingdom people. The world would try, through distortion and confusion, to pull us back into its own kingdom. As it does, we lose our way as stewards and consequently our purpose and our joy in life.

In the face of all of this, how is it that we fall back so easily into the sin of absolute ownership? This sin—this tendency to use ownership as power, the hoarding of resources as a form of self-definition and the sin implicit in all attempts to be stewards—culminates in the greatest single challenge to the church with regards to stewardship: the creation of a two-kingdom mentality among God's people. This is the subject of the next chapter. To set the scene let us just say here that this two-king-

---

[14]Fred Van Dyke, David Mahan, Joseph Sheldon and Raymond Brand, *Redeeming Creation: The Biblical Basis for Environmental Stewardship* (Downers Grove, Ill.: InterVarsity Press, 1996), p. 143.

dom understanding of reality is the result of sin at all four levels. It is a distortion of our relationship to God, to our neighbor, to our selves and to God's creation. It is a plastering of a vague and ill-defined notion of stewardship over the rotting walls of self-centeredness and sin.

In chapter four we have laid the groundwork for understanding the prevalence of its roots throughout every level of our existence. In this chapter we have understood how all brokenness has been assumed and redeemed in Christ. We have seen that we are called to live now as stewards in the joyous work of participation. Yet our lives remain marked by the vestiges of sin already redeemed and by brokenness already assumed and healed. The root cause of this latent sin is the persistence of a two-kingdom mentality that permeates the church and that threatens our witness as stewards in the kingdom of the triune God of grace. For that reason it stands as a modern-day Jericho. Until its walls come down, stewardship programs, events, teaching and even theological writings will have little impact in this vital area of discipleship. Let us now look squarely at this evil among us.

Chapter 6

The Myth of the
Two Kingdoms

"I did it my way."
FRANK SINATRA

HOW WONDERFUL IT WOULD BE TO HAVE ENDED THIS BOOK WITH
the last chapter. Imagine everyone in our world living in
the reality of healed and reconciled relationships at all four
levels. There would be no distortion in our understanding
of God as our gracious Creator and Lord. There would be no self-doubt or
empty arrogance in our own self-understanding. There would be no
enmity in our relationships one to another. There would be no exploitation of our creation but a godly care and nurture of our world. And there
would be no need for books on stewardship.

The reality in which we live, however, is somewhere between the coming of the kingdom of God in the life, death and resurrection of Jesus
Christ and the final universal establishment of that kingdom that we
await in his second coming. We live in that time of the "now" and the
"not yet." Now we see through a glass dimly. In this world the kingdom
of God has come in power and authority to those who believe on his
name. The powers and authorities of evil have been disarmed and

defeated by the cross of Calvary. We, the church, live as citizens of a new kingdom, and we believe that the reality of Christ's work is the basis of our existence and the substance of our hope. But for a little while, in this "time of the church," the kingdom of God has come in provisional form, and the powers and authorities of evil are still given the time and place to work. The focus of this study is not to understand why this is the case but to deal in real terms with the effects of these times on our call to be stewards in the kingdom of the triune God of grace.

In this time of the church in which we live, sin continues to eat away at our relationships at each of these levels, seeking to negate the reality of their full reconciliation in the work of Christ. It cannot do so. But it can so distort this reality that these relationships continue to have the most profound marks of absolute brokenness. We must never succumb to the temptation to believe that the brokenness we see is the reality. We must see this brokenness for what it is: a perversion of what has been set right by Jesus Christ. At the same time we must not underestimate the extent of the damage caused by this perversion.

One profound and insidious characteristic of the perverted state of all relationships is the rise and triumph of a second kingdom alongside the kingdom of God. We must be clear at this point. We are not talking about a phenomenon of the world outside the church. We are talking about a form of idolatry that has been allowed to rise in the midst of the church. It is those in the church who are called to be stewards in God's kingdom. It is to us that the good news of the restoration of all relationships in Jesus Christ has come and been heard and met with faith. And to our detriment and shame it is among those of us who are children in this new kingdom that this second, counterfeit kingdom has been given place and power to rise.

The Kingdom of This World

The basis of this new kingdom is the centrality of human existence and experience. The hope of this new kingdom is the glory and fulfillment of humanity as the central player in the created world. This is not a new story. From Adam and Eve, humanity has sought to carve out its own kingdom next to, on top of, or in place of God's. We have seen how this fundamental shift away from the kingdom of God caused a radical distortion in relationships at all four levels of human experience. We saw it in Eden, and we see it today. We can better understand this second kingdom by setting it side by side with the kingdom of God in terms of how both kingdoms view "reality." We will consider this earthly kingdom in this chapter and the kingdom of God in chapter seven.

Our Birth-to-Death Reality

The kingdom of this world operates exclusively on the understanding that human reality is marked by birth as its beginning and death as its end. We live our lives in a birth-to-death reality. In these few years that are given to us, we search for that which will satisfy, fulfill and bring us happiness, contentment and peace. In these years between birth and death we build our own kingdoms made up of this stuff of life that we look to to bring us what we desire and provide us with some sense of meaning. This is a lifelong quest. Although experiences vary widely, for most Americans this quest has common characteristics for us all.

In our younger years we try to understand who we are and where we fit in this world. We decide what we want to do with our lives, or at least we try. We look for a mate for life. We prepare for our future by getting an education, deciding on a career, finding a satisfying job, building a good marriage, buying a first home and starting a family. Our kingdom consists of careers, hopes, health and the early years of relationships focused on marriage and family. If we do not find some fulfillment in our younger years, we can begin down a path of insecurity, self-doubt and anxiety.

Our midlife years find us caught up in rearing children and trying to keep our marriages together. We make advances in our careers and often find our jobs overwhelming our lives. We are pressured by the financial challenges of providing a home, saving for college and retirement, and facing the threat of job changes and the financial burden of caring for aging parents. Our kingdom includes a struggle to keep our health, to find time for meaningful relationships with our children and our spouse, not to mention friends and family. It is a time for building equity, for amassing possessions, for establishing investment accounts, for keeping up with the Joneses, and for finding meaning amidst it all. If that meaning eludes us, these years can be overwhelming.

In our older years we face retirement and a new search for meaning and purpose. Our families include grandchildren, daughters-in-law and sons-in-law, and parents in need of our care in their final years. Our kingdom consists of a major focus on issues of health, finances, safety, security and peace. If we look back on our lives and find them void of real purpose and meaning, these final years can collapse into bitterness and depression.

In every phase of life we build our worldly kingdom in order to find the stuff that will provide us with what the world around us tells us we must have if our life is to have worth. If we are honest with ourselves, we must admit that we are all kingdom builders. We all seek a life that brings us happiness, security and satisfaction. We all seek meaning in these years between birth and death. This is reality, we say.

This struggle to build our own kingdoms has a frenetic and unsettling impact on our life. We do not build these kingdoms with an air of peacefulness and calm. We do not go about this work at a measured pace nor in a carefree manner. We do not build this worldly kingdom with a quiet confidence or a joyful heart. The kingdom of the world is built at a breakneck pace that pits us against our neighbor. It dangles the carrot of contentment always tantalizingly just out of reach. It drives us without rest and rewards us with a constant, nagging anxiety that despite our frenzied efforts we will always be lagging behind. In a very real way the kingdom of this world is never built, but it acts like a black hole constantly demanding more with no hope of ever having enough. The irony of the kingdom of the world is that it does not let us stop long enough to enjoy what we have amassed. Instead it fills us with anxiety that what we have may be lost. It fills us with desperation by telling us that what we do not have is what is necessary for our final happiness. And it fills us with despair because no matter how hard we strive we realize that the stuff that brings real happiness and peace may remain forever out of our reach.

And yet the message of this emptiness in pursuit of riches is being lost on our youth. David Myers raises the alarm in citing an annual study by UCLA and the American Council on Education. The study shows that among college freshmen, those that considered it "very important or essential" that they become "very well off financially" rose from 39 percent in 1970 to 74 percent in 1996. Myers goes on, "Among nineteen listed objectives, becoming 'very well-off financially' is now ranked number one. It outranks not only developing a life philosophy but also 'becoming an authority in my own field,' 'helping others in difficulty' and 'raising a family.' "[1]

Comedian George Carlin has a routine denouncing our consumerism

---

[1]David Myers, "Money and Misery," in *The Consuming Passion*, ed. Rodney Clapp (Downers Grove, Ill.: InterVaristy Press, 1998), p. 52.

where he talks about our pursuit of "stuff." He depicts us Americans as frantically buying and storing more and more "stuff." And then we all buy big houses so we have a place to put all of our stuff. And on our big houses we put big locks so our stuff can be kept safe while we go to the mall and buy more stuff. Carlin has put his finger on it. We are builders of kingdoms made up of stuff.

Ray Van Leeuwen speaks about the sinner's desire for consumption and gain without the threat of penalty, "Sin wants freedom from limits, forbidden acts without consequences. Sin wants something good, some luxury, some joy, some thrill or power or intimacy. But it wants that good at the expense of reality. The sinner seeks to expand his little kingdom at the cost of the order and total goodness of God's righteous kingdom."[2] In all of this we are constantly reminded that death is an ever-present reality that may cut short our years of kingdom building and leave us woefully short of having achieved that place where life finally fulfills and our existence finally attains its goal. Is it not ironic that our lifestyles of anxious kingdom building have led to increased health problems and premature death? Our hectic pace and our anxiety and fears over dying before we "have it all" contributes to diseases and illnesses that indeed cause thousands to die early in life. How many of our modern killers—cancer, heart disease, alcoholism, stroke among others—are greatly exacerbated by our stress-filled and fear-driven lifestyles? In our drive to find purpose and happiness within the confines of our earthly kingdom before we die, we undertake an agenda of kingdom building that kills us. Such is the nature of the perversion of this second kingdom.

To some, the kingdom of this world is comprised not of possessions but of experiences. Today we are learning that generation Xers are abandoning a hunger for material possessions in favor of amassing experiences through which they hope to achieve the meaning in life that they have seen elude their well-to-do yuppie parents. The thirst for purpose through experience has caused the evolution of an entirely new realm of human activity. It is marked not by a quest for new and meaningful experiences of artistic beauty, human goodness or the triumph of the human spirit. Nor does it seek after the enriching qualities one derives from world travel, volunteerism, philanthropy, education and meaningful rela-

---

[2]Ray C. Van Leeuwen, "Enjoying Creation—Within Limits," in *The Midas Trap* (Wheaton, Ill.: Victor, 1990), p. 30.

tionships. Instead it is marked by a somewhat twisted desire to experience life at the edge. The word that most clearly defines these experiences is *extreme*.

People seeking fulfillment through experience eagerly vie for the admiration of their peers that comes from acts defying death. What seems apparent is that when life loses its meaning, the only kingdom left to build is one that is constructed of moments where life itself is in the balance. Perhaps one needs to go to the very point of losing life to be assured that there is still some reason to keep it. In this way too this kingdom is never built, for there is always one more experience slightly beyond the last that may hold the key to the elusive meaning of life. And so we move from extreme to extreme.

Whether it is through possessions, accomplishments, power, experiences or any of a myriad of ways we seek for meaning, life lived between birth and death is truly what Thoreau called a life of "quiet desperation." Yet this is all the kingdom of this world offers. The world through television, magazines and other media wants to tell us is that the good life is attainable and true happiness and peace are found in the biggest kingdoms made up of the grandest "stuff." In the end our earthly kingdoms are like so much cotton candy in the rain, and we are left to face the reality of death with the sticky mess of shattered dreams, broken relationships, unfulfilled hopes and gnawing despair.

Finding a Place for Our Spiritual Kingdom

We said at the outset that our concern here was for those of us in the church who understood ourselves to be children in the kingdom of the triune God of grace. The question then is, "Where does our faith fit into the building of our worldly kingdom?" As Christians, what do we do with our faith commitment as we spend our time building our earthly kingdoms? We must assume here that we take our faith seriously. The deceptive nature of this myth of the second kingdom is based on the sincere desire of those of us in the church to live as Christians and to build our earthly kingdom side by side with our non-Christian neighbor.

To accomplish this we build a spiritual kingdom alongside our earthly one. Perhaps it would be more accurate to say that this is our first kingdom, the kingdom of our faith. If we are trying to live as Christians, this kingdom has priority in our lives as it pertains to those things that we assign to this kingdom. That is the key. This spiritual kingdom contains those things that belong to our spiritual life. Here we find our church life, our prayer and devotional life, our Christian service and our eternal security. In this kingdom we may be heavily involved as deacons, elders, Sunday school teachers and choir members. We may attend the church faithfully, give financially, serve on committees, volunteer to chaperon youth events and attend adult Bible classes. We may even try to have our spiritual kingdom intersect our earthly kingdom from time to time. We may take seriously our obligation to share our faith, to live like a Christian in our work, to rear our children to have Christian values, and to be a witness in our world. Yet all the time we see "reality" as divided between that which is part of our spiritual kingdom—and thus belongs to God—and that which belongs to our earthly kingdom—and rightly belongs to us. The myth of the second kingdom convinces us that the desire to be faithful in the former kingdom frees us to live as we wish in the latter.

The church plays along with this seemingly good and pure desire. It preaches to us that our goal as Christians is to work at ways in which our spiritual kingdom can more often intersect our worldly kingdom. It may not use such terms, but that is the effect of Christian teaching that talks of discipleship without calling into question the very existence of our earthly kingdoms. It is teaching that allows us to remain comfortable in our kingdom-building activities, as long as we are sincere when we work in our spiritual kingdoms as well.

Jeorg Rieger warns that the new mammon in the world is the emergence of the market as the center of world economies. He sees rightly the power that such a new religion demands: "The market now pushes its own theology, preached not only on Wall Street but also in everyday relationships. Some economists, clearer on this issue than many theologians, begin to understand that Mammon is displacing God."[3] More disturbingly, Rieger goes on to ask, "What if our theologies and our churches have, at least unconsciously, become part of the religion of the market? What if the God worshiped on Sunday mornings looks more like Mammon everyday?"[4] This is the insidious nature of the rise of the second kingdom when it is not challenged from the pulpit, taught in the seminary classroom or modeled in our nation's Christian leadership.

---

[3]Jeorg Rieger, *Liberating the Future: God, Mammon and Theology* (Minneapolis: Fortress, 1998), p. 7.
[4]Ibid.

The church also supports this bifurcation when it allows us to deal with sin in an abstract way. When we only conceptualize sin but never see it actually in us, we can live comfortably in between these two kingdoms. Wuthnow found this exact tendency in his research regarding the sin of greed.

> It appears, however, that regarding greed as a sin is quite easy for most Americans to reconcile with the desire for a lot of money. Thus, while 86 percent of weekly churchgoers say greed is a sin, only 16 percent of them say they were ever taught that wanting a lot of money was wrong, and in fact 79 percent of them say they wish they had more money than they do. Most churchgoers can thus deplore the greed they see in others but remain insensitive to its impulses in themselves.[5]

For too long the church has accepted this two-kingdom worldview, which is the product of a deficient doctrine of salvation. As Protestants we have allowed ourselves to accept an understanding of salvation that assumes a strict division between body and soul. As we saw in chapter three, we have lost the richness of the Old Testament's use of *nephesh* and its understanding that our humanity is a unity of body and soul. The new creation in Christ is not just a detached, spiritual creation but a holistic transformation of everything we are and everything we have. If the kingdom of God is occupied by the people of God who are this new creation, then there is simply nothing left with which we can build a second, earthly kingdom. Yet if we separate the two, we grant a very tidy and timely credibility to the whole two-kingdom scenario. We grant and perhaps even encourage our people to place spiritual things in their spiritual spheres, and we back away from the church interfering too much in their earthly affairs. If Christ assumed our fallen humanity only for a spiritual purpose, if only our souls have been redeemed, and if we are only called to be people of God in a portion of our lives, then the church has no answer for this two-kingdom dichotomy. Consequently, the church has no theology in which to train up stewards.

We have reached this point because we have lost the significance of the incarnation in which Christ assumed the totality of our humanity, body and soul. We have forgotten that Christ rose again not as a spirit only but with a redeemed body that bore the marks of the cross. As a result, our doctrine of salvation has focused too exclusively on the salvation of our

---

[5]Robert Wuthnow, *God and Mammon in America* (New York: Free Press, 1994), p. 126.

detached souls at the expense of an understanding of the redemption of the whole person.

The cost for this loss of balance has been the devaluing of everything that is material in lieu of the spiritual. We see only how Christ's salvation for us changes our inner-self, bringing us eternal security, but we do not see it touching our earthly existence. This salvation affects only our spiritual kingdom of prayer and church and faith, and therefore it saves our souls. It does not, however, touch our earthly kingdom, and therefore it does not redeem our wallets, our careers, our greed, our experiences, our relationships, our health or our anxieties. Again Wuthnow's research is telling. He cites that while 86 percent of weekly churchgoers agree that greed is a sin, 67 percent also agree with the statement "Money is one thing; morals and values are completely separate."[6] As long as we allow this split between the spiritual and material to prevail, we will continue to provide a theological justification for the existence of these two kingdoms side by side. We will continue to preach and teach as though the Christian life should be made up of the peace and hope of the spiritual kingdom side by side with the franticness, the emptiness and the despair of the earthly kingdom.

What is even more disturbing is that we will continue to allow the children of the kingdom of God to have a dual citizenship. We will condone the idea that one need not make an absolute commitment to either kingdom but that our lives can be marked by a vacillation between the two. We will contradict Scripture and lead our people to believe that they can indeed serve two masters. We will let our people move comfortably between one kingdom and the other and applaud them for those moments when the two are brought closest together. We will even secretly rejoice when their success in building earthly kingdoms brings financial benefit to the spiritual kingdom. We will give our people the message that they can be both "in" the world and "of" the world. This is the message the church sends when it refuses to deal with the scandal of this second, counterfeit kingdom.

This two-kingdom reality is nothing more than a return to the sin of Adam and Eve. It is a return to a distinction between that which is God's and that which we seek to judge for ourselves, to take under our control, and to use for our own gain. It sets out a clear dichotomy between what is

---

[6]Ibid., p. 129.

rightfully God's and what is rightfully mine. To God we gladly give all that belongs to our spiritual kingdom—as long as God is equally glad to leave us alone with the stuff of our earthly kingdom. We are even so "Christian" that we will share some of what is "ours" with God. And for doing so the church will thank us profusely, put our names on plaques, treat us like the really good Christians that we are, all while keeping its nose out of the way in which we build and use our earthly treasure. What a great arrangement.

Postmodernism and the Social Context of the Two Kingdoms

This bifurcation of our lives into separate compartments is gaining even greater support from the emerging worldview known as postmodernism. So powerful is this new mindset and its effect on our call to be stewards that we must look at it more closely.

As we saw in chapter two, for the postmodernist, truth is not something you discover, it is something you create. Truth is created locally by communities for which that truth makes sense. The truth of any given community is binding only for that community, for there is no basis upon which we can accept a "universal truth" equally binding on everyone. The reason for the lack of this basis is the perceived absence of a meta-narrative. That is, there is no one story that unites all humanity. Instead our existence consists of the accumulation of countless individual stories, each of which carries equal value and truth. To find our way in the post-modern world we must respect everyone's story and tolerate all local truth. The concepts of one sovereign creator God, the universal atone-ment of Christ, the Great Commission and the kingdom of God are not only foreign to the postmodern world, they are anathema.

One of marks of postmodernism is eclecticism. If every person's story and every local truth have equal validity, then we must create a world where all the stories and truths can exist side by side, each operating freely and without influence on each other. This calls for absolute toler-ance, moral relativism and the abandonment of every form of judgment and assessment that may lead to the devaluing of any story or the ques-tioning of any truth. David Green calls this, "A new 'Eleventh Command-ment': Thou shalt not judge."[7] In order to carry out this nonjudg-mentalism it requires that we create compartments into which we place

---

[7]David Green, "One Nation, After All," *U.S. News and World Report*, March 16, 1998, p. 84.

stories and truths and insulate them for their own protection. Not only can there be no judgment of what may exist in any given compartment, but people must be allowed to have contradictory compartments in their life existing side by side. And people must be given the freedom to move freely and comfortably among these often contradictory compartments without judgment.

Gene Edward Veith noted that the 1998 presidential sex scandal involving Bill Clinton is a perfect example of the compartmentalization of life in our postmodern world. At the same time that the president was under intense scrutiny of his personal sex life, the polls showed an all-time high in his popularity rating as it pertained to his work as president. The American people were quite happy to allow the president to be almost a completely different person in his private affairs than he was in his public office. The article pointed out that in postmodernism each of us should be allowed and encouraged to maintain numerous compartments in our life and that it is mentally healthy to be a different person in each of these compartments. "Instead of having a single core identity, human beings are free to have many identities, compartmentalizing them so they do not impinge on each other. Religion, sexual desires, job demands, family role, and political beliefs are all part of one's makeup, but none of these compartments need have any bearing on any of the others."[8] Not only is such compartmentalization allowed but it is normative for a truly healthy life. Veith concludes, "Those who are consistent in their beliefs, who try to live according to a specific set of principles, and who imagine that they have a single core identity are, according to postmodernist psychologists such as Mr. (Robert Jay) Lifton, mentally ill."[9]

This postmodern view provides a social context for a two-kingdom understanding of reality. When this social context is added to the timid, pallid and superficial teachings about the Christian's relationship to the material world that comes from the church, the two-kingdom view of reality is all but impossible to unseat.

The Rise of the Second Kingdom
This two-kingdom view of reality is the greatest single challenge to a theology of the steward. It affects in the most profound ways our relation-

---

[8]Gene Edward Veith, "A Postmodern Scandal," World, February 21, 1998, p. 24.
[9]Ibid.

ships at all four levels. By doing so it sets all attempts at stewardship in a context that is alien to the biblical norm, and it thereby renders stewardship studies ineffective from the outset. Until we are willing to face the reality of this second kingdom and move to expose it and renounce it as an alien and counterfeit edifice, our otherwise good and well-meaning books, programs, courses and sermons on stewardship will never make it inside the walls of our worldly kingdoms. No actual transformation will ever take place. We will not raise up godly stewards for the work of the kingdom of God. And the church will continue unwittingly to lend credence and context for this two-kingdom reality. This is what is at stake if we are not willing to lay siege to the worldly kingdoms we have built. The devious nature and ultimate damage that such inaction causes can be seen at all four levels where the true reconciliation of all things in Christ is relegated to only one portion of our lives.

The Second Kingdom and Our Relationship to God

As stated earlier, the sin of Adam and Eve brought about the consideration of the human *in abstracto* from its created relationships with God, self, neighbor and creation. At the heart of this sin lies the birth of this second kingdom. Just as the first sin immediately threw humanity into conflict with its Creator, so the rise of the second kingdom is marked by a fractured understanding of the creature's relationship with its Lord.

At creation, humanity's existence was bound up with its creator. The only kingdom that could be posited was the kingdom of the one who called everything into existence. Humanity and God were coinhabitors of this kingdom, albeit in profoundly different ways. Yet they were there together, "walking in the cool of the evening" and having perfect fellowship. Man and woman were part of God's kingdom. That was a fundamental aspect of their self-definition and self-understanding. They were children of the triune God of grace: nothing less and nothing more—for they could never be anything more.

As we seek to understand our post-fallen state, we have seen that the brokenness of the relationship between God and humanity brought about a coup d'état of the central place in the existence of the human. God was displaced by the human "come of age." A new "reality" had taken shape. No longer were the man and woman identified solely by their relationship to God and his kingdom, they now stood on their own two feet with their destinies in their own hands. They had grasped for this warped, pseudoindependence, and they had gotten it. They were, in some way, "like God," able to know right from wrong and decide for themselves. They had found a place outside of God's kingdom to dwell, and that place called for a new kingdom to be built. It called for a kingdom that had all the trappings of this new age that would recognize the exalted state of the man and woman and that would hail this new royalty. It called for a kingdom that would stand side by side with the kingdom of a God. With the old kingdom of God now set aside, it was time to make a place to mark the rise of human ingenuity, wisdom and reason.

The moment the kingdom of God was abandoned as the only proper place for the creature of God, this second kingdom became inevitable. The created state of peace and contentment, of meaning and joy, was dependent upon a relationship with the Creator who now had become the deity that could only be approached in repentance, humility and self-lessness. This was no role for the newly independent creature outside of Eden. So humanity desperately needed a place for itself. It needed a new place to find meaning, a new place to know itself, a new place to be comfortable, secure and at peace. It did not actually need to do this, of course. It could have found for itself all it needed in a return to God in faith, repentance and obedience. However, humanity chose another route. When Eden was lost, humanity in its arrogance turned to a second kingdom.

Again, we must remember that we are speaking here of the people of God. The existence of this second kingdom does not preclude the reality of God in our lives. It does not diminish our belief in God, our faith in God or the sincerity of our desire to worship him. It does not mean that we are not Christians, that our salvation is in question or that our faith is ingenuous. It simply means that we keep God in his rightful place—in our spiritual kingdom. There our God reigns supreme. There our faith in Jesus Christ calls us into a relationship with God. There we worship, fellowship with our Christian brothers and sisters, pray, serve and give. If anyone were to look at us in the our spiritual kingdom, they would say, "Ah, there is a fine Christian fellow," or, "Now there is surely a godly woman."

The problem lies not in our general faith in God, nor in the way in which God is active and present in our lives as we operate as people in our spiritual kingdom. The problem is what we do with God as inhabitants of our kingdoms of this world. The question here is not one of faith but of *lordship*. The question is not whether we believe in God as strongly in our earthly kingdom, but who is Lord and master here. The very fact that we build a second kingdom means that the ultimate lordship is ours. In building our kingdom we reenact the sin of Adam and Eve. We demonstrate that we have also grasped at power and sought to be like God. We too seek a place for ourselves that lies just beyond the reach of God.

We must be careful here to understand how subtle this shift may be. Many of us may believe that we have not built such a kingdom. After all, we acknowledge that all good things come from God, and we thank him and praise him for everything we have. We may pray over purchasing decisions, give generously to the work of the church and affirm that everything we have belongs to God. In this we may be sincere and our heart may be truly seeking after these things. However, we must be ready and willing to look carefully at our lives for signs that indicate that we too are kingdom builders. If we allow the Holy Spirit to work in our lives, our eyes can be opened to the subtle ways in which we quietly gather to ourselves those things in life that we ultimately label as "ours." We will see that each of us entrusts some portion of our contentment and joy in life to things that we keep in our control. They may be possessions, relationships or experiences. They may represent a latent, unacknowledged greed or desire for power and fame. We know that they will manifest themselves in the guise of godliness, but underneath they are nothing more than the trappings of a second kingdom.

If we as a church will admit that we all fall victim to the temptation to build our own kingdoms, we can begin as a church to change. Unless change takes place at this fundamental level, we will not raise up a new generation of stewards. The reason is simple: you cannot be a steward of something that is yours. Ownership and stewardship are mutually exclusive. As soon as anything becomes a part of "our" kingdom, it ceases to be an asset that can be stewarded. This is not a matter of rights and privileges; it is a matter of lordship. Therefore, it may be more accurate to say that lordship and stewardship are mutually exclusive. Where God is not Lord, we are not stewards. As long as our relationship to God is seen in wholly spiritual terms—that is, as belonging only to our spiritual kingdom—we will retain a lordship for ourselves and deny our calling to be stewards in the kingdom of the triune God of grace.

We have seen how Jesus Christ came to heal the brokenness of our relationships at all four levels, including and particularly our relationship with God. In doing so he has ushered in the kingdom of God and called us into it as his children. This brings these two kingdoms into sharp conflict. Before we became Christians, we dedicated our lives to building this earthly kingdom. We saw our lives hemmed in by birth and death, and we defined our existence according to the content of this kingdom of ours. How do we now deal with these two kingdoms?

If we are left to ourselves, we will find convenient ways to allow them to coexist. This is the deceit of the enemy, that we need not abandon our earthly kingdom because of our Christian faith. It deceives us into believing that God's kingdom only requires a portion of ourselves, leaving more than enough to continue to inhabit our earthly kingdom. We can be Christians, generous, good neighbors and active laity without abandoning our earthly kingdom. We can keep the lordship of God restricted to our spiritual lives and there we can worship, pray and serve with the best of them. We can accommodate ourselves to our postmodern world and compartmentalize our lives in dramatic or subtle ways. We can become very comfortable in our dual citizenship and even believe it to be blessed by God. We can do all these things, but we cannot be stewards in God's kingdom. The rise of the second kingdom has caused this split in our understanding of our relationships to God, and it will keep us from ever being stewards as God has called us to be.

The Second Kingdom and Our Relationship to Ourselves

We have seen how our relationship to ourselves has been redeemed in Christ's restoring to us a sense of self-worth and self-identity as children of the God who created us. We are stewards of this special relationship as we understand our place and role in this world, and therefore our purpose for being. In that renewed sense of purpose we have also found the peace and fulfillment that was lost in Eden. All of this is dependent upon our recognition that our entire existence is wrapped up in our identity as children in the kingdom of the triune God of grace.

The rise of this second, counterfeit kingdom wreaks havoc on this self-identity. Yet it does so according to form; that is, it does so subtly, deviously and almost as a sleight of hand. It shifts our focus just enough to skew our entire self-image, almost without our knowing it. Quietly, bit by bit, the rise of the second kingdom calls to us to base our self-understanding on a second set of criteria. It lures us into seeing ourselves not *only* as children of God but also as citizens of this world who must rise to meet a second set of standards for "success" and "happiness" as defined by this secular context.

At first, it may simply set these alien criteria side by side with the fruits of the spirit and the marks of servanthood that demarcate our lives as children of the kingdom of God. It may ask only that we pay some attention, that we give even a small bit of notice to this second set of standards. It asks only this because the enemy knows that the lure of our worldly kingdom is strong. It will not take long for us to make the shift in part or even in full. Soon our lives that were defined by grace and our identities that were adorned with the joyous response of the faithful steward bear evidence of the need to find our identity *also* in how much we make, what we possess, where we live, who we know and what we do. We carry in us the two sets of criteria that result from our dual citizenship. We must live according to our allegiance to two masters. This is the necessary result of our two-kingdom worldview. This is what the church often does not understand. If we are deficient in our teaching and preaching against this second kingdom, if we allow our people to live comfortably in this dichotomous pseudoreality, then we must live with the results. We must expect them to put as much value on their place in society as their place in the kingdom of God. We must expect that our people will seek ways to reconcile their quest to be people of God and people of the world. We must expect that the children in the kingdom of God will develop a schizophrenia of sorts, trying to be different people in different situations. What we teach and what we preach will be filtered through this bifurcated self-identity, sifting out only what makes sense for our lives inside the church. Our people therefore appropriate Christian teaching on a "take it or leave it" level, treating Christian doctrine and biblical preaching like a smorgasbord where they take what appeals and leave what seems distasteful.

The problem, however, is worse than this. In the very best case we Christians will seek an internal harmony between these two radically different sets of standards. For awhile this may be possible, but the internal angst it renders will soon cause the balance to be destroyed. What does a Christian do when this balance fails? As subtly as the first invitation to take notice of this counterfeit kingdom and its alien standards, the balance will shift to the side of the worldly kingdoms we have built. The most committed of us will struggle all of our lives to keep the two in balance. The slightly less committed will make room for the construction of a self-identity along worldly lines. The weakest will sell out almost completely, ending up with nothing more than a Christian veneer over a wholly secular agenda. In every case, if this second kingdom is left to itself, our self-identities will more and more conform to its standards over and against the marks of the children of God. That is the result of sin and fallenness and misplaced pride.

We cannot be stewards of that which we own. We cannot be both lord and steward. As our self-identity shifts from our gracious existence as ones bought with the price of the Son of God to an existence measured by the size of our kingdom and the price of its contents, the relationship we have to ourselves shifts from the steward of a gift to the owner of an asset. If the kingdoms we build in this world rightfully belong to us, then our self-worth and our self-understanding that are based on our success in these kingdoms are ours as well. Both stand alongside and therefore outside of and alien to the kingdom of God and our self-understanding as children by grace of the triune God. In this dichotomy, stewardship is impossible. We will, according to Scripture, either love one and hate the other, or hold to one and despise the other. We cannot keep these two radically different self-identities together.

The result will inevitably be conflict. That is a good description of the place of the gospel in the church today. The gospel is both good news and an offense. The cross is both the seminal symbol of hope and a serious stumbling block. The values of the kingdom of God will come crashing headlong into the values of our earthly kingdoms. How do we respond to the biblical call to be people who give in a world that measures us by how much we have? How do we respond to God's call to be humble servants in a world that rewards the shrewd entrepreneur, the cutthroat executive and the aggressive self-promoter? How do we hear that the "first shall be last" in a world that derides the loser, forgets the second-place finisher and exonerates only the winners? The list of questions could go on endlessly. Insert your own set of dilemmas that pertain to the struggle you feel in trying to live as a real Christian in a world that values so much that is the polar opposite of Christian living. Look at your own earthly kingdom, that which you call "yours," and ask yourself how much pressure you feel to maintain and build this kingdom because of what it means to you and your self-identity. Do not scoff at the rich young ruler in Matthew who "went away sad for he had many possessions" until you have taken inventory of your own possessions and their link to your own

understanding of who you are and how you want to be viewed in this
world.

The point to be made here is this: We cannot give place to a second
kingdom alongside our "spiritual kingdom" and not see our self-identity
become wrapped up in it. We cannot spend our lives building our earthly
kingdoms without having our self-worth become enmeshed with its standards. And therefore, we cannot be stewards of our relationships to ourselves as children in the kingdom of the triune God of grace if we have
sworn allegiance to this second kingdom and serve as its master and lord.

The Second Kingdom and Our Relationship to Our Neighbor

Much that has been said in the two categories above can now be applied
to our relationship to our neighbor. We have seen that if our relationship
to God is effected by our giving place to a second kingdom, then our relationship to ourselves will inevitably and tragically also be effected. This
happens in so many ways that space does not permit us to list them all
here. What is important is that each of us look at our own lives and determine how this second kingdom, and the process of building and maintaining it, impacts on our relationship to our neighbor, and how this
impact is in contradistinction to our role as neighbor in the kingdom of
God. For the sake of clarity, we will lift up three such areas.

Gift versus means. In God's kingdom, our self-identity is tied up in part
by our place among and with our neighbor. We were created in the image
of a triune God to be in fellowship with one another. Our being as God's
children is relational at its core. And this is not relationship for its own
sake, but it has a goal. To be in fellowship with our neighbor is how we
bear witness to our world that the kingdom of God has come. Jesus prays
to the Father that we would be united in love and purpose "that the
world may believe that you have sent me" (Jn 17:21). This fellowship is to
be so radical in its nature and so outstanding in its witness that its shines
out in the darkness of our world as a light to all humanity.

This is what it looks like to be a neighbor in the kingdom of God. It is
based on our common understanding of our relationships with God and
with ourself. It is the product of the equality that rules at the foot of the
cross of Christ. It leaves no room for hierarchy, class, racial, ethnic or gender divisions. It seeks only the best in each other, and it sees the elevation
of the individual as possible only through the elevation of the entire fellowship. It cares for people out of selfless love, and it is not afraid to see a

brother or a sister lifted up. After all, we are all one and the same before the throne of God. These are the relationships we are called to steward. They are not ours; they are precious gifts to be cared for and shepherded with the utmost care of a faithful steward.

How radically different this understanding of neighbor is to that which comes to us from the values of our earthly kingdom. As we go about our work of kingdom building, we soon realize that our neighbor is not always a gift. We soon see that what is in our best interest is often not in the best interest of our neighbor. We certainly see that hierarchy and class are tools we need to rise above and succeed, to measure our kingdom against our neighbor, to come out on top. Therefore, subtly, we come to see our neighbor as a means to an end. We see how our kingdoms rely on our proper use of others, and relationships become the vehicles we use to get what we need from others to build our kingdoms. The bottom-line question we seek in relationships is, "What am I getting out of this?" We weigh our relationships in the balance, maintaining those that "pay off" and jettisoning those where debits outweigh credits.

This may sound harsh, but this is the way in which kingdoms are built. To whatever extent we buy into it, we are common users of others for our own means. The point is that we cannot build earthly kingdoms without at some point using others as instruments or vehicles that are critical to the process. If our self-definition comes from the size of our earthly kingdom, then we have redefined our relationships to our neighbor. No longer is our self-understanding tied up with our *being with* our neighbor, but it is constituted on the extent to which we can *use* our neighbor to better ourselves. As Christians we may seek very good ways to do this. We may try to have the best intentions, and we may seek some good for our neighbor as well. However, the undeniable fact is that if we are about the building of an earthly kingdom, we will inevitably see our neighbor as a means to that end. As means, they will play a distinctly different role in our lives outside the kingdom of God than they must as fellow members of God's kingdom.

With versus against. From this first distortion of our relationship to our neighbor comes the second. Our self-definition is to be defined in part in relationship with our neighbor. The key word here is *with*. That is, as we function in these relationships, as we lift up our neighbors, care for them and live with them as the coredeemed of God, we *are* the children of God. It is only in being with our neighbor in this fellowship in this kingdom in honor of the grace of this God that we have self-definition as children of God. We are defined by the term *with*.

Again we face a radical shift as we look to our lives in our worldly kingdoms. Suddenly our self-definition does not come in our identity *with* our neighbor but solely in distinction *against* our neighbor. That is, we are now measured not by how well be live among our neighbors but by how well we have done in competition with our neighbors. We define success in our kingdom-building work according to the standards of this world. Therefore, we are successful to the extent that we stand out as having amassed more, achieved more, experienced more, earned more and enjoyed life more than our neighbor. That is the only true standard by which our world measures success. It is an "over and against" context for creating a positive self-identity. I can only be seen as having self-worth, and my life can only be seen as having meaning and purpose if I can compare myself favorably to you, if I have done better than you.

There is an insidious nature to this competition that seeps into the church. As Christians we seek to take the high road in this kingdom building activity. Therefore, we may not accept that our success must come at the cost of finding ourselves better than our neighbor. Yet we do it in the church all the time. It comes in the form of spiritual pride. It is a "holy" way of setting our own spirituality in contrast to others. We may believe that it has a holy purpose, but praying more, working on more committees, going to more church events and even giving more can all be just Christianized ways of defining ourselves in terms of how much better we are than our neighbor. Perhaps that is why we spend so much time quietly tearing each other down. It is so much easier to tear down another than to better ourself in comparison. In both cases the culprit is spiritual pride that sees our neighbor not as someone to be *with* but someone to *compete* with and ultimately to be over and against.

Jesus used the parable of the Pharisee and the publican to make the point. Only the publican—a despised tax collector—could ever see himself *with*, for he came in repentance, seeking to be right with God and his neighbor. The Pharisee says verbally what we must admit to in quiet shame. We are the Pharisee whenever we allow the thought or motivation to overtake us and say, "I am glad I am not like that man."

We cannot be stewards of relationships that we use to better ourselves. They cease to be gifts to be stewarded, and they immediately become possessions to be used. Again the question is lordship versus stewardship.

Until we see our neighbors and our relationship with them as essential to our own self-identity as a child of God, we will never be stewards of our relationships with them.

Caring versus competing. A third example we will offer is the quality of the relationship with our neighbors in these two kingdoms. In the kingdom of God we have the opportunity and the responsibility to build relationships based on a true openness and vulnerability. That is, if we are not interested in using our neighbor, and if our self-identity is tied up with the quality of our relationships, then we will be motivated to be open, honest, caring and even vulnerable before our neighbor. Why not? We have nothing to lose and everything to gain. After all, our self-worth is wholly tied to who we are as a child of God. Why should we not be open and vulnerable? Why should we not seek close and caring friendships? If being *with* is the key in the kingdom of God, then the quality of our relationships is of paramount importance. When we read all of the Scriptural commands as to how we are to love our neighbor, we can only begin to understand them when we see how vital they are to our own being as children in the kingdom of God.

Therefore, our call to be stewards of these relationships has great power, for it is a call to a wholly committed way of relating. It truly calls us to "love our neighbor as ourselves," for as we do so, we continue to define our love for ourselves as children in the kingdom of the triune God of grace. Here we see again how these different levels of relationship are all tied together. In loving God we have the opportunity to love ourselves. In that real love for self as a child of God lies the secret of the great commandment, that we love our neighbors *as ourselves.*

It is from this understanding that we can be empowered to stand in solidarity with the poor, the marginalized, the oppressed and the forgotten. It is the call to stand *with* our neighbor that sets the steward out from all others. It calls us to advocacy, to active protest and to lifestyle change. It calls us to love our neighbor in deed as well as word. It calls us to become intentionally uncomfortable as we step out into our neighbor's world. It calls us to give and to give sacrificially of all that God has entrusted to us. For most, that sacrifice will be measured more in terms of time, reputation, safety and power than in dollars. Standing with our neighbor is far more than writing a check, yet it is also writing a check. The question we must return to is, "How do we love ourselves?" If we answer in terms of Christ's love for us, then our agenda to be *with* our neighbor is set out in all its clarity and challenge.

This is another area that is foreign to our earthly kingdom. If we are defined not *with* but *in comparison to* and therefore *over and against* our neighbor, then the last thing we will seek is openness and vulnerability. Consequently, the last thing we will do is stand *with* our neighbor. We will, in fact, seek after that which will put us in the best possible light vis-à-vis our neighbor. We will put on a mask of strength, self-assurance, confidence and poise and never let our guard down. We will keep relationships at the superficial level where talk of kingdoms thrives. We will play the role we need to play in order to maintain the image of our place over and against our neighbor. We will do all we can to make our kingdom as big and bright as possible, or at least a little bigger and brighter than our neighbor's. In the midst of this competitive environment, there is no place for openness and vulnerability. What we leave in our wake are scores of superficial relationships and very few true, intimate friends. We know little about our neighbors beyond "kingdom talk," and therefore we are never able to be truly a neighbor. We are so busy being "better than" that we cease to be able to really care. Gustavo Gutiérrez says with great clarity, "Added to the idolatry of money is that of power that overrides all human rights. To these idols an offering of victims is made, so that the biblical prophets always link idolatry with murder. Those excluded in the present international economic order are among these victims."[10]

These relationships, too, become impossible to steward. They are not valued as a divine gift, but they are used and exploited for our own good. As such, they again become "ours," building blocks in the construction of our earthly kingdom. We cannot be stewards of relationships that make people into means, relationships that measure worth based on self-serving outcomes and that operate according to the values of the world.

These are just three examples of how the rise of the second kingdom has devastated our ability to be stewards of our relationships with our neighbors as God has called us to be. It sets the understanding of neighbor in the kingdom of God on a collision course with the world's view. Our allegiance to these two kingdoms will render us impotent as true, godly neighbors and therefore as stewards in the kingdom of the triune God of grace.

---

[10]Gustavo Gutiérrez, "Liberation Theology and the Future of the Poor," in *Liberating the Future: God, Mammon and Theology* (Minneapolis: Augsburg, 1998), p. 117.

The Second Kingdom and Our Relationship to the Material World

We have reached the conclusion that no one aspect of the Christian life is more grievously damaged by this two-kingdom worldview than the call to be the steward. In fact, stewardship makes little or no sense at all if these two kingdoms are allowed to stand side by side. Despite the devastating picture we have painted in the three areas above, the place where this two-kingdom thinking is most prevalent is in our relationship to the created world. Here we seem to have found the most peace with cordoning off a space that is "ours." We must see here again how this is a product of the brokenness in the three levels above. If our relationship to God is distorted by being divided into two segments along kingdom lines (level one), then our understanding of who we are (level two) and how we are to live with our neighbor (level three) is equally distorted. If we do not know who we are and how we are to live with our neighbor, we will not understand our role in this creation. Put more directly, if we limit God's lordship to a spiritual kingdom, we will divide our self-understanding the same way. We will see our neighbor as a means to an end, and we will see creation as a commodity to be used and abused for the building and enhancing of our own kingdom. It all begins with a loss of lordship in all areas of life, and it is manifest most fiercely here as a sanctioning of the exploitation of creation for our own use. It is the ultimate end product of the dichotomy between spiritual and material.

Here again we reenact the sin of Adam and Eve. Vera Shaw writes,

> The story of Eden gives amazing insight into environmental problems. While surrounded by the abundance of the perfect environment, enjoying all of its wonderful resources, Adam and Eve decided that no restrictions should limit their control. This fascination with evil polished the forbidden fruit. Humans believed all creation was for their satisfaction, and they alone should decide how to use it.[11]

This grasp at control and the desire to decide for ourselves is the rejection of the lordship of God in this area of our life. It is the move from being steward to being lord. It is the product of a two-kingdom view of reality. In this framework, the privilege of dominion given to us as one-kingdom people in our relationship to God is now redefined by an alien domination of creation as part of a second kingdom set apart from God. Here *subdue* becomes *exploit*, *rule* becomes *lord over* and *use* becomes *abuse*.

---

[11]Vera Shaw, "The Ecology of Eden," *Green Cross*, winter 1995, pp. 4-5.

We no longer seek to "have dominion" as God has dominion over us, but we understand dominion on our own terms. When our relationship to creation is no longer defined by the characteristics of God's lordship over us, then sin will distort Scripture's intent, and we will subsume creation under our earthly kingdom and use it as was never intended. Our creation has suffered intensely from this two-kingdom thinking.

Think for a moment what happens to all of our teaching on Christian giving in this scenario. We begin by affirming that the assets that make up our earthly kingdom are rightfully ours. We may pay lip service to the idea that in the end God owns everything, but this is nothing more than a view of reality that affirms a kingdom of stuff we have accumulated and, therefore, of stuff that belongs to us. We measure our self-worth, our success and our place among our neighbors according to the value of this kingdom. Therefore, we do not take lightly the request to reduce its value or decrease its size. Giving away what has taken us a lifetime to amass and what defines us in this world is no small request.

Giving belongs to this second kingdom. It may be taught in our churches, it may hold out eternal benefits, and it may have some connection with Christian obedience, but as long as it requires a decision that will reduce the size of our earthly empire, it belongs to this second kingdom. That is a reality we must face if we are willing to go about Christian fundraising without challenging the very existence of this worldly kingdom.

Given this scenario, Christian giving can only mean the decision to make a transfer of assets from one kingdom, the earthly kingdom of what is "mine," to another kingdom, our spiritual kingdom. Put in accounting terms, Christian giving becomes the debiting of our earthly kingdom and the crediting of our spiritual kingdom. One decreases in order to increase the other. The primary "stewardship" question in this asset transfer is, "How much of my assets should I give to the church?" Or put another way, "How much is enough: 5 percent, 4 percent, 3 percent?"

Defining *enough* becomes the work of the church stewardship committee. Is *enough* defined by how much the church needs? How much the pastor is worth? How much I am receiving back from the church for my investment? Or is *enough* defined by how much it takes to keep me from feeling guilty? How much I need to improve my tax return or how much it takes to keep the pastor from calling? In its more heinous guise, *enough* can be measured by how much it takes to buy me the power I want to have over the church. How much do I want the church to need me? How much do I want to be known as the "big giver"? Or how much do I want everyone to know just how large my earthly kingdom really is?

If the church is willing to allow us to serve two masters without challenge, the result will be that our definition of *enough* in our earthly kingdom will always drive us to get and keep the most that we believe we can, while our definition of *enough* in our spiritual kingdom will always motivate us to give the least that we feel we must. In every case the question of "Christian giving" will always revolve around the decision to decrease the assets in our earthly kingdom in order to "give joyfully" to the kingdom of God.

The challenge that arises for Christian leaders then is, "How do we motivate our people to make such a transfer of assets?" That is, what must we say and do to bring about this act of decreasing the value of an earthly storehouse of treasure in order to enrich the work of the kingdom of God? Unfortunately, most of the answers that "work" are borrowed from the fundraising techniques of the world that does not bother itself with this two-kingdom thinking. The result is that the church finds itself using such motivations as guilt, a distorted understanding of "Christian obedience" and appeals to altruism, to tax advantages and to tradition. We find ourselves using techniques that rely more on the pride of ownership and the reward of greed than upon the role of the Holy Spirit in Christian giving.

What's Wrong with This Picture?

As Christians when we read the descriptions of the effects of this two-kingdom view of life on all four levels of relationship, it should cause us to be uneasy and even alarmed. If we look to the commands of Scripture for how we are to live, this scenario is indeed troubling. If we look to the world for evidence of the fruit of this two-kingdom lifestyle, what we see should cause us grave concern. Whether viewed from Scripture or from the testimony of the world we are unequivocally led to one conclusion: There is something terribly wrong with this picture. We will close this chapter by looking at a few clues as to what might be so very wrong with the two-kingdom view of reality.

A View from the Winner's Circle

One clue from Scripture comes to us from Ecclesiastes, where Solomon looks back over his life in search of meaning and finds only vanity and meaninglessness. For all of us who toil and struggle to build our earthly kingdom, for all of us who are caught up in the pressure and franticness of kingdom building, and for all who hope that one day there will be meaning to it all before death comes, these words are a dousing of cold water.

First, Solomon looks to wisdom, his great gift from God.

> I, the Teacher, was king over Israel in Jerusalem. I devoted myself to study and to explore by wisdom all that is done under heaven. What a heavy burden God has laid on men! I have seen all the things that are done under the sun; all of them are meaningless, a chasing after the wind. . . . I thought to myself, "Look, I have grown and increased in wisdom more than anyone who has ruled over Jerusalem before me; I have experienced much of wisdom and knowledge." Then I applied myself to the understanding of wisdom, and also of madness and folly, but I learned that this, too, is a chasing after the wind.
>
> For with much wisdom comes much sorrow;
>   the more knowledge, the more grief. (1:12-14, 16-18)

If we look to wisdom and knowledge in our earthly kingdom to provide us with meaning and purpose in life, Solomon warns us that these means will fail us. For all of the importance of godly wisdom and knowledge, if they are our hope, we will be greatly disappointed.

Solomon goes on to look for purpose in life in other areas.

> I thought in my heart, "Come now, I will test you with pleasure to find out what is good." But that also proved to be meaningless. "Laughter," I said, "is foolish. And what does pleasure accomplish?" I tried cheering myself with wine, and embracing folly—my mind still guiding me with wisdom. I wanted to see what was worthwhile for men to do under heaven during the few days of their lives.
>
> I undertook great projects: I built houses for myself and planted vineyards. I made gardens and parks and planted all kinds of fruit trees in them. I made reservoirs to water groves of flourishing trees. I bought male and females slaves and had other slaves who were born in my house. I also owned more herds and flocks than anyone in Jerusalem before me. I amassed silver and gold for myself, and the treasure of kings and provinces. I acquired men and women singers, and a harem as well—the delights of the heart of man. I became greater by far than anyone in Jerusalem before me. In all this my wisdom stayed with me.
>
> I denied myself nothing my eyes desired;
>   I refused my heart no pleasure.
> My heart took delight in all my work,
>   and this was the reward for all my labor.
> Yet when I surveyed all that my hands had done

and what I had toiled to achieve,
   everything was meaningless, a chasing after the wind;
      nothing was gained under this sun. (2:1-11)

This lament comes from the heart of a man who lived out to the fullest the fantasies of every kingdom builder. Unlimited pleasure, inconceivable riches, music and culture, fame and stature, wisdom and laughter—and a harem to boot. How many people today are striving for a level of financial success where they would be able to say, "I denied myself nothing my eyes desired, I refused my heart no pleasure"? Is that not a restatement of the American dream? Is that not the end result of all kingdom building? Is that not what the world is telling us will bring us ultimate satisfaction and final contentment? Is that not what we envy of the rich and famous? If we were honest with ourselves, would we not like to be in Solomon's shoes, even for just the while? Could it be that we may come to a different conclusion given the opportunity? Maybe, just maybe, for us it would not be meaningless. Maybe for us it would bring real contentment and not be a "chasing after the wind."

The truth of course is that Solomon speaks for all of us. The witness of the world and the teaching of Scripture speak unequivocally to the emptiness and meaninglessness of pleasures and possessions when they are sought after as the source of real meaning in life. As we admit to ourselves and to God that we are indeed kingdom builders, we must not let this truth escape us. For all of the lure and temptation in this world, we must come to the stark realization that this stuff of our kingdom will in the end be bitterly disappointing as we look back on our life.

Finally Solomon considered his death in light of all that he had worked to accomplish in his life. He concludes,

> So I hated life, because the work that is done under the sun was grievous to me. All of it is meaningless, a chasing after the wind. I hated all the things I had toiled for under the sun, because I must leave them to the one who comes after me. . . . So my heart began to despair over all my toilsome labor under the sun. For a man may do his work with wisdom, knowledge and skill, and then he must leave all he owns to someone who has not worked for it. This too is meaningless and a great misfortune. What does a man get for all the toil and anxious striving with which he labors under the sun? All his days his work is pain and grief; even at night his mind does not rest. This too is meaningless. (2:17-18, 20-23)

Solomon had live his years in a birth-to-death reality. As he looked back over what most would consider to be an ideal life, he saw it all as empty and meaningless. The kingdom he had built for himself had failed him. What could not bring him ultimate joy and contentment in life was rendered even more impotent in death. How sad, futile and desperate are the years of our lives that we spend building our kingdoms with stuff that is supposed to bring us everything we desire because we can call it "ours." These words of Solomon should serve like a flare in a dark night signaling to us that something is indeed very wrong.

The Great Equalizer

A second indication that something is terribly wrong comes from that moment when our relatives and loved ones look back over our lives and remember us. In my profession I attend a lot of funerals. I find eulogies to be very enlightening more for what they do not say than what they do. In light of the fact that we spend our entire lives building our earthly kingdoms, it should come as a shock and surprise that little if any time is spent talking about that kingdom by those we leave behind. I am reminded of the bumper sticker that reads, "The one who dies with the most toys wins." I have always wanted to attend the funeral of someone with that bumper sticker. When the remembrances are finished, I would like to jump up and yell, "But did he win?" Imagine living your whole life according to a standard that is rendered meaningless at your death. Imagine striving your whole life to achieve a goal that is completely ignored at your life's end. What a tragedy.

Instead of replaying our accomplishments or listing our assets, family members and friends will remember us for who we were and the difference we made in their lives. The summation of our life will not consist of a listing of the contents of our earthly kingdom. How did we get to the point where all that seems so important during our life is seen as substanceless and vain at our death? I find that at every funeral I attend I ask myself, "What do I hope people will say at my funeral?" When I answer that question honestly, I realize how disconnected that answer is from the things that drive me each day. Clearly something is wrong with a worldview that consumes us with passion to invest our entire life in building a kingdom that will ultimately and inevitably disappoint us in life and be forgotten in death.

The Dark Side

Finally, if we are honest with ourselves, we will see that behind each desire to build a portion of our earthly kingdom lies a dark side. As Christians we may be successful for time in keeping this dark side in check. We may be able to rise above the temptations that come in the striving after this earthly kingdom. Even so, we must admit that they are there and that from time to time they manifest themselves even in our most innocent acts. The accumulation of material possessions cannot be carried out without recognition that greed, sinful pride and selfishness hover around the edges. The drive to succeed is enmeshed with issues of power and status on one side and fear on the other. The quest for meaningful relationships as part of our earthly kingdom also invites manipulation, plays on insecurity and tempts us to use others for our own self-betterment. Even the amassing of experiences has its dark side and its lure into self-gratification, its temptation to devalue people and its unsatisfying nature that draws us into an unending need for "more and greater and deeper" like a treadmill without an off switch.

These are just a few indicators that lead us to the conclusion that this second kingdom, this earthly empire built side by side with our spiritual kingdom, is not what God desires for his people. It is more than a myth; it is an outright lie and deception by the enemy. It is a grand illusion that our world has bought in toto and that the church has allowed to creep into its theology either overtly or through mere negligence. As a result, we are just as likely to see champion kingdom builders in the pew next to us as we are anywhere in the world.

For there to be real change we must come to conclusion that the only kingdom builder that matters is the one we see in the mirror. Until we acknowledge for ourselves that this is a worldview that describes *our* lives, there will be no permanent change. It must begin with us. As Christians, as church leaders, as teachers, as seminary students, as children in the kingdom of the triune God of grace, we must stand up and renounce with all our heart the place that has been given to the rise of the second kingdom.

Stewards are not owners. Stewards are not lords. Stewards are not kingdom builders. If we are called to be stewards in God's kingdom, we must begin by denouncing our ownership and lordship over any and every dimension of our life. Nothing can be held back. Nothing can be excluded. That which is not given over totally to God's lordship will continue to be part of an alien second kingdom. There is no freedom in such a kingdom. There is no joy in such a kingdom. There is no peace in such a kingdom. And ultimately there is nothing but meaninglessness in such a kingdom. Only when we are ready to acknowledge such can we move on to understand what it means to be faithful stewards in the *one* kingdom of our Lord and Savior Jesus Christ.

The first step in this direction is the incredible truth that our lives are not marked by the same boundaries as the world. We do not live according to a life-to-death reality. As Christians we live according to the gospel of Jesus Christ. Therefore, the joyful, meaningful and productive life of the steward in the kingdom of the triune God of grace is one that is lived in a new and ultimately transformed reality. Our existence in God's kingdom, our "reality" is not marked by birth behind us and death ahead of us, but as children of God our lives are marked by *death behind us and only life ahead*. In this one reality of our existence as God's children lies the key to our ability to live as stewards in God's kingdom. It is perhaps the ultimate paradigm shift. It is the final piece to our study, and it will be the foundation for the next chapter.

Chapter 7

The One Kingdom
of the Steward

"When Christ calls a man, he bids him come and die."
DIETRICH BONHOEFFER

T HE CALL TO BE A STEWARD IN THE KINGDOM OF GOD IS ALL ABOUT
death. Before it is about giving, sharing and investing, it is
about death. Prior to it being about commitment, obedience
and sacrifice, it is about death. The fact that we do not hear
much about death in the church's teaching on stewardship may point us
to why such teaching has been so ineffectual.

We have seen how the existence of two kingdoms renders true, godly
stewardship impossible. Whatever happens that looks good and seems
right about our acts of giving, if we have dichotomized our lives into two
spheres, where lordship remains ours in one, then we have not been stewards in the kingdom of God. The reason is not that we have been evil, that
our faith is not real or that our motives are not genuine. The reason is that
we have bought into a birth-to-death view of reality and therefore have
failed to take our death seriously.

The death we are talking about here is not the physical death that
awaits us all. That, if you will, is only a secondary death. It is a passing of

a sentence from which we have already been reprieved. It is a transition, a passageway and a gate, but it is not an event around which we organize our lives or one that gives definition to all that came before. These are the marks of the world's view where physical death is the end of all things. It is the finish line at which one must be in first place (or at least not in last). It is the final curtain, and as it falls, the rest of the play must make sense and bring purpose, meaning and fulfillment. It is the ultimate moment of stock-taking, of accountability and of "reality." Therefore, it is an ominous and foreboding time that people approach with either fear for all the things left undone or with resignation for all the futility of a life of accomplishing so much and enjoying so little. This is what death means to those locked in a birth-to-death worldview.

This is not, however, what Scripture is speaking of in many places where it deals with death. It is not what Deitrich Bonhoeffer meant when he wrote those powerful words. And it is not the death that is so important to the call to be a steward in the kingdom of the triune God of grace. To understand this biblical idea of death we must return to the vicarious humanity of Christ.

Vicarious Death

In chapter five we saw how the work of Christ for us was a vicarious work. That is, Christ bore the totality of *our* humanity, and therefore he truly lived *our* life of obedience, was baptized *for us*, suffered the judgment for *our* sins, paid the penalty *we* owed, died *our* death, and descended into the hell waiting for *us*. We praise God that he also defeated the evil that bound *us*, overcame *our* sin, rose triumphantly *for us*, returned to the right hand of the Father representing *us*, and will return to claim *us* and establish the kingdom of God in its fullness. It was the faithfulness of Christ as prophet, priest and king that has handed us back our life and opened up to us our future.

It is the vicarious nature of this work that is the key for us here. Christ did not come as a heavenly guide to "show us the way" that we might now stride into heaven down the right road. He did not come as a physician to provide us with a remedy for sin that, once we have accepted it and taken it, heals us and fits us for heaven. He did not come as a teacher to impart wisdom to us that, once enlightened, we might find heaven within us or through self-transcendence. In all these ways the atoning work of Christ remains detached from us and ultimately throws us back upon ourselves to work out our own destiny. In this way, it plays into our self-centeredness, which so badly wants to find a role for us in our own salvation. It returns us to Eden in a grab for power where we can know the options and choose for ourselves. These are popular notions of the work of Christ, and all lead to the same dead end. They fix what is wrong, but they bring about no ultimate transformation in our lives. They buy us eternity but leave us mired in life. They deal with sin in an abstract, transcendent way, but they ignore its effects on us in this life. In the end, they are the religious formulae that support the building of a second kingdom and a bifurcation of our view of earthly reality.

We simply must not miss the critical importance of the vicarious nature of the work of Christ. It is a view that is a radical departure from all other ways of understanding the work of Christ. As such it has a profound effect on how we see ourselves as children of God and therefore on how we seek to live and what it means to be a steward. Plainly stated, everything we have said about the call to be a steward will stand or fall on this one primary point.

The reason for this is that the vicarious humanity of Christ calls us to an all-encompassing, no compromising, wholly committed life of joyous response. We have made the case for this in chapter five, so we will only reiterate the main point here that Christ bore our humanity in his incarnation, life, death and resurrection. Therefore, as a result of what was done for us two thousand years ago, *we have been changed.* Not because we are smarter, holier, more biblically literate, or because we are Presbyterian, Baptist, Methodist, Lutheran, independent, Pentecostal and so forth. We have been changed because of what Christ did for us.

The reason this point is so incredibly important is that our response is wholly wrapped up in our understanding of what has come before and therefore what motivates us to respond. If indeed Christ bore our humanity, and in that bearing atoned for us in his life, death and resurrection, then the one word that describes our response to his work is *participation.* We do not ever again act on our own. We are never again thrown back upon ourselves to "act properly" in order to receive the grace of God nor to be workers in his kingdom. Our work as stewards is not the fulfillment of certain expectations of "good church people" who should be generous. We do not live as Christians out of fear or guilt or resigned obedience, nor out of the hope of temporal or eternal reward.

The reason we must eschew these counterfeit forms of "Christian living" is made plain in Scripture. Simply put, "You are not your own; you were bought at a price" (1 Cor 6:19-20). When we understand that by the vicarious work of Christ, our whole existence becomes wrapped up in Christ's work for us, the Scriptures come alive.

What we learn is that our life as Christians begins with our knowledge that death precedes life. Not the second death that is merely physical but the far more heinous death that marked the lives of Adam and Eve as they fled from Eden. It is the spiritual death that comes from separation from God. It is the real death that is to be feared for its eternal consequences. It is the "first death" that is the sentence of eternal separation from our Creator and an eternal consumption of us by the evil we have chosen. It is this death that Christ overcame in his work for us, and it is our participation in this overcoming, our own "death to death," that must mark our first step of living according to that atoning work. Before we can "live to righteousness," we must "die to sin."

Yet we must be careful here not to see that dying as *our* act, or else we fall back into all that we are seeking to lay aside. It is not our work, but it is our participation in the work of Christ for us. When Christ died our death, he conquered sin for us. For us to live free from that sin we must participate in the death of Christ in our own dying to sin. When the Holy Spirit calls us to faith, we are truly called to "come and die."

And what a glorious dying it is! I believe so many have never learned to really live joyfully as Christians because they have never learned what it means to die. Christian dying to sin is a setting aside of all that would stand between us and our walk with Jesus Christ. It is an acknowledgment of our sinfulness and our need for the salvation won for us on the cross. It is a repenting of our attempts to go it alone. It is a renunciation of our self-centeredness, and therefore it is truly a "dying to self." It is an unlocking of the chains that bind us, the fears that press in on us, the anxieties that keep us down and the despair that renders our life meaningless. It is a turning away from our own agenda, a laying aside of our own selfish striving for a worldly version of success, place, honor and happiness. It is a surrendering of our own lordship over all four levels of our relationships. It is the abandonment of our earthly kingdoms and the renunciation of our thirst for kingdom building. It is death to everything that obstructs and prohibits us from living joyfully as beloved, free and empowered children in the one kingdom of God into which we have been called as stewards. This is the death that marks the beginning of life, the death that opens the doors to the kingdom of God, the death that sets us free.

Death as the Life of the Steward

The point that we must make is that *we cannot be stewards in the kingdom of the triune God of grace until we have died this death.* In Christ we have died this death. "He himself bore our sins in his body on the tree, so that we might die to sins and live for righteousness" (1 Pet 2:24). Sin has been broken for us. "For we know that our old self was crucified with him so that the body of sin might be done away with, that we should no longer be slaves to sin—because anyone who has died has been freed from sin" (Rom 6:6-7). In our lives we must die this death in our participation in the work of Christ for us. Through it we are set free to really live for Christ. This dying and rising is symbolized in baptism. "Don't you know that all of us who were baptized into Christ Jesus were baptized into his death? We were therefore buried with him through baptism into death in order that, just as Christ was raised from the dead through the glory of the Father, we too may live a new life" (Rom 6:3-4).

The new life in the kingdom of God is the "life after death" for the Christian. Again it is marked by participation. Hear these amazing words from Ephesians, "Because of his great love for us, God, who is rich in mercy, made us alive with Christ even when we were dead in our transgressions—it is by grace you have been saved. And God *raised us up with Christ and seated us with him in the heavenly realms in Christ Jesus.*" (2:4-6, emphasis mine). Everything we are as Christians is bound up in the vicarious work of Christ. And everything we are called to do as Christians must be equally bound up with our participation in that great and ongoing work of Christ through the church.

This means our lives are freed to be marked by the fruits of the Spirit, and our worldview is re-centered on the reality that God came to establish one kingdom and to call us as his children to live in it. This is how we participate in Christ's work for us. We die to sin—and thereby participate in Christ's death for us, and we live to righteousness—and thereby participate in the righteousness of Christ for us.

Dying and rising has "once-for-all" and "daily discipline" aspects to it. We have seen that in the salvific work of Christ, atonement was completed for us all. That can never be undone, and nothing ever needs to be added to it. Remember the words of the writer of Hebrews,

Because Jesus lives forever, he has a permanent priesthood. Therefore he is able to save completely those who come to God through him, because he always lives to intercede for them. . . . He sacrificed for their sins once for all when he offered himself. . . . But now he has appeared once for all at the end of the ages to do away with sin by the sacrifice of himself. . . . And by that will, we have been made holy through the sacrifice of the body of Jesus Christ once for all. (7:24-25, 27; 9:26; 10:10)

This is the ultimate reality that keeps us from wandering into a dangerous self-serving form of righteousness. All our acts of living for Jesus are responses to what has already been done for us. Our lives are therefore truly a response! We need to be reminded of this daily, for it is the basis of our hope, the motivation for our faithful obedience and the source of our joy. It is the good news, it is freedom, and it is light shining in the darkness.

We now are given the privilege of living out this reality in our lives. Yet we are called to do so in a world that still believes it is under bondage to evil and in which sin still reigns in a distorted hope that the cross will not ultimately prevail. The kingdom of God has come in provisional form. It is no less the reality of our existence, but it has yet to be revealed to a world that rejects its claims and rebels against its grace. For that reason, Paul reminds his church in Colossae that the result of this dying to sin also has a provisional nature, "For you died, and your life is now hidden with Christ in God. When Christ, who is your life, appears, then you also will appear with him in glory" (Col 3:3-4).

We live in a kingdom that is both "now" and "not yet." This provisional nature provides us with the opportunity to live as children in God's kingdom and thereby to announce the grace of God to all the world. If we hear the "not yet" nature of the kingdom in Hebrews 2:8, "Yet at present we do not see everything subject to him [Jesus]," we must also hear the very certain "now" reality of the kingdom in the words of Jesus in Matthew 28:18, "All authority in heaven and on earth has been given to me." It is this kingdom into which we are called to be stewards, and the entrance into this kingdom comes through death. Moltmann gives us a word of warning about maintaining this balance: "It would be one-sided to see the lordship of God only in his perfected kingdom, just as it is misleading to identify his kingdom with his actual, present rule."[1]

Our call is to live as stewards in this present and coming kingdom.

---

[1]Jürgen Moltmann, *The Way of Jesus Christ* (London: SCM Press, 1990), p. 97.

That means that we bear witness to a world that views reality as those years lived out between birth and death by proclaiming with lips and lives that our true reality is indeed exactly the opposite. Our lives begin not with birth but with death. If this is the case, then the hope and joy we have to proclaim to the world is that with our true death behind us, *all we have ahead of us is life.*

The Life Ahead

June is always a magical month in our household. As the final days of school wind down, there is a quiet euphoria that sweeps our hallways and resounds up our staircases. The first day of summer recess is like the beginning of a never-ending vacation. In those first few days of "freedom," nothing can stifle the enthusiasm of the anticipation of countless weeks of summer kid stuff. A few years ago it rained on the first day of the official summer break, and I commented to my oldest, "Too bad you have to spend your first day of vacation inside." To which he replied, "Dad, who cares about one bad day when you have you whole summer ahead of you!"

This outlook of hope and joy is seen at a different level in the survivors of supposed terminal illnesses who now have been given "new life," a second chance to live. They report that their entire outlook on life is radically new. Every day is a gift, and should their life end tomorrow, they would be thankful for the days that they have been given in this new life.

This attitude of new life and a freedom for the future is the defining mark of the Christian and therefore of the steward who has died to sin and now looks ahead as God's new creation. The story of our redemption is the story of life coming out of death. It is Easter's resurrection after Calvary's cross. It is a story of release from bondage, of pardon for a sentence of death, of atonement for guilt and of victory out of defeat. Therefore, the story of our salvation is the pronouncement of our freedom.

No one word better describes the life we live in a "death-to-life" kingdom reality than the word *freedom.* And no phrase better describes the life of a steward in the kingdom of God than "freed for life." Our salvation is our freedom from all that the enemy would use to bind our hearts and minds, keeping us from knowing the truth that sets us free. Jesus Christ professed himself to be "the way, the truth and the life." For the steward he is the way in that our salvation and our Christian life are found only through faith and participation in grace. He is the truth that sets us free through our death to sin. If you know the truth, the truth will set you free. And he is the life, the abundant life that can only be lived on the far side of death, and therefore it is a life of freedom lived in and through the Son. "If the Son sets you free, you will be free indeed" (Jn 8:36). This freedom can be described as freedom *from* and freedom *for.*

Freedom *From*

Our freedom in Christ is both reactive and proactive. It is reactive in that it is a freedom from the bondage we have incurred through sin. George Barna has found that 50 percent of respondents to a survey who identified themselves as "born-again" Christians agreed that "the main purpose of life is enjoyment and personal fulfillment."[2] How desperately we need to be freed from such views that only serve to bind us. It is a freedom won for us on the cross that seals our liberation from a life of mindless pursuit of self-interests. It is a freedom from the deceit of self-idolatry and the allure of kingdom building. It is a freedom from everything that we would like to place in our second kingdom, lock up with a key and call "ours." It is a freedom from the dual standards of success that plague the Christian life. It is a freedom from guilt that settles in with each attempt to meet the world's criteria for self-acceptance and self-worth. It is freedom from the confining, angst-driven pursuits for meaning and happiness in these years between birth and death. It is a freedom from all of these things that make up the "real world." Therefore, it is also a freedom from fear, anxiety, hatred, prejudice, envy, bitterness, cynicism and depression that haunts the halls of our second kingdom.

In a financial sense this is a freedom from the endless pursuit of meaning through materialism. It is a breaking of the bondage of needing more to be happy and wanting more to be secure. Wuthnow found in his research that the one single largest influence on how much people gave to religious work was the *perceptions* they held about their own personal wealth. That is, "Whether they have needs or not, those who value money less give more, and those who value it more give less."[3] Only when we have been freed from the lure of financial gain for the building of our earthly kingdom can we be the "cheerful giver" so loved by God.

The freedom from all of the baggage of the second kingdom does not

---

[2]George Barna, *Virtual America* (Ventura, Calif.: Regal Books, 1994), p. 81.
[3]Robert Wuthnow, *God and Mammon in America* (New York: Free Press, 1994), p. 237.

come from a new "outlook on life" that allows us to see beyond them with rose-colored glasses. Nor does it come from some supernatural source of power that magically removes them from our lives so we no longer have to deal with them. The change comes at a more fundamental level. Here we can understand the words of Doug Hall when he writes, "Stewardship is no longer concerned with matters—including religious matters—on the periphery of existence; it belongs to the essence of things . . . for the call to responsible stewardship encounters us precisely at the heart of our present-day dilemma and impasse."[4]

In dying to sin we have become a new creation, and therefore we have had our feet set on a new path. Our new being has been freed from the deceptions that marred our understandings of who God is and therefore of who we are and how we should live. We no longer struggle for meaning in life before death because we have already died. We no longer face fears and anxieties because we no longer grant eternal value to temporal things, nor do we judge ourselves according to our ability to gain and keep what can only be lost. We no longer agonize over our kingdom building with its pressures and standards because we have abdicated our hollow throne and entered the new kingdom already built for us.

It is the context of this new journey that frees us. For this journey sees only life ahead of us, and therefore it frees us to be life-givers and life-sustainers in all we do. We no longer fear for our lives, for they have been bought with a price and given back to us on the far side of our death. In this way we are already experiencing life after death. It is here for us in provisional form, and it will be ours in its fullness at our second, physical death. In between we are freed to live for Christ in every fiber of our being. No wonder Paul could proclaim, "For to me, to live is Christ and to die is gain" (Phil 1:21). No wonder he could take joy in saying, "I have been crucified with Christ and I no longer live, but Christ lives in me" (Gal 2:20).

Imagine what life would be like if every day was seen as an incredible gift in a life that was guaranteed to last forever. Imagine what it would be like to be so certain about tomorrow that you could be free to invest every hour of today doing whatever was most pleasing to God. Imagine being so certain about who you were in the eyes of God that you could give yourself away in service to others with real joy. This is not only possible,

---

[4]Douglas John Hall, *The Steward* (Grand Rapids, Mich.: Eerdmans, 1990), p. 95.

it is our calling as stewards in the kingdom of the triune God who has freed us for just this kind of rich and abundant life. We are freed from all that would keep us from being joyful stewards at all four levels of our relationships. This is what it means to be freed *from* through our death in Christ.

Freedom *For*
The proactive side of this freedom in Christ is the substance of the calling to be stewards. We look back to what we have left behind in our dying to sin, and we look ahead to our vocation in the kingdom of God as his free, new creation. The pattern of our vocation follows the pattern of the redemptive work of Christ for us. Remember, our work in God's kingdom is participatory work. Therefore, we must see our calling as stewards as a freedom to carry out the work of reconciliation on all four levels of our relationships in which we were created.

First, we are freed for service to God. This freedom comes in our yielding all lordship to God alone. It is a freedom from the pressures and attitudes that draw us into the vicious cycle of claiming lordship over our own kingdoms that we might find meaning there, only to find that the more lordship we claim, the less meaning we really experience. We have been freed from this devastating downward spiral, and now we can humbly submit all of our lives to the lordship of the God of the one kingdom in which we serve as joyful stewards.

Along with a lordship issue this is also a power issue. We are freed for a new understanding of power. Our commitment to the one kingdom of God and our consequent denunciation of our worldly kingdoms, bestows upon us a power that may surprise us. We have seen that one aspect of the quest to build our own kingdoms is the thirst for power to control—control others, ourselves, our environment and even God. By rejecting this kingdom we are freed from the tentacles of this self-centered understanding of power. By dying to sin we have made impotent the temptations to seek this power and to use this power in our mad scramble from life to death.

This is true freedom. However, our obedience as stewards in God's one kingdom is not devoid of power. Powerlessness is not the antithesis of the world's understanding of power. What we find as stewards in God's kingdom is a godly power that radiates from every person who can stand in the midst of this broken world with a mind of peace, a heart of joy, a clear sense of self-purpose and an unbridled hope for a future in Christ. God grants to us a power that brings transformation into every relational area of our lives. People who come in contact with stewards in the kingdom of the triune God of grace witness transformation and are therefore in some way touched by God's power to become transformed.

This is real power but it is never *our* power. This transforming power comes to us and through us as the work of the Holy Spirit. It is controlled by God alone, and it is the product of the life that has been freed for fellowship with God in Christ. How ironic that it is only by giving up all forms and claims to power that we become the conduits of the greatest power in the universe. It is only by becoming powerless in the world's eyes that we are given the high calling to be stewards in God's kingdom and therefore ambassadors for reconciliation and transformation. This is what we have been freed *for* in our relationship to God as his stewards.

Second, we are freed for true love of self. From the sin of Adam and Eve, our lives have been marked by a sinfulness that splits our loyalties and distorts our self-understanding. If we do not see ourselves as solely and wholly created as God's children, fitted for work in his kingdom and freed from the bondage of self-delusion and doubt, then we live with brokenness in our self-image. If we measure ourselves in our neighbor's eyes, then we have lost our identity. If we look to our earthly kingdoms to show us the meaning for our lives, then we have lost our hope.

To be freed to love ourselves is to be freed to see ourselves in God's eyes. What a freedom this is! We no longer see ourselves *in abstracto* but as children of God—redeemed, forgiven, embraced, empowered and called into service. Our self-worth is wholly wrapped up in our vocation as stewards in the one and only kingdom that claims our allegiance. A favorite saying of mine states, "It doesn't matter if the world knows, or sees or understands; the only applause we are meant to seek is that of nail-scarred hands." Therein lies the focus of the steward, and this focus brings to us the freedom to love ourselves as God's beloved creature. Our very being is once again wrapped up in relationship, and therefore our self-love comes from the source and partner in that relationship, the loving God we know in Jesus Christ. By denouncing our divided loyalties and by rejecting the lure to consider our selves *in abstracto*, we are freed to love and accept ourselves in Christ.

Third, we are freed for service to our neighbor. This freedom results from a denunciation of the sin that demanded that all of our relationships with our neighbor must be self-serving; that is, they must contribute to the construction of our earthly kingdoms. We have seen how relationships become means to this end and how we become manipulators to bring about these ends. Freedom in our dying to sin is a freedom from the need to use others because it is a freedom from kingdom building. With no kingdom to build, with allegiance to the one kingdom of God, we enter into our earthly relationships with a whole new focus. Suddenly words that carried no meaning to us before become a core of our response to our neighbor: "selfless service," "sacrifice" and "joyful giving." None of these concepts can be considered seriously if we are kingdom builders. But if we are free, if we are stewards in God's kingdom, then our lives are God's gift to us to invest in service to our neighbor.

We make this investment joyfully, regardless of the temporal costs, because we know that all we have ahead of us is life. How else can missionaries invest decades of life in our world's most hostile areas than if they see their lives from an eternal perspective? How else can we consider sacrificial service than if we have understood our lives as a gift to be stewarded and in that sense to be given back to a world in need of the transforming grace of God? Why else would a Samaritan risk his life for a stranger at the side of a dusty Judean road? Why else would a woman give her entire life to caring for the desperate plight of the poor in Calcutta? Because they have died to the bondage of sin, they understand that their life has been given back to them as a gift to be stewarded, and all they see ahead of them is life.

When we are freed from the fear of physical death and the bondage of a birth-to-death worldview, we are freed to see our lives in this dramatically new light. And so we are freed to see our neighbor in this wonderful new way. We then are called to be stewards of these precious relationships, not counting any cost but investing ourselves with joy in God's work of human transformation. We will also be recommitted to care for creation, for as Ray Van Leeuwen reminds us, "One cannot love one's neighbor without taking care of creation."[5] Here we see the interconnectedness of our work at these levels. We have treated them separately here for clarity, but they are all intertwined, and together they represent one offering of worship to God.

---

[5]Ray C. Van Leeuwen, "Christ's Resurrection and the Creation's Vindication," in *The Environment and the Christian* (Grand Rapids, Mich.: Baker, 1991), p. 69.

Finally, we are freed to be stewards of our relationships with our creation. In dying to sin and rising with Christ we destroy the value of creation as a component in our kingdom-building activity. We are in turn given the freedom to reclaim the original intent of the terms *rule over* and *subdue*. "To subdue Eden apparently meant to retain the goodness and beauty that God gave it, while actively serving Eden through managing (cultivating) it to better enhance and manifest the qualities hidden within it."[6] We are reminded that in Christ we hear God's words and follow God's commands in a distinctly new and transformed way. When we hear that we are to "keep" creation, we know that this keeping is the godly care with which God keeps us. We will seek no counterfeit definition that will thrust us back into our old kingdom paradigm, but we will embrace the new life in Christ and the new, restored relationship with God's creation that must and will naturally follow.[7]

We will seek to be stewards of creation in the same way we understand God's stewardship of creation. We will "rule over" and "subdue" creation as we see God's ruling and subduing work in our own lives. Therefore, we will understand the role of grace, compassion, selflessness, wisdom and faith in all of our dealings with the stuff of creation.

But we must go beyond this. If we are truly a new creation in Christ, then we will develop a heart for a creation that was made "in, by and for" Christ. The "Evangelical Declaration on the Care of Creation" is a fine example of a balanced, Christ-centered and unapologetic statement for the church. It lays out ten principles of biblical faith for the care of creation. Among them are the following affirmations: "God's purpose in Christ is to heal and bring to wholeness not only persons but the entire created order. . . . The presence of the kingdom of God is marked not only by renewed fellowship with God, but also by renewed harmony and justice between people, and by renewed harmony and justice between people and the rest of the created world."[8]

---

[6]Fred Van Dyke, David Mahan, Joseph Sheldon and Raymond Brand, *Redeeming Creation: The Biblical Basis for Environmental Stewardship* (Downers Grove, Ill.: InterVarsity Press, 1996), p. 96.

[7]In *Redeeming Creation,* Van Dyke, Mahan, Sheldon and Brand offer a helpful symmetry of the use of the Hebrew word *shamar* in God's command to "keep" creation and his blessing, may the Lord bless you and "keep" you. They conclude that clearly humankind is instructed to "keep" the garden as the Lord "keeps" us.

[8]"An Evangelical Declaration on the Care of Creation," published by the Evangelical Environmental Network, a ministry of Evangelicals for Social Action.

When kingdom building ceases to be at the core of our life, we are freed to consider all things temporal as a part of that redemptive work of Christ and therefore as undergoing the same transformation that marks our lives. For that reason we must again understand our relationship to creation as a participation in the work of Christ in creation. We are called to make the radical transition from seeing the created world, our possessions and our time as temporal commodities with only a utilitarian value to understanding all creation as part of a world that is being transformed by the grace of God. Therefore, every use we make of this creation carries with it an opportunity and a responsibility. In exegeting the great hymn of Colossians 1:15-20, Ray Van Leeuwen concludes, "This passage stands against every sinful Christian attempt to divide reality into secular and secular realms. All of reality is Christ's good creation, all of reality is redeemed by him; therefore, all of reality is the responsibility of God's people."[9]

The opportunity is to glorify God and to demonstrate the transforming power of the grace of God in every use we make of the temporal things in our world. The responsibility is to undertake each use with prayer, with care and with an attitude of a true steward. On this earth we sow and reap; we use animals for food and clothing; we harvest natural resources for energy and products; we invest our money and our time. In all these activities and in the choices represented in each we must bear witness to this opportunity and this responsibility. This we are freed to do when we die to the sin of kingdom building and the distorted use of God's creation that it breeds. This we are freed to do when we are raised to new life in Christ, a death-to-life joyous existence that gives itself over to serve God, our neighbor and our beloved creation.

This is what it means to be a steward in the kingdom of the triune God of grace. Stewards pay homage to only one Lord. Stewards serve in only one kingdom. Stewards look ahead and see only life. For this reason, stewards are joyous, stewards are people of hope, stewards are free.

The Steward as Worshiper
The final word that can and must be said about a theology of the steward brings us back to the beginning. We contended at the outset that stewardship was ultimately an act of worship. Our journey now brings us back to this all-important point. Only from all that has been said can we now

---

[9]Van Leeuwen, "Christ's Resurrection," p. 62.

understand the true nature of stewardship as worship. Only here can we see why stewardship cannot be something pasted on to the Christian life, just as preaching and teaching stewardship cannot be pasted on to the end of the church calendar (more on this in chapter eight). Being a steward in God's kingdom is not an activity we do alongside our other roles as Christians, but it *defines our roles as Christians.* We must no longer split the terms *Christian* and *steward* as if the latter were one of many options available to the believer. The very term *steward,* understood as we have developed it here, carries with it the essence of what it means to be a follower of Jesus Christ.

If we are truly stewards in God's kingdom, then we have died to sin, repented of our old, kingdom building ways, come under the one lordship of God in Jesus Christ, and accepted the call and vocation of living a death-to-life existence marked by love of God and selfless service to our neighbor and creation. Being a steward in this sense is simply a definition of the new creation in Christ. For this reason we must see our call to be stewards as wrapped up wholly in our lives as Christians.

The reason this is so critical is that it is only at this point that we can consider our work as stewards as authentic worship. By authentic worship I mean a lifestyle that intentionally seeks to glorify God in every moment, act and decision. We worship God every day, every waking moment when we seek to be stewards in his kingdom in this dynamic way. Worship becomes an offering back to God of all that we are, all that we have and all that we do. It is a conscious striving to reflect the grace of our Lord and Savior Jesus Christ in our lives, to bear witness to the majesty and love of God and to be agents of reconciliation and transformation through the power of the Holy Spirit. Therefore it is trinitarian worship, and it is participatory worship.

We have demonstrated how all our work as God's children is our participation in the vicarious work of Jesus Christ for us. Because it is participatory work, it is authentic worship. That is, it is never our work, our act, our worship *in abstracto.* We can only be the steward and our stewardship can be authentic worship only as it is our participation in Christ's work for us. That is why it must be free. That is why it can only be carried out on the far side of our death to sin and resurrection to the new life in Christ. On this far side of death, everything we have, everything we are and everything we do is a gift by the grace of God. How else can we live than as stewards of these gifts in the freedom of our new lives in Christ?

And what else can this new life be but worship?

The Oneness of Worship

This lifestyle and therefore this worship is characterized by a "oneness." We serve *one Lord*, we are citizens of *one kingdom*, and we offer *one service* as stewards. We have renounced shared lordship, dual citizenship and divided service. As such our lives have a determined sense about them. We are not thrown about by competing passions or by the various suitors vying for our allegiance. We are not distracted by various pursuits of self-actualization or kingdom expansion. We are not passionless about our future or insecure about our status in life. We are focused, determined and forthright. We have a sense of confidence that gives way to compassion and sacrificial service without ever losing that determination and certitude. This sense of freedom and purpose is also our worship. It bears witness to the steward who has been set free to render one service in one kingdom to one Lord. Therefore, it brings our God great joy.

The Wholeness of Worship

As this worship is trinitarian, focused and manifest in all aspects of our lives, it is also worship at all four levels of our existence. We worship God in our stewardship of our relationship to God. We worship and glorify God in our self-love that is the love of one created by God. We worship and glorify God in our selfless service to our neighbor. And we worship and glorify God in our care of creation. Worship happens in the local church, in the home, in the workplace and in the community. Worship happens in cleaning up a stretch of highway, taking meals to shut-ins, caring for our health and gathering together on Sunday in our churches. Worship also happens in our participation in dialogues for racial reconciliation, in our protests against immorality that brings brokenness, in our work for justice for the poor and in our advocacy for the voiceless, the sick, the forgotten and the outcasts. Worship happens when a husband and wife sit down to discuss their budget and seek to make God-pleasing decisions with their money. Worship happens when leaders of Christian institutions seek to make God-pleasing decisions about the use of funds entrusted to them for ministry. And, dare I say, worship happens when a Christian fundraiser meets with a donor to discuss an opportunity to give to further the work of the kingdom. I will make the case in chapter nine that this is a uniquely Christian moment that should cause us to see

Christian fundraising as a critical ministry in the kingdom of God. Commenting on 2 Corinthians 9, Bassler concludes, "Giving to others thus glorifies God (v. 13), and an act of charity is thereby transformed into an act of worship."[10]

To the extent that each of these glorifies God, they bear witness to the freedom of the steward to live the new life in Christ, and they create an opportunity for the transforming work of the Holy Spirit. These are indeed acts of authentic worship.

New Lenses for Reading Scripture

One-kingdom living provides us with a new set of lenses with which to read Scripture. This is a powerful statement, but one that must be made if we are not to miss the holistic effect that our new freedom in Christ is to have on every aspect of our lives. We cannot seek to live the new life in Christ as stewards in God's kingdom if we continue to read Scripture through the lenses of our old, two-kingdom worldview. One of the joys of the new death-to-life vocation of the steward is the opportunity to go back and reread Scripture with this new set of lenses. That is, when we understand the transformation that marks the Christian life, we can understand the challenging verses in Scripture that, frankly, make little sense in the two-kingdom mindset.

The goal here is not to undertake an exhaustive exegetical analysis of every difficult or misinterpreted verse in Scripture. Our goal is to provide some examples of how one-kingdom living changes our understanding of Scripture. From these examples one can create a new mindset for reading Scripture. We acknowledge that the role of inspiration is the Spirit's alone; however, we are called to be responsible in how we come to Scripture. Our goal is to provide a context for such a responsible approach.

The Rich Young Ruler

The Bible is rich with references to the stewardship of our money and talents. While many seem straightforward, some are more enigmatic. Take for example the story of the rich young ruler in Matthew 19. When read through the lenses of our two-kingdom lifestyles, the request of Jesus seems singularly unfair. The young man only wanted to know the way to

---

[10]Jouette Bassler, *God and Mammon: Asking for Money in the New Testament* (Nashville: Abingdon, 1991), p. 108.

eternal life. Why did Jesus not give him the "I am the way" speech or demonstrate the kind of compassion and forgiveness he had shown to the woman caught in adultery or the woman with the hemorrhage? Why this seemingly impossible temporal request in response to a spiritual question? The church has struggled with various explanations of this text that have ranged from a literal interpretation that leaves us hopeless to an allegorical interpretation that gets us off the hook completely.

Now how does this story look through our new lenses that have emerged from one-kingdom living? What we see is that this rich, powerful young man had become a champion kingdom builder. His question to Jesus could be paraphrased as, "What must I do in my spiritual kingdom to assure eternal life, without bothering my earthly kingdom building?" In other words, what are the minimum requirements that will allow me to have peace about my spiritual future so I can continue to focus on my temporal well-being? We can read this into the young man's inquiry because we have been through the same set of questions with God. In our own kingdom building we have sought the dual citizenship that allows us to ask deep spiritual questions in the understanding that the answers will impact only our spiritual realm.

Jesus would have none of this. He saw the question for what it was, and he forced the young man to consider that the call of Jesus would have implications far beyond his spiritual kingdom. Keeping one's spiritual house in order, which in this case was keeping the law of Moses, is not all that is required for eternal life. Jesus was forcing a shift of paradigm. He was asking that the young man denounce his earthly kingdom and enter into the joy of one-kingdom living. He was offering him "treasure in heaven" in place of earthly baubles, a chance to follow the giver of life instead of the anxious existence that sees ahead only death.

This call comes into sharper focus when we set this story alongside Jesus' parable of the treasure hidden in the field. Jesus tells us that the discovery of something so utterly invaluable, so precious and so unique led the discoverer to the joyful act of "selling everything he had to buy the field" and thus acquire the treasure. The contrast here is staggering. The farmer recognized the true worth of the treasure and counts nothing as too costly to obtain it. The rich young man however missed the value of what Jesus was offering him, and so it was deemed too light on the scales when compared to his own kingdom. In the face of their respective decisions, the farmer knew unequalled joy, and the rich young ruler went away sad.

It is imperative that we see therefore that the call to this young man from the lips of Jesus was a genuine call. We must be careful not to soft-sell Jesus' response in order to maintain some support of our two-kingdom lifestyles. Jesus said what he said. The young man heard and went away sad. And Jesus let him. Jesus did not run after him shouting, "Wait, wait, I was only speaking metaphorically!" Jesus was serious. Jesus was bidding the young man to "come and die." The young man knew it and so did the disciples. That is why they responded, "Who then can be saved?" Jesus' answer is the door that opens up to us the new life in Christ. He proclaims that while this dramatic shift seems impossible to us, "For God all things are possible." Even the transformation of a generation of kingdom builders into truly one-kingdom people? Even the transformation of our churches into true stewards and trainers of stewards? Yes, even this.

The Widow's Mite
A second passage worth noting is the small story of the widow's mite from Luke 21. Jesus' words of commendation of the woman's gift reminds us again that being a steward is an affair of the heart and soul first. The two small copper coins represented to Jesus a woman who trusted in the Lord with all her heart. How else could she give away her sustenance? Compelled to give she does not hold back but places her trust in God. This is a one-kingdom response. It demonstrates the heart of a steward. For this Jesus commends her, setting her gift side by side with those who would give only "from their wealth." That is, those who give what they can afford to transfer from their earthly kingdom. The widow had no such kingdom, so her giving was uninhibited. This is what it means to give generously as a steward in God's kingdom. It is not the percentage of our giving, for Jesus asks us for nothing less than everything we have. It is a free act of love and trust that would have us give it all.

The Sermon on the Mount
This same teaching comes through Jesus' Sermon on the Mount. He instructs us that our giving should be done so quietly that our left hand may not know what our right hand is doing (Mt 6:1-4). He warns us not to build earthly kingdoms filled with treasures that moth and rust can destroy, but to store up "treasures in heaven" (6:19-21). He bids us not to worry about the stuff of this world like clothing and food but to "seek

first the kingdom of God and his righteousness" (6:25-34). Finally, he promises God's provision for our every need (7:7-11) if we will but ask in faith. If we read these verses with our new lenses, we will see the theme of one-kingdom living come shining through. All that God has for us in the way of the abundant life is predicated on our death, which marks the transformation of our lives from the myth of the two kingdoms to the joyous one-kingdom reality of the steward.

The Macedonian Collection

The apostle Paul picks up this theme and carries it forward in his teachings on the Macedonian collection in 2 Corinthians. In our old paradigm, imagine how odd the following verse sounds: "Out of the most severe trial, their overflowing joy and their extreme poverty welled-up in rich generosity" (8:2). Severe trial and extreme poverty are not usually considered to be the best precursors for a generous donation. Most fundraisers would avoid calling on someone who they knew to have endured severe trial and extreme poverty. If a gift were given, these two characteristics would hardly be credited as the motivators as Paul seems to do. Of course, these are our old lenses. If we pick up our new lenses, the picture makes more sense. If there are two experiences that throw us completely at the foot of our God in total trust and dependence, they are severe trial and extreme poverty. The history of the church throughout the ages is rife with stories of incredible faith, church growth, and dynamic transformation and renewal that emerged from severe trial and extreme poverty. Those who have worked among the "poorest of the poor" are continually blessed by the depth of faith and joy so many know as they depend upon God for their daily life.

In describing the church in Macedonia in this way Paul lets us know that these people are faithful, trusting and wholly committed stewards in God's kingdom. Why then should it surprise us that their giving was both generous and joyful. Why should we be amazed that they "pleaded with us for the privilege of sharing in this service to the saints"? Is it not fitting that Paul should record, even to his own surprise, that they "gave themselves first to the Lord, and then to us"?

Bassler concludes,

> It is clear in all of this that it is not the monetary contribution *per se* that Paul celebrates in Macedonia and urges in Corinth, but the giving of *self* that the

giving symbolizes. Thus he can say that zealous participation in the concrete collection gift is not merely one good deed among many, but an act that confirms the transforming presence of more intangible spiritual gifts.[11]

That is the sequence followed by stewards in the kingdom of the triune God of grace. It is wholeness on the vertical level, followed by selfless service to our neighbor and our creation. It is generous because it comes in response to God's immeasurable generosity to us in Jesus Christ. What a model of one-kingdom living!

The Man with the Donkey

One more example of godly stewardship must be mentioned here. It is seldom if ever cited among the chief models that we have listed above. However, this one simple instance in the life of Jesus may speak more about responding as a true steward than all the others.

Imagine the scene. A man has his colt and his donkey tied up in their usual place, probably either ready for their daily work or for a rest from the morning work already completed. In first-century Palestine as well as in most developing rural nations today, one's animals are the most important single asset to one's survival. They are transportation, farm machinery, hauling vehicles, food and clothing producers, trading pieces and so on. As such they are guarded and cared for, protected from disease, theft and injury.

On this particular day a man had tied up his colt and his donkey in a secure place out of harm's way and in plain sight to discourage any would-be thieves. Now into this safe scenario come two strangers who, to the man's surprise and anger, stop and begin to untie his animals, his property, his very livelihood. The Gospel of Mark records that those who witnessed this asked, "What are you doing untying the colt?" In Luke it is the owner who asks the question. We can only imagine that this was not a passive query but a defiant protest to the two thieves. We can even conceive of the owner reaching for his club as he is asking the question, ready to attack and defend his property.

Given this scenario, the response of the two disciples and the reaction of the owner seem incredible. The disciples say what they were instructed to say and nothing more. They simply respond, "The Lord needs it" (Lk 19:34). They added no excuses. They made no additional pleas. They did

---

[11]Ibid., p. 103.

not defend the request or try to persuade the owner with explanations. They did not apply any "making the big ask" techniques. They had no giving charts, no video presentation, no campaign booklet and no brochures. They quoted no Scriptures on rewards for cheerful giving, and they did not promise the animals would be returned or paid for. They did not try to inflict guilt, incite sympathy or conjure up omens of tragedy if the gift were withheld. They discussed no tax advantages for the owner, no special benefits for the gift and no naming opportunities in the coming kingdom. They said nothing more than the simple words the Lord had given to them.

We can assume from the story—recorded in all four Gospels, although much abbreviated in John—that the owner knew who "the Lord" was. He was not put into a trance, nor was he the victim of a mind-controlling "Force" à la *Star Wars* fame. From all we can tell from the story, he simply heard and accepted the words of the strangers. He stood and watched without protest as they untied his two animals and led them away. And it was over. Two precious animals lost all because two strangers said, "The Lord needs them."

Is this not for us today an image of the true steward? We are called to care for all the Lord has given to us just as the owner cared for his animals. Yet we are also called to be ready at any time to give them away to strangers if and when we believe the Lord has need of them. Our assets are to be in this constant state of readiness to be used in the kingdom of God. Therefore, they can never belong to a worldly kingdom, but they must again be placed squarely in the realm of the one kingdom in which we live and work as stewards.

As the stewards of these assets we must be ready at a moment's notice to part with them for the sake of the kingdom and in the name of the Lord. And this we must be prepared to do not because of the way we are asked, the rewards we are promised, the advantages our giving will bring us or the guilt we will assuage. We must be prepared to give only because we believe "the Lord has need of it." In this way the simple story of the man with the donkey and colt is a story of true stewardship. What a joy it must have been when the man later saw Jesus ride into Jerusalem on that same donkey! What a joy it will be for us when we see how God will use the resources entrusted to us in the work of his kingdom!

There are numerous other examples we could cite that take on new meaning when seen through the lenses of one-kingdom living. We have a new and richer understanding of why it is more blessed to give than to receive (Acts 20:35), what motivates us to be truly cheerful in our giving and why that is so pleasing to God (2 Cor 9:7), why giving so clearly marks the life of a true disciple (Is 58:7; Jas 1:27 among many others), and why greed and covetousness bring such death to our souls (Jer 17:11; 1 Tim 6:10; Jas 5:3 among others). I challenge you to read through Scripture with these new lenses and see how the theme of one-kingdom living emerges throughout the entirety of the text.

We have traced our way from an understanding of who our God is (the triune God of grace) to an understanding of who we are (stewards in the kingdom). We have seen God's design for our relationships on all four levels. We have seen the effect of the Fall with its brokenness and deception, and how Christ's redeeming work brought wholeness back to each level of relationship. We traced the devastating effects of the myth of the two kingdoms, and we have considered the joyous life of one-kingdom living.

For the first time, we are now prepared to talk about stewardship. Therefore, we will conclude our study with a look at the role of the church and the family as both a steward and the training ground for the formation of stewards, and then we conclude with a look at the ministry of Christian fundraising.

Chapter 8

The Family, the Church & the Future of Stewardship

S TEWARDS ARE NOT BORN, THEY ARE MADE. WE DO NOT COME BY stewardship naturally. We are not brought into this world with the heart of a steward. We do not have the innate ability to engage in the relationships we have with God, our self, our neighbor and our creation with a sense of wholeness, a willingness to sacrifice, nor a heart of selfless service. Instead we must be taught from our earliest days to share, to be nice to others and to take care of our toys. From earliest childhood we set apart what is "ours," and we spend our time adding to it and protecting it. Left to ourselves, we are natural-born kingdom builders.

If we are to be taught to be stewards, it must happen first in our homes. There we must not only hear the right words, but we must see the right behavior and experience the right attitudes if we are to overcome the sin of self-centeredness into which we were born. Parents have the primary responsibility to teach and model the life of the steward in God's kingdom. If it does not happen there, it is extremely hard for it to be learned later in life.

Beyond our family we must also learn it, see it and experience it in the church. Here at the focal point of our worship of God, we must learn that stewardship and worship are synonymous. In the church we must receive the instruction that will guide us and hear the admonition that will challenge us to be stewards in God's kingdom. It is the family's responsibility to teach stewardship, and it is the church's responsibility to form stewards.

The Family as Steward and Teacher of Stewards

The family is the primary place where we learn about relationships. The very term is relational, defining individual persons living in relationships where the relationships define the individuals. *Father, mother, son, daughter, grandparent*—these are all far more than descriptive terms, they are relational terms. None of them can be considered *in abstracto* for they have meaning only in their relationship to the one for whom we are father, mother, son, daughter.

Now that we have seen that *steward* is also solely a relational term, we can see how important the family is to the work of training stewards for God's kingdom. Families have a formative effect on children in those first crucial years of life, and the Scriptures place great importance on families for the training up of children to be disciples of Jesus Christ. Therefore, the family has a special call and a unique responsibility to be a steward and to prepare a new generation of stewards.

"One Flesh" Stewardship

The model for the family begins at the very first moment that the family is inaugurated. In the marriage service of every Christian couple is the reminder that God ordained marriage as a special union unlike any other human relationship in Scripture. Only three places does the Bible teach us of an absolute unity and an absolute diversity held together in one entity. The first is ascribed to God in two places: the nature of the Trinity (three persons, one God) and the nature of Christ (fully God and fully human in one person). This mystery of unity and distinction is then pronounced, second, on the union of one man and one woman who leave their father and mother, cleave to one another and in the sight of God become "one flesh." The basic building block of the family is the miracle of the oneness of male and female that reflects the image of the God in which both were created. The third place this unity in diversity is found is the mystery of the church, where individual members become the one body of Christ. This we will consider in the next section.

All four levels of relational wholeness are to be experienced in the special union of male and female. Since it is God who has *joined together* these two, he not only exists at the center of their relationship, he defines their relationship. If you take God out of marriage, you lose the miraculous oneness that marks it as bearing the image of God. With God at the center of marriage, the couple become stewards of the relationship they have with God both as individuals and as "one flesh."

The miracle of *one flesh* also redefines the two individuals. It is a return to the prefallen ideal of finding one's self-definition in the eyes and heart of another. As one flesh, man and woman now commit to be defined by the union rather than the individuality of the two members separate and apart from that union. The husband can no longer consider himself in abstraction from his wife nor the wife from her husband. This does not mean that marriage is a loss of personal identity but exactly the opposite. We gain an identity in marriage that more closely reflects the image of God than any other relationship. If our God is defined as Trinity, unity in trinity and trinity in unity, then this triune God's creatures reflect that nature as they come together under the miracle of marriage where they, too, become "one flesh" and are redefined as a "duality in unity." If we believe that it is in God that we live and move and have our being, and if God is truly at the heart of this marriage miracle, then it is also appropriate to talk of marriage in a triune way, again reflecting the image of God. However this is described, in marriage our self-identity becomes redefined according to the miracle of "one flesh," and as such it too must be stewarded.

Here we must take on a very difficult issue with regards to our tendency to be kingdom builders in every area of our life. As we see our spouse as a gift from God, and therefore our marriage as a relationship to be stewarded with care and grace, we reflect the one-kingdom living we have been seeking. However, at the very moment we begin to see our partner as somehow being "ours," as belonging to us and therefore under our control to bring about our good, then we not only slide into two-kingdom thinking, but we deface the image of God our marriage was meant to reflect.

How many marriages have failed because one partner saw the other as a means to building a bigger and better earthly kingdom? We do not talk

about it in these terms, but when we consider our spouse as an "other" to
be used in our own plans for success and achievement, we have lost the
oneness of the marriage covenant. Again the shift that occurs mirrors the
sin of Eden when we no longer want to be defined "in relationship." Once
we step outside of that self-defining relational context, we can only see
the other as a tool to be employed in our kingdom-building activity. For
this reason it is imperative that Christian couples renew their commitment to each other at every opportunity. It is vital that their commitment
to one-kingdom living be constantly at the heart of their prayers and their
conversations. The small, subtle movements away from this common
commitment must be watched for, named and expunged from the marriage. This takes work, constant prayer and total commitment. These are
stewardship terms, and healthy marriages bear witness to God's grace
working in and through two people committed to be godly stewards of
this most precious of all human relationships.

It is easy to see from here how our changed relationships to God and
self in marriage work their way out in our relationships to others and to
our creation. Relationships to our neighbor are now conditioned by the
new reality of the "one flesh" of the marriage partners. Decisions on the
whole array of relationships, ministry activity, career, finances and the
like now involve both partners seeking to live out their oneness in obedience to God. Each of these relational pieces requires a new understanding
of "one flesh" stewardship. As the couple works out these new ways of
relating, they not only build a solid marriage, but they begin creating a
context into which their children will learn from their earliest days what
it means to be a steward in the kingdom of the triune God of grace.

This "one-flesh" understanding of the steward does not mean that single adults are not called to be stewards and in that call to reflect equally
the image of God. It does mean that it is to married partners that God has
entrusted the work of procreation, and the oneness of the miracle of marriage is the backdrop for that important work. It also does not mean that
single parents, whether by divorce or the death of a spouse, can no longer
raise up stewards or model godly relational values. It does mean that this
role and responsibility must be carried out with a determined intentionality that can bridge the gap left by the absence of the second person in the
marriage union. Many single Christian parents do an outstanding job of
creating a family setting where marriage can be modeled and stewards
can be trained for God's service. However, each would tell you that it

requires a devoted effort to fill in the spaces left vacant by the other member of the marriage. Thank God for those models of godly single parents!

Christian Family Values

Because of the political realities of our day, the term *family values* has taken on a negative and distorted meaning. I use it here to define those values that are learned in the context of a Christian home that prepare children for lives as disciples of Jesus Christ. At the core of these values must be an understanding and commitment to be a steward of our relationship at all four levels in God's kingdom.

This work of training up stewards does not begin where we would think. It does not begin with the vertical relationship of the child to God, but it begins at the horizontal relationships of parents to parent and parent to child. This is because in their earliest and most formative years, children learn much more from what they experience and see than from what are told. They learn first about the value and content of healthy relationships with their parents and between their parents as marriage partners. Parents have the initial responsibility to model relational wholeness at these two levels from the first day of life. Resetting our priorities around the needs of the other, sacrificial giving, supporting each other, caring for the needs of the other above our own, taking joy in the wellbeing of the other are all ways in which we model relational wholeness and therefore create an understanding for the need to steward our relations with one another.

Parenting is a stewardship responsibility. Children are a gift from God (even in their twos and those teenage years). They are never "ours" in the sense that we have an absolute right of ownership of them. Again we see the subtle influence of two-kingdom thinking. Our children can never be considered *in abstracto* from their relationship to us as God's gift to be stewarded and cherished. How tragic is our human history of abusing, manipulating, devaluing and ultimately destroying the lives of the children entrusted to us by God. What impact would it have on our world if parents saw their children as precious gifts from God that require our loving and committed stewardship? How many young lives would be spared if we never allowed a child to be considered a piece of property to be owned and used for our own success and enjoyment? The issues of child safety and well-being that face us as a country and a world are stewardship issues.

The role of godly parenting that takes seriously our responsibility to train up stewards will include the introduction of our children to our own personal relationships with God in Jesus Christ. This relationship will have been modeled through our family time of worship, prayer and love. It will be evident in our values, the use of our resources and our treatment of our neighbor and our creation. However, there will come a time when we as parents are called upon to introduce our children to the God we serve. In a sense, parenting on an earthly level is a preparation for a lifetime of parenting on a spiritual level. That is, our goal in being earthly fathers and mothers must be to prepare our children to know and follow their heavenly Father, who also cares for us like a mother cares for her newborn child. In a sense, there is a time when we step aside in our role as parent, and with incredible joy see our children embrace God as "Abba, Father." Of course, our roles and responsibilities as parents never end. However we must have as our goal the shifting of our children's focus away from us as the source of their well-being to the loving heavenly Father who has been revealed to us in Jesus Christ through whom we come to have personal relationship with God, the Holy Spirit. In this way we teach our children that their relationship to God in Jesus Christ is the ultimate relationship in life. In fact, it is the very purpose for their existence, and now that relationship requires their commitment as disciples and stewards. We introduce them to the kingdom of God that they enter upon their baptism, and we teach them that this membership requires our stewarding of relationships at all four levels.

Perhaps the final relational area that is taught is our stewarding of our creation. It may be the most difficult for children growing up in our materialistic world, and so it can come only as a result of a personal faith that now seeks to live as children in the kingdom of God. Here we can introduce our children to the call to one-kingdom living. Here we can open up to them the motivations behind our actions. Here we can help them understand why we recycle, tithe, become involved in issue of justice, advocate for the poor and under-represented in our society. Here we can share with them the joy of giving in a world that values the hoarding of resources for the construction of personal kingdoms. Here we can give them lenses through which to see the world God created and gave to us to *rule over* and *subdue* as our God rules over and subdues us. Here we can give them a new vocabulary for living with the other creatures God put in this world in a way that glorifies God. Here we can help them understand that their new life in Christ required their death to sin, and therefore here we can open up to them the unspeakable joy in the knowledge that all they have ahead of them is life. In all these ways we can teach our children to be stewards in the kingdom of the triune God of grace and thereby fulfill our responsibilities as parents.

Finally, we must teach our children how to worship. They will soon learn that life in this world is very hard. They will soon understand the devastation caused by a nation consumed with personal kingdom building that sets us against our neighbors and our creation in a fruitless pursuit for meaning. They will learn what it is to be used and abused by others, disappointed by things that promise fulfillment and happiness, and discouraged by the loss of direction that comes from navigating your way in a society that is morally and spiritually adrift. In the midst of all these "realities" we can give our children a most precious gift if we can instill in them a sense that their work at being stewards of the relations entrusted to them by God is a constant and abiding act of worship.

Worship has a way of lifting our eyes to see beyond the present. It reconnects us with our God and recognizes his lordship in every area of our life. It reassures us of his presence and reminds us that all of our work is meaningful. It causes us to look for his hand in all we do, to expect good to come out of evil, to believe in miracles and to not lose sight of our goal. It also keeps in front of us that this life we live is not our own, that it has been bought with a price, and therefore we render our lives in service back to God. All of this and more is kept in front of us when we understand our daily work as stewards to be acts of divine worship and praise. What a gift to give to our children.

The Church as Steward and Former of Stewards

If it is the parent's responsibility to train up stewards, it is the church's responsibility both to be stewards and to *form* stewards. First, the church must be a steward. The local church is formed to carry out a call by God to be the bride of Christ for his work in the world. This call includes the following four responsibilities.

First, the church is called to be the gathering place for the worship of God. As such it creates fellowship for believers and unites them in a common, public declaration of faith and worship. In this way the church is responsible to deepen and strengthen the relationship of believers to God. The church has a stewardship responsibility to create worship opportunities that can be indwelt by the Holy Spirit, strengthening the faith of the parishioners in their common act of worship. The church does not control the outpouring of the Spirit, but it does bear the responsibility to provide the setting and give the direction to meaningful worship experiences, believing that God will be faithful in pouring out his Spirit on the worship.

Second, the church's call includes the responsibility to train up disciples. The church is called to be the place where Christians can be fed by the Word of God, challenged in their walk with Jesus Christ and encouraged in their commitment to joyful Christian obedience. It must therefore be the place where the Bible is taught, where discipleship is the goal for all Christian education, where knowledge is passed on, where open discussion can take place and where spiritual growth is nurtured and experienced. The church, as the priesthood of all believers, has a stewardship responsibility for all of the people in its local expression. The church is a faithful steward when it takes with the utmost seriousness the responsibility to make disciples of all nations, beginning with "Jerusalem."

Third, it is the church's call to serve the community in which it finds itself. The church plays the role of servant, neighbor, prophet and advocate in the midst of a world in need of the transforming power of the gospel. The church is called upon to be a steward of its relationship to its neighbors near and far. It therefore must be a church engaged in the community. It must be a church committed to serve the physical and spiritual needs of its neighbors, advocate for justice and morality, and speak out for the neglected and oppressed. It must seek to be a light shining on a hill, a sprinkling of salt in an unsavory world, and a source of healing and reconciliation in a society marked by brokenness and strife. The church is the godly steward to the extent that it invests its time and resources in its relationship with its neighbors.

Finally, the church's call includes a responsibility to steward creation in all of its forms. This includes not only an environmental advocacy and active involvement in the care of our created world but also the stewarding of the resources of the church itself. On the one hand the church must be on the leading edge of efforts to rescue our environment from pollution and misuse, to use land wisely, to produce energy responsibly, to care for animals both domestic and wild, to manage population growth and so on. The church must be committed to its role as advocate and activist for the caretaking of God's world if it is to be faithful to its call to be a steward of this relationship.

On the other hand, the church is called to be a steward of its own resources. That is, it is called to use its own land responsibly, spend and invest its own funds wisely, and employ the talents of its people efficiently. In this way the church not only fulfills its calling, but it models for its people what stewardship looks like.

In these ways the church is called to be a steward, and in being true to this calling, the church bears witness that it is indeed the bride of Christ. It models the one-kingdom living that typifies one who is wholly committed to Jesus Christ and the singular lordship of the kingdom of God. It does so because it is the church of Jesus Christ and as such its work as steward is a participation in the work of Christ already done for her. How else can the church act than to participate in Christ's ongoing work? As the church acts in this way, the "one flesh" miraculous union of the male and female in marriage is realized in the church as the bride of Christ. And all the world sees in the church the grace and love of Christ. In this way the church is the beacon of the gospel, not so much by what she says but by *who she is.*

Tempting the Bride of Christ

We have made the point that being a steward in the kingdom of God requires a death to sin and the embracing of a new "death-to-life" view of reality. It requires a denunciation of the two-kingdom life and a commitment to the one lordship of the kingdom of God. This is as true for the church as it is for the individuals who make up the church. Just as we struggle against the temptation to become once again kingdom builders, so the church must be a caretaker of its own attitudes and actions lest it, too, becomes swayed by a worldly view of success.

The temptation for the church too often comes from within the greater organized church. That is, it comes from a comparison with other churches both within and across denominational boundaries. In so many ways churches can abdicate their responsibilities to be stewards and fall victim to their own version of kingdom building.

These temptations come in many forms. One form is the numbers game where church "success," and therefore the success of the pastor, is measured by the size of the congregation. Attend any gathering of pastors and you will hear the question asked a hundred times, "So, how big is

your congregation?" Pastors with large congregations simply reply with a
number. Those with small congregations must add a qualifier to save
face. "Well, we have only seventy-five in worship, but our church is . . ."
You can fill in the blank with any number of qualifiers that are offered in
an attempt to mitigate against the conclusion that the church, and therefore the pastor, is unsuccessful.

The numbers game can also come in the form of church budget, or
in its more insidious form, in the garb of missions giving. How many
of us have seen pastors use the level of their missions giving as a gold
badge, boasting of the attitude of "humble servanthood" on behalf of
their congregation? When numbers are used to measure success, even
success in ministry, we are beginning to build earthly kingdoms side
by side with the spiritual kingdom that should demand our complete
allegiance.

A second temptation the church faces is the facilities game. Akin to the
numbers game, measuring success in terms of the size and quality of our
physical plant is a form of kingdom building. In some ways it seems closest to the idea of kingdom building as now people can drive by and actually see the kingdoms we have built. This is not to say that large churches
and quality buildings are inherently bad. Again, it is a matter of attitude
and lordship. Buildings erected to the glory of God should be excellent
and worthy of the kingdom of God. However, they should also reflect
kingdom values including care for creation, judicious use of resources,
balance in funds for buildings vs. missions and ministry and so forth. It is
when these values become unbalanced and when facilities are built to
glorify human accomplishment rather than God that we have slipped
into kingdom building.

Other forms of kingdom building include the prestige game where the
church's place in the community and the fame of its members drive it
more than mission and stewardship. Prestige has blinded many a congregation from pursuing ministry to the poor or advocating for the voiceless
in our society. The church cannot be an agent of God's transforming
power if it values its prestige over its mission. Along with prestige comes
every form of self-centeredness that creates a spiritual pride that destroys
rather than stewards relationships. It comes in worship where congregations argue over who has the best choir, the best preacher, the best bell
choir or the most-acclaimed organist. It can come in our discipleship programs when we seek to have the most famous guest speakers, the most

publicized vacation Bible school program or the biggest daycare center. It may come in big ways, such as which church has the largest facilities, to small ways, such as which pastor drives the biggest car. While none of these are wrong in and of themselves, they are all places where the temptation toward kingdom building can manifest itself. For these reasons, we must constantly be watching for the attitudes and motivations that drive this temptation and be strong enough to take action against them if we are going to be faithful to our call as the church of Jesus Christ.

There is also the temptation of the church to identify its success with its adherence to tradition. This is a debilitating form of kingdom building. Tradition serves the church like an anchor serves a boat. At times it is invaluable in keeping us in place and helping us not drift aimlessly on every wind that blows. However, when it is important for the church to move in the direction that God has called us, that same anchor now holds us back, slows us down or even stops our progress altogether. It is this latter misuse of tradition that falls into the realm of kingdom building. Keepers of tradition have prided themselves in thwarting every new idea that may make them uncomfortable, labeling most as "liberal," "modern" or "compromising." Their earthly kingdoms consist in the familiar surroundings of dead and dying traditions that they guard with great tenacity to the very death of the local church. This too is a self-centered form of kingdom building that the church must overcome if it is to be a true steward in God's kingdom.

The local church, just as the members who comprise the church, is called to a wholly committed one-kingdom life. Therefore, its worship must be pure in a desire to steward the precious relationship between the children of God and our heavenly Father. Its discipleship must be focused on the one goal of glorifying God in the raising up of a community of knowledgeable, mature disciples who will denounce their own kingdom building and seek to follow Jesus Christ in the entirety of their existence. The church's outreach must be uncompromising in nature and unambiguous in its actions. It must embrace the whole gospel and seek to minister in all ways to every person the way Christ taught us to serve. And finally, the church must be bold in its commitment to care for creation, in the effective and unblemished use of its resources, and in its decision-making regarding building versus missions, saving versus investing and the host of other challenges it will face in the management of its resources.

If the church is to be the church of Jesus Christ, it must do so by resist-

ing the temptation to kingdom building and instead recommitting itself
to carrying out its responsibilities to be the steward or the relationships
that define all four areas of its calling.

The final piece we will examine is the role of the church as the former of
stewards. We will look at this important work of the church in four areas:
teaching stewardship, *preaching* stewardship, *modeling* stewardship and
inviting stewardship.

Teaching Stewardship

One of the main points of this book has been to show that the concept of
the godly steward is not an add-on to the "proper" teachings on the life of
the Christian, but instead it lies at its very heart. To be a Christian is to be
a steward in the kingdom of the triune God of grace. These are not two
options, two paths one can take. They are inextricably bound together,
and as such they define one reality called the "Christian." If we have
made this point successfully, then what must follow is that all teaching by
the church regarding the Christian life must consequently be teaching
about stewardship. Not one after the other but both together as one teaching.

If this is the case, then we must begin to infuse all of our Christian education curricula with stewardship language and concepts. From Sunday
school to adult Bible classes to lay training programs to seminary education to the Christian popular press, we must recapture this key teaching
as the rubric around which Christian education must be formed. As long
as we allow it to be an add-on, it will continue to get short shrift in our
church teaching. It will continue to be seen by parishioners as an optional
part of the Christian life, and it will again be both feared and misunderstood by the vast majority of pastors and congregants alike. What is
worse is that this neglect will never force the issue of kingdom building to
be dealt with in our churches, and our giving, living and serving will suffer immeasurably as a result.

Christian education from the earliest days with our youngest children
up through the rigors of seminary training must recapture the paradigm
of the steward. We must be willing to reclaim jettisoned vocabulary and
infuse it with new meaning for the church today. We must be willing to
debunk long-standing myths about our two-kingdom lives and replace
them with careful and accurate instruction about one-kingdom living in a
death-to-life reality.

This must take place in the church. The church cannot form stewards unless it recaptures this holistic understanding of our call to be stewards in God's kingdom. Stewards are formed through a process of consistent, learned, biblically based teaching. This teaching must be supported by the modeling of stewardship and through the challenge for personal transformation. This is the church's role and responsibility. It can happen elsewhere, but it must happen first and most consistently in the church.

What will it require for us to take this teaching to heart, to change the direction of our Christian education programs and to call the church to teach it boldly? What would it mean to the church to raise up an entire generation of stewards committed to caring for relationship at all four levels? What kind of dramatic transformation would we see in our families, our communities, our churches and our world? The church has the responsibility to form stewards. It must do this through a systematic approach to Christian education that dares to name the steward as the central paradigm of the Christian life.

Preaching Stewardship

As in our teaching curricula the preaching on stewardship has a woeful history in the church in America. Most of the reasons are obvious by now. As a detached and misunderstood feature in the Christian life, preaching on stewardship has never found favor among pastors. Because it has been almost solely associated with money, it has found less favor in the congregation. So every November or so, most churches resign themselves to the fact that they will need to endure the annual stewardship sermon. The pastor does not like to preach it, and the congregation does not like to hear it, but everyone is willing to "take their medicine" as long as it only comes once a year. I find I am asked to preach on many a "stewardship Sunday," to which I usually agree to the relief of the pastor. A guest preacher, especially one who is a fundraiser by profession, can get away with strong talk about giving once a year or so. The regular pastor can then go back to focusing on more "spiritual" things, perhaps referring back a few times to "that stewardship sermon" when giving gets low. And so the cycle is perpetuated. To the unfortunate pastor who dares preach on stewardship for several Sundays comes the charge, "Obviously he is only interested in our money." How dare we be forced to sit in such a spiritual setting and listen to a series of sermons on how we handle the stuff of our earthly kingdoms!

The problem, of course, comes from preaching on giving without challenging the two-kingdom lifestyles of those in the pews. In doing so we are only afforded a limited amount of territory in this private domain before we are seen as meddling in the personal affairs of our parishioners. As long as these second kingdoms are allowed to stand unchallenged, our stewardship preaching can only be an attempt to motivate a little larger transfer of assets. We may choose to use guilt and fear on the one hand or rewards on the other to inspire this motivation. But it can only be for a brief time, within a limited scope and always with the realization that we are trespassing on private property the whole time we are preaching. It is no wonder that it is so uncomfortable and so unsuccessful.

The proper response to this dilemma is to jettison wholesale the entire approach to "stewardship" and to start over. The intent of this book is to provide the content for this starting over. It is to make the case that our call to be Christians is commensurate with our call to be stewards. Therefore, Christian preaching must be preaching about what it means to be stewards in the kingdom of the triune God of grace. It is about the call to one-kingdom living that is the central imperative in the gospel. It is about challenge, death, freedom, joy, obedience and life. It is a message that fosters transformation and brings about renewal. It is preaching that is true to our creation-redemption-glorification theology that transcends denomination and culture. It is the most desperately needed word in our world today, and it is the sole responsibility of the church to proclaim it, teach it and model it.

Such preaching would incorporate the steward paradigm into its teaching year around. Advent, Christmas and Epiphany are filled with images and theology that declare the incarnation of Jesus Christ as the starting point of the life of the steward. Lent, Palm Sunday, Holy Week and Easter bring us the story of the work of the faithful high priest, the obedient servant and the faithful steward in the victorious risen Lord in whom we participate in our call to be stewards in God's kingdom. Pentecost and the celebration of the life of the church provide the context in which the life of the steward is carried out, as well as the eschatology that brings us hope in our death-to-life reality. Every moment in the church year is filled with opportunities to preach the centrality of the steward to the joyous and obedient life of the Christian. And when November comes around, preaching on stewardship in terms of our financial giving to the work of the church will be the most natural thing we could imagine. It will fall on ears already attuned to its message and on hearts that already embrace its tenets.

This preaching will also provide the necessary challenge to its listeners. Preaching on the role of the steward in God's kingdom requires courage and conviction. It will most certainly be met with hostility, anger and confusion. When we move to challenge people's kingdoms that they have invested a lifetime to build, that provide them with their self-worth and that define their place in this world, we are playing with dynamite! However, nothing short of a direct, caring but uncompromising challenge will free our people to be the people of the kingdom of God. Nothing else will unlock them from their bondage to kingdom building. Nothing short of this will bring them to the moment of death that opens up the abundant life in Christ. If we are truly to preach the call to be stewards in the kingdom of the triune God of grace, we must accept this challenge and move ahead in the power of the Holy Spirit, trusting that God will do great things through our obedience and faithfulness.

Modeling Stewardship

Undergirding the church's work of teaching and preaching the call to be stewards must be the church's own modeling as steward. The responsibility for this falls first to the pastor. If the pastor is himself or herself striving to be a steward in the kingdom of God, then there is already a model for church leaders. There is substance behind his preaching and her teaching, and there is leadership that has the potential for transformation. This does not mean that the pastor must be perfect, but in this vital area more than perhaps any other the pastor must accept the mantle of responsibility to model the life of the steward as the first step to the renewal of the church and the formation of a new generation of stewards.

The pastor models the ethics of the steward both by private decisions and public witness. Privately, the pastor's own decisions that support the stewarding of relationships at all four levels will determine his or her effectiveness in leading the congregation in dynamic change. There are certainly limitations to this because pastors, like the rest of us, feel the temptation to be kingdom builders and fall victim to them from time to time. It is *not* necessary that the pastor be perfect. It *is* necessary that the pastor strive to be consistent, admit mistakes and demonstrate a commitment to kingdom values. By identifying the areas of kingdom building in our own lives, we as Christian leaders model in a most powerful way what repentance, transformation and renewal look like. The opportunity lies not in our being perfect models but in letting our congregation see our own process of change and growth. As our own second kingdoms come crashing down, we earn the right to challenge the same in the lives of others. The command is not that they "do as we do," but we know that they will never take on in their own lives what they see missing from ours. That is the burden and the opportunity laid at the feet of every pastor and Christian leader.

Perhaps most important is the pastor's modeling of the stewarding of their relationship to God through insistence on time for reflection, prayer and personal worship. Congregations must be trained to understand that this relationship is not "part of the job." It is a personal need that falls in the realm of the vocation of steward, and it is not part and parcel of the daily responsibilities of the pastor. Christian leaders who do not insist in setting aside that personal time to steward their relationship with God are modeling a destructive lifestyle for their people. This is the first and most important component to the responsibility of the pastor.

Pastors model other aspects of this transformation process in different ways. It is not a call to turn down pay increases, improvements to the parsonage or upgrading the pastor's car. Modeling that is most effective does not come from the premise that money and possessions carry some inherent evil. Instead pastors model the vocation of steward by their use of their resources, their involvement in the well-being of others and in their care of creation.

From the pastor there emerges the responsibility of church leadership to make decisions and lead the church in ways that model this same steward paradigm. How we handle our budgeting, how we treat our employees, how we prioritize our time and resources among the various needs of our people, how we choose to invest our mission dollars, how we choose the partnerships we will enter into, how we handle church discipline, how we raise money, how we invest our endowments, what we pay our pastors, how we care for our facilities and property, how we welcome visitors, how much we invest in our Christian education programs and so many other decisions and processes are opportunities to model for our people what it means that the church is a steward in the kingdom of the triune God of grace. It is a chance to demonstrate a defiance of two-kingdom thinking. It is a chance to show how faith and the decisions about finances fit together. It is a chance not only to model right decisions but also the processes that led to those decisions.

If we are to take fullest advantage of these opportunities, it is essential that we choose men and women for leadership positions who are of the highest spiritual maturity and who are committed to personal transformation. I have long contended that the most spiritually mature members of a congregation should be serving as trustees. If the church allows a split between the temporal and the spiritual, what usually follows is a deacon or elder board comprised of spiritual leaders and a trustee board made up of business and finance people where their spiritual maturity is a secondary concern to their business acumen and financial expertise. If transformation is to take place in all areas of the church around the paradigm of the church as steward, the strongest spiritual leaders need to be in control at the place where such transformation is most difficult, namely, at those points of decision about property and finance. If the trustee board makes the shift, if the church becomes the steward at this place in its life, then it has a chance to model what it teaches and preaches.

A final opportunity to model the vocation of the steward is in the weekly worship services. We have made the case that in the life of the steward all work is worship. In the same sense we can say that all worship is an act of stewarding our relationships at one or more levels. When worship is seen as stewardship and stewardship as worship, we can begin to model this in how we worship. This requires education, taking us back to the importance of teaching and preaching stewardship. This is supported by worship experiences that lift up the stewardship aspect of coming together as community, hearing the word spoken, the word sung and the word preached, partaking in the sacraments, and praying and praising God together as the body of Christ.

These are all acts of the faithful steward. These mark our participation in the Son's worship of the Father in the power of the Spirit. For that reason we pray to the Father in the name of the Son and by the power of the Spirit. We hear the Word of God that points us to Jesus Christ who came to reveal to us the Father by the illumination of the Spirit. We are baptized in the name of the Father, Son and Holy Spirit. We partake of the Eucharist that is a participation in the salvific work of the Son for us who presents us clean before the Father and empowers us for life by the Spirit. We come together as the church, the bride of Christ, to worship the Father and to be led by the Spirit for service to our neighbor and our world. This trinitarian understanding of worship is the model for the steward who sees all work done for the kingdom as a participation in the work of the Son empowered by the Spirit for the glory of the Father. Every church service presents us with the opportunity to model for our people that the church is a steward in God's kingdom, and the work of the steward is participatory worship.

Our decisions as Christian leaders provide opportunities to model our own commitment to be stewards in God's kingdom. As pastor, as lay leader, as worship leader, as youth leader, as teacher, as trustee, as deacon and elder, as church treasurer, as missions director, as Christian education director, as worshiper—we are given the command and the supreme privilege to be agents for the transformation of our churches and our communities. It requires first our personal transformation. Then it calls us to model this transformation in every area of our lives, both as individuals and as the church. As we do, our teaching and preaching on the vocation of the steward will have the power to bring about real transformation throughout out churches and beyond.

Inviting Stewardship

A final word must be said about the intentionality of this work. Central to our teaching, preaching and modeling, stewardship must be a constant invitation to personal engagement in this transformation process. That is, this whole effort cannot be left on a theoretical level or offered as only a need in one's spiritual kingdom. Even here at the very last we can fall victim to two-kingdom thinking. It is not enough to teach and preach if there is not a constant inviting and a system of discipleship-building for those who accept the invitation. We must be clear with our people that the call to be stewards is not just one selection among many on the smorgasbord of Christian attributes, but it is a direct call *to them*. To support this we must have Bible study groups that take on the responsibility to educate those who answer the call and to help and support them during the long, hard process of dismantling their earthly kingdoms. This process requires death, repentance and a turning away from a lifestyle that has defined success, happiness and life itself. This kind of radical change does not happen overnight nor does it happen alone. It requires a commitment by a community to support one another for the long haul.

It is also a process that never actually ends. While milestones can be reached, becoming a true one-kingdom steward is a lifelong journey. We must take this journey together as a community, as a family, as a couple, as disciples. This journey will certainly be marked by lapses, challenges and obstacles. But it will also deepen our faith and bring new meaning to the command, "Trust in the LORD with all your heart and lean not on your own understanding" (Prov 3:5). It may put us in conflict with friends and relatives who do not understand this call or condone its requirements. It may make us look odd to the world. But it will also draw us closer to the one who said, "But take heart! I have overcome the world" (Jn 16:33).

Because it is so radical and hard, and because it brings such freedom and joy, we must be intentional about our invitation to the journey and in our support of those along the way. This invitation must also become part of our weekly worship. It must be offered to all who come together to worship the God who calls us to be his stewards in his gracious kingdom. How natural it should be to invite all those assembled at worship to begin the journey of faith into the new life as stewards in the one kingdom of God. The church is called to teach, preach, model and invite. The church is called to be a steward and to form stewards for the work of the kingdom. This is our privilege; this is our mission; this is our hope. May God grant to us the wisdom to see and embrace this as our calling and the courage to carry it out with passion and joy.

Chapter 9

A Theology of
Asking & Giving
The Ministry of Fundraising
in the Kingdom of God

THE GOAL OF THIS CHAPTER IS TO PROPOSE A THEOLOGICAL FOUNDation for Christian fundraising. As such, this chapter is written for all pastors, trustees, stewardship committees and board members who carry responsibility to raise money or to oversee the raising of money for the cause of Christ. It is also written for all who give generously to the work of the kingdom of God. To build such a theology, a case will be made as to how our Christian fundraising must proceed if our work is truly to be a part of the advancement of the kingdom of God. We will seek here to establish the urgency and importance of this discussion in order to help move it to the top of the agenda among Christian development professionals, parachurch organizations and the church. It is hoped that this chapter will prove adequately provocative and compelling to foster dialogue on these key issues.

Kingdom Thinking

Let us begin by formulating a central question to this chapter, namely, "What's so Christian about our fundraising?" We who are responsible to raise money do so with the assumption that there is a link between our Christianity and this work. We assume that our personal faith not only does but *should* and even *must* have an impact on the way we go about this work. If we are not to become kingdom builders, we cannot create an artificial dichotomy between faith and work, between the ethics of the kingdom of God and the ethics of the workplace.

Let us be sure before proceeding that this assumption is valid. There is a truism that states, "You cannot be *sort of* pregnant." Biologically, pregnancy is an absolute. It is not a state that one can choose to move in and out of depending on one's feelings at any particular moment. It is not a state in which one can decide to accept some of its features and decline others. It is a whole, complete and absolute state of being.

Using this absolute, total biological commitment to the state of pregnancy as a metaphor, let us ask what it really means that we are children in the kingdom of the triune God of grace? It is a critical question for us who work as Christian fundraisers. The coming and the anticipation of the final coming of the kingdom of God are the most dominant themes in Scripture. They permeate the Bible from beginning to end telling us not only that we live in anticipation of a final coming of the kingdom of God in its fullness (and thus we are instructed to pray, "Thy kingdom come") but also that in the resurrection of Jesus Christ it has already come in its provisional yet wholly real form (and thus Jesus proclaims repeatedly, "The kingdom of God is at hand"). When we hear Jesus describing for us time and again the various marks and characteristics of this kingdom, we are like immigrants being introduced to the country in which we are now to live. As God's children we are being introduced to our new home, even while we are still residing in the old neighborhood.

The provisional yet wholly real form of the kingdom of God creates the tension in which we are now to live as the people of God. We are still in the world, yet we are to be called out, distinct and not "of the world." Indeed, we are to live according to the ethics of the kingdom of God, and those ethics are in almost every way a radical departure from the norms and values of the world. What we have described as the "One kingdom of God" Donald Kraybill has termed the "Upside-Down Kingdom."[1] It is the kingdom where the first will be last, where the humble will be

---

[1]Donald B. Kraybill, *The Upside-Down Kingdom* (Basingstoke, U.K.: Marshall, Morgan and Scott, 1978).

exalted, and the mighty will be laid low. It is the kingdom where to be the greatest you must become the least, to lead you must serve, to gain your life you must lose it. It is the kingdom where to be filled up we must empty ourselves, where richness is found in poverty and where the meek will inherit the earth.

It is the kingdom that calls us to turn the other cheek, to walk the extra mile, to give the cloak as well as the coat. In this kingdom we are called to love our enemies and hate our sin in the midst of a world that loves its sin and hates its enemies. It is a kingdom whose central symbol is a mark of humiliation and defeat, and whose ethics seem to be utter foolishness. It is precisely at this point where the totality of our commitment is brought into sharp focus. For citizenship in the kingdom of God does not provide us with a passport to journey in and out as we find it expedient and useful. There is no dual citizenship in this kingdom and the world, allowing us to move back and forth at our own discretion. We have been bought with a price, and it is no longer we who live but Christ who lives in us. We are not to be conformed to this world but transformed by the renewing of our minds in the Holy Spirit. The kingdom of God is like a treasure hidden in a field. When we find it, we sell all we have and leave all behind to purchase it.

When we survey the scriptural evidence on what it means to be citizens of the kingdom of God, we can only conclude that this citizenship carries with it the kind of spiritual absolute akin to the biological absolute of pregnancy. You cannot be "sort of" or "occasionally" a citizen of the kingdom of God. It is an all or nothing proposition, a state that permeates every area of our life. It changes us profoundly and completely, sets us in a new direction, grants us a new hope and a distinct future. It calls us into a lifestyle that reflects the values and ethics of our new citizenship, and it requires of us our fullest commitment in the very midst of a secular and pluralistic society. Futurist and author Tom Sine reminds us of what discipleship meant for those first called by Jesus.

> To be a disciple of Jesus didn't mean just getting one's spiritual life worked out and viewing discipleship as the maintenance of that compartment of life while continuing the rest of life pretty much as before. No. Following Christ meant that His grace began changing his followers in every compartment of life. . . . Those first disciples understood that even as Christ incarnated the kingdom of God in his life, they were called as the body of Christ in society to be the presence of that kingdom in every dimension of life. . . .

Those early Christian leaders seemed to understand more fully than we do today that following Jesus Christ means actively living all of life under his lordship. It means placing his kingdom at the very center of our lives, and it means actually becoming a foretaste of that kingdom in our culture to the extent that the Spirit fills us and grace transforms us.[2]

As this book has sought to show, everything we do as Christians and therefore as Christian fundraisers and donors is wholly dependent upon the understanding that being a Christian is nothing less than a total commitment to live according to the ethics of this new kingdom in which we have our sole citizenship—the kingdom ushered in through the life, death and resurrection of Jesus Christ. Once we open even the slightest crack in the door of the absolute nature of this commitment, we place ourselves on the slippery slope of assimilation, cultural conformity and, ultimately, ethical relativism with the result that we fail to be the kingdom of God in and for the world. We then fall back into our citizenship of this world and once again become kingdom builders with perhaps a thin veneer of religiosity pasted over our otherwise unchanged lives. We live as lords of our own kingdoms and offer our limited worship in the sphere of the church. And this we pass off as true Christianity. To be a citizen of God's kingdom in and through Jesus Christ is to be singularly committed to following him. This is where we must start if we are to have any basis upon which we can hope to answer our question, "What's so Christian about our fundraising?"

Christian Institutions and the Kingdom of God

We now face a dangerous and all-important transition because here we must deal with the reality of the second kingdom in our lives as fundraisers. It is possible, and experience has shown it may even be probable, that we can agree with all that has been said thus far as it pertains to our personal, private lives in our vertical relationship with God. That is, the ethical demands of our citizenship are wholly binding on us as we seek to grow in our relationship with God. But how much further are we to take our discipleship, our commitment to follow Jesus? I believe for most there is a level of comfort that this citizenship also carries over to the church and our relationships with our Christian sisters and brothers. In the church's business of preaching, worship, Christian education, evangelism

---

[2]Tom Sine, *Taking Discipleship Seriously* (Valley Forge, Penn.: Judson Press, 1985), pp. 41-42.

and missions, these radical ethical demands surely also apply. The church is, after all, the body of Christ, and should therefore conform not to this world, but to him exclusively and completely.

From here we may find it difficult to jump to the secular world of business and commerce, of politics and law, of social service and leisure. Here we enter into the modern debate of the place and efficacy of the ethics of God's kingdom in a world that rejects him, feels no obligation to him, and indeed feels disdain for the ethics of his kingdom. I believe there is a limit at which secular organizational ethics can be expected to conform to kingdom ethics. If the institution does not see itself as a part of the kingdom of God—even if many or most of its employees do—then there is no basis upon which the ethics of the kingdom of God can be normative to that institution. Therefore, while individual employees may feel called to live their own lives according to kingdom ethics, it is not expected that the institution will embrace those ethics as its own. In fact, just the opposite will likely occur. The institution will pay full allegiance to the ethics of the kingdom in which it resides and reject the ethics of the other kingdom, just as individuals who reject their place in the kingdom as God's children will also reject the ethical implications of that citizenship. Therefore, it is relatively clear that while the church surely is called to live out its citizenship through its adherence to kingdom ethics, secular institutions can hardly be expected to do the same.

But now we come face to face with the gray area that lies between these two poles. With the church on one side and the world on the other we must ask, "What of the Christian organization, agency, school, mission or institution?" The vast majority of Christian fundraising is done on behalf of Christian institutions that support the local church but are separate from it. Where do such organizations stand when it comes to a commitment to the ethical standards of the kingdom of God? And further, do our churches truly reflect kingdom ethics, or are these questions also needing to be asked in our churches?

I believe that this is *the* question of our day as those involved in Christian fundraising. Everything else we discuss and plan and teach is ultimately and invariably tied to how we answer this question. Let me ask it this way, "What is the relationship between the standards and qualities of a Christian organization and the ethical imperatives of the kingdom of God?" The reason this is and must be a watershed question for our day becomes quite clear as we examine the two common but problematic answers to this question.

Separate but Serving

We can answer this question on the one hand by seeing our institution as somehow serving the kingdom of God while not being itself a part of that same kingdom. Instead of understanding ourselves as a faith community of God's children seeking after his will and conforming to his ethical standards for our work, we can view ourselves primarily as a business that must be fiscally secure and financially prudent. This may be as an educational institution that grants degrees and therefore must adhere first and foremost to accreditation standards, as an employer who must set and follow personnel policies, as a not-for-profit agency that must undertake aggressive fundraising, and so on. If we as Christian institutions are not part of the kingdom of God, then we are part of the kingdom of this world, and we will adopt the trappings of our citizenship. Let us remember that citizenship in God's kingdom is an all or nothing proposition.

If this is who we are, if we belong to the world and only serve the kingdom of God, then this places us in a rather staggering paradox. For then we are serving the church as institutions that are operated in allegiance to the relativized ethics of a kingdom that, by its very nature, is opposed to the church. We may be training leaders of a faith community in institutions that replace faith and trust in God with reliance on the projected performance of the market, the ability to read demographic trends and the shrewdness of our business practices. We may be preparing men and women called by God to be servants of God in institutions that measure the success of our preparation system by standards that are products of a post-Enlightenment philosophy of education. We may be preparing missionaries to go out and transform our society with the gospel of Jesus Christ in institutions that hold as normative a set of values that in large part support the society into which these missionaries are sent. This is a strange situation indeed.

It is precisely here where the compromises come in our profession. If we are not committed to the ethical implications of the kingdom of God, then we will, de facto, take a completely different approach to the whole area of fundraising. The overriding question we will ask of every program, technique or scheme will be, "Will it work?" Fundraising is a highly utilitarian profession that operates under the pressure of an incredibly objective set of measurements of success. An "off year" by a faculty member may show up in a few negative course evaluations; a poor performance by an administrator may mean a program objective gets delayed. However, a bad year in the development office is posted in absolute objective detail in the annual report for all to see, and it may mean programs are cut and jobs are lost. Such work is not more important than these others, it is just more publicly measurable. If you do not believe me, imagine a fundraising officer telling the board that they missed their annual fund goal by 50 percent but the year was a success because they held some *really* great events. Oh yes, fundraising is a highly utilitarian profession.

For this reason there is immense pressure on all those who raise funds to "do what works." There are ethical standards for fundraising outside the kingdom of God, and we surely would not choose clearly questionable techniques even if we were not guided by kingdom ethics. Yet our starting point and standards for measurements of success are wholly influenced by the ethical underpinnings of the kingdom in which we believe we reside. For this reason, if we are operating in the kingdom of this world, then we find it acceptable to look to secular institutions and glean from them techniques and programs that work. We may find it expedient to "Christianize" these techniques to make them more acceptable to our donors and more palatable to our boards. Bible verses inserted into otherwise secular appeal letters, the use of premiums of a religious nature that have the same goal as the state college's football regalia or school logo merchandise, and the ever-present request for "financial *and prayer* support" are but a few ways in which we paint a coating of religiosity onto techniques that we borrow from other institutions.

Please do not misunderstand me here. I am not saying that techniques and programs used by secular institutions and adopted by religious institutions are inherently unethical. What I am saying is that how we see ourselves in relationship to the kingdom of God influences to the greatest degree how we assess the ethics of these techniques and of our entire profession and its mission. It is one thing to use a technique based on its apparent success and then dress it up in Christian clothing to make it acceptable. It is quite another to build a development program from a biblical, kingdom perspective, and then to incorporate only those techniques that are a clear and honest fit.

For that reason I am grieved that this all-essential starting point seems to be systematically omitted from so many of the Christian training con-

ferences and seminars on Christian fundraising. You can sometimes find
the odd session on biblical stewardship or the ethics of fundraising, but I
have yet to see this critical issue given the central place it simply must
have. The point I want to make is this, if Christian institutions and missions entrusted with the task of furthering the work of the church of Jesus
Christ for the upbuilding of the kingdom of God do not see our very institutions as part of that same kingdom, then this question of the "Christianity" of our fundraising practices is superfluous. If this is so, then let us say
what we are with the clarity it is due: we are secular institutions serving a
religious client. If this is the case, then we can go back to holding work-
shops on annual giving and donor relations using the successful programs at Stanford, the United Way and the Red Cross as our models. We
can copy that clever major donor program that worked so well for the
local symphony, and we can put in place the membership and gift club
scheme that was so effective at our area hospital. But if we choose this
route, then let us also stop asking the questions about how "Christian"
our practices are. Let us stop believing that we still need to seek some sort
of biblical support for our work. Let us stop pretending that faith and
prayer are integral and essential components of our success. And let us
quit telling the churches we serve that they are partners with us in our
work.

In all these ways we are seeking to slip in and out of the kingdom of
God, and we must stop it, for it is impossible. This is the reality of what
we must say if we see our institutions as operating outside of the kingdom of God. There simply can be no other conclusions. There can be no
comingling of kingdoms. There can be no pick and choose ethics. There
are no dual citizenships.

In the Kingdom but Not of the Kingdom

Now let us turn to our other option. Perhaps we see our institutions as
partners with the church and as part of the kingdom of God. Perhaps the
mission statements of our organizations clearly indicate that we are not of
this world but belong to another. Perhaps the employees and leadership
of our institutions are committed to the church and the advancing of the
kingdom through our given work. Perhaps our boards are made up of
dedicated women and men who hold these same ideals. These are all distinct possibilities, but they do not go all the way in answering our question. For there can exist an institution of faithful people who feel called to

a Christian purpose and who are themselves citizens of God's kingdom and who espouse its ethics, and yet the institution, in its policies and practices, remains outside. This can happen even in the church. In these cases, the dichotomy that existed earlier between the kingdom of the institution and that of the client it served now reappears in a more insidious form. For we now have a dichotomy between what the institution stands for and what it actually does, between intent and content, between mission and operation.

This is the locus of much tension at nearly every level of institutional life when people of God attempt to live according to the ethics of the kingdom of which they are a part, while the institution remains somehow almost mysteriously connected to the other kingdom with its juxtaposed ethic. There is in so many of our Christian organizations and churches a kind of institutional schizophrenia. On the one hand we bear the marks of a faith community: reliance on faith, seeking God for our future, a sincere effort toward wholly committed discipleship, lifestyle evangelism, social concern and outreach, servant leadership and so on. And yet in the midst of this community there is a set of institutionally accepted norms and practices that seem simultaneously essential and yet wholly out of place. This paradox emerges almost everywhere we look. For instance, what do we do when following the leading of the Holy Spirit appears to run counter to conservative and careful financial planning? What do we do when customary and acceptable personnel policies seem to be in conflict with kingdom ethics? What do we do when aspects of a new degree program that are deemed to be essential in building servant leadership do not meet with accreditation standards? How do we project our fundraising income when we acknowledge that all gifts are from God through the work of the Holy Spirit in the lives of our donors? And how do we live in anticipation and urgency as if Christ were coming back tomorrow while continuing to add to our stockpile of tens of millions of dollars in endowments?

Again I must explain my intentions here. I agree that it is part of our Christian stewardship to plan carefully, be financially prudent and fiscally wise, follow the laws of our land and prepare our institutions against lean years. Yet despite all of this, throughout our institutions there are countless places where the call to be the children of God and live according to the radical commands of his kingdom run headlong into our assimilation of what the world has deemed acceptable, logical, sound and even legal. How we make decisions at each of these points of conflict will indicate clearly in which kingdom we truly reside. We may say that our organization is part and parcel of the kingdom of God, but our institutional ethics may say otherwise.

Nowhere is this truer than in our fundraising. It is here and only here in this context that we can now seek to answer the question, "What's so Christian about our fundraising?" You and I as those responsible for raising money for the kingdom of God are in an industry shot through with these ethical dilemmas. To some people both inside and outside the kingdom the very term "Christian fundraising" is an oxymoron. Yet each of us has come to some level of comfort in how we go about our business, what we have chosen to include and what we have chosen to reject in our fundraising practices. I want to examine just how we go about that task, how we decide what is Christian about what we do. This can only be done once we have established the all-or-nothing nature of the kingdom of God and its ethical demands on us. Only in this milieu as we seek to be faithful citizens of this kingdom can we ask these questions.

The Christian Development Program

To discuss our work in this context we almost immediately confront an issue that impacts this discussion profoundly and is perhaps the greatest single challenge in the process of evaluating and building a truly Christian development program. I will state it this way: from beginning to end the ethical demands of the kingdom of God as they relate to money and fundraising are, to the eyes of the world, foolish and even naive. Much of what we must say in Christian fundraisng will sound like absolute nonsense to our colleagues who live and work according to the standards and ethics of the kingdom of the world.

To illustrate this point I want to make a case for how we must begin this investigation. If we have ruled out the process of looking to what works in the world and Christianizing it for our use, then we must substitute a more appropriate process. The way I believe we must proceed is to ask this question, "If we were to start from scratch, with no preconceived ideas with regard to what works in fundraising but only with a firm commitment to the ethics of this kingdom of God in which we live, what kind of development program would we build?" What would it look like, what techniques would we use and, most importantly, what would be the assumptions upon which this program would be based?

Let me share with you five teachings that I believe we must look to in Scripture if we were to build such a new system. In each we must keep in mind that we will have to fight against much of the baggage we carry from the effect of the world's ethics on us. We will use the lenses we introduced in chapter seven, and we will strive to ask only for the eyes of faith and the wisdom of the Spirit as we begin this process.

Money and Power

First, we learn from Scripture that when we deal with money, we are dealing not with a neutral medium of exchange but with powers that operate behind, in and through money. If we use the Bible as our guide, we immediately find that we are dealing here with major themes in Scripture: Jesus spoke most frequently about two things—the kingdom of God and money. Almost exclusively when he calls us to be faithful participants in the former, he warns us of the dangers of the latter. Richard Foster points out,

> Discussions of stewardship, almost without exception, view money as completely neutral and depersonalized. . . . What all this talk about stewardship fails to see is that money is not just a neutral medium of exchange but a "power" with a life of its own.[3]

There is, behind money, a power that seeks our devotion above all else. The words of Jesus in Matthew 6:24 are no doubt familiar. Listen to them again, "No one can serve two masters. Either he will hate the one and love the other, or he will be devoted to the one and despise the other. You cannot serve both God and Money." In this remarkable passage Jesus dispels the myth that money is a neutral medium of exchange, and instead he ascribes to it incredible power. This passage is the clearest indication not only of the power behind money to inspire devotion but also of the strict dichotomy between the two kingdoms we have been discussing. The quest for money seeks to inspire our devotion to the extent that we will shift our worship and service from all other masters to serve it alone. Richard Foster concludes, "Mammon is a power that seeks to dominate us." In view of the first commandment Jesus directly attacks one of humanity's greatest forms of idolatry, the worship of money and all that it brings.

---

[3]Richard Foster, *The Challenge of the Disciplined Life* (San Francisco: HarperCollins, 1989), pp. 24-25.

Part of our jobs in Christian fundraising is to understand that each day our donors stand before these two gods just as Jesus defined them two thousand years ago. They know the temptation of trying to serve the one while holding on tightly to the other. Jesus says this is impossible. To serve a master is to make it the priority in your life, to submit to it fully, to trust in it, to let it permeate every part of your life and, finally, to be transformed by it. To serve God as our only Lord and master is the foundation of kingdom ethics that requires of us that we have an attitude toward money that leaves no room for compromise. The lure of money must have no priority in our lives. We must not submit to its power, put our trust in it, allow the pursuit of it to permeate our lives or be transformed by it. According to Matthew 6, if we serve God as our only master, we are left only to hate and despise the power of money and its quest to dominate us. We must take the Bible seriously when it says, "The love of money is a root of all kinds of evil. Some people, eager for money, have wandered from the faith and pierced themselves with many griefs" (1 Tim 6:10). As we have shown, it was this total submission to God alone that Jesus was demanding from the rich young ruler of Matthew 19. For him, only the total abandonment of his earthly kingdom that demanded of him the worship of money could free him fully to embrace the living God. To love one master, we must despise the other.

Now we may be tempted to label such a view as an archaic superstition or a nonsensical overreaction. And this is where we stand once again at the crossroads of the two kingdoms. Outside the kingdom of God this kind of talk is ridiculous. Within the kingdom of God it is an essential truth that has major implications for building a Christian understanding of fundraising. For if at this crucial point we are willing to let the Bible speak, it leads us to a fundamental teaching of how we are to understand our mission of raising money in the kingdom of God.

We must never for a single moment lose sight of the stark realization that whenever we deal with money, we are dealing with dynamite. What is one day that which we control, the next day becomes the controller. Such dynamite must be defused, and the greatest defuser that we as Christians have at our disposal is the opportunity to take that which seeks to dominate us and simply give it away. Think about it. There is no greater expression of money's total lack of dominance over us or of its low priority in our lives that when we can, with joy and peace, give it away for the Lord's work. You cannot worship the god of mammon and be a free and cheerful giver. Likewise, you cannot serve the living God and be a hoarder of his resources. Giving, both how we give and how much we give, is the clearest outward expression of who our God really is. Our check stubs speak more honestly of our priorities than our church memberships.

If this is a right and proper understanding of what Scripture says about money, then this must guide everything we do. True, godly Christian fundraising encourages and enables God's people to give. When this giving is done with joy and out of a spirit of obedience, it helps free people from the dangers associated with the handling of money. It keeps priorities straight, and it breaks the bondage money continually fights to put us under. Robert Wuthnow comments on the response of a woman who participated in a comprehensive study on the issue,

> In a way that she considers curious, she says that giving "freely" makes her feel more secure. By giving some of her money away, she convinces herself that she is not really dependent on having money and material goods. She is just herself—and could be happy even if she lost all her money.[4]

Obedient Christian giving is a liberating act of joy that renews us each time we do it. In building our development programs let us begin by asking what kinds of approaches and techniques we can use that will lead our donors to give joyfully, to break bondage in their lives and free them to serve their one and only master. This is the starting point and framework for our new Christian development program.

Gracious Rewards for Obedient Giving

This leads us to a second teaching, one that is problematic only when it is seen through the eyes of old, secular lenses. There is a clear teaching that godly giving brings with it rewards. Only by giving can we receive the fullest of what God has in store for us. As you read the vast array of Scriptures that speak about money you cannot help but notice that nearly every command or directive to give has a reward or blessing attached. Listen to a few. "'Bring the whole tithe into the storehouse, that there may be food in my house. Test me in this,' says the LORD Almighty, 'and see if I will not throw open the floodgates of heaven and pour out so much blessing that you will not have room enough for it'" (Mal 3:10). "He who gives to the poor will lack nothing" (Prov 28:27). "For even when I was in

---

[4]Robert Wuthnow, *God and Mammon in America* (New York: Free Press, 1994), p. 231.

Thessalonica, you sent me aid again and again when I was in need. Not that I am looking for a gift, but I am looking for what may be credited to your account" (Phil 4:16-17). "Give, and it will be given to you. A good measure, pressed down, shaken together and running over, will be poured into your lap" (Lk 6:38). "Command them to do good, to be rich in good deeds, and to be generous and willing to share. In this way they will lay up treasures for themselves as a firm foundation for the coming age" (1 Tim 6:18-19). In the Philippians and the 1 Timothy references the gifts are described as those in the coming age, as gifts and treasures in heaven. Others are described as temporal gifts or blessings. In either case, God clearly attaches rich and abundant blessings for obedient Christian giving.

This could lead to the temptation that the reward may become our motivation for giving that, ironically, puts us back under the same bondage from which giving was to free us. To give a little for the purpose of getting more back is regarding tithing the same as investing in the stock market. It is a return to two-kingdom giving. If the motivation is net profit, the gift is not free and the reward is lost. The same can be said for the temporal rewards of prestige or public honor. Jesus warns of this false motivation in Matthew 6:1: "Be careful not to do your 'acts of righteousness' before men, to be seen by them. If you do, you will have no reward from your Father in heaven." Whether out of pride or greed, wrong motivations nullify the reward. This should not stop us, however, from understanding that God does seek to reward the obedient giver. He even asks us to put him to the test and see if he is not faithful to his promises of abundance and provision.

The question we must ask here is the purpose of such abundance and provision. Is it simply a reward for our obedient giving for us to use as we wish? Bassler's study suggests something quite different. In 2 Corinthians 9, Paul speaks three times of God's provisions for those who support the collection. Bassler rightly concludes,

> Each time, however, the provision is presented not as a *reward* for the giver's generosity but as an *enabler* of it, not as a result of generosity but as a source for continuing generosity.[5]

Here we must also cite a teaching in Scripture that turns the conven-

[5]Jouette Bassler, *God and Mammon: Asking for Money in the New Testament* (Nashville: Abingdon Press, 1991), p. 109.

tional donor-donee on its head. Consider for a moment the often misunderstood passage that Paul ascribes to Jesus in Acts 20:35, "It is more blessed to give than to receive." In the transaction of giving and receiving, Jesus is saying that the *giver* comes out ahead. The one who receives gets only that tangible and perishable gift that the giver bestowed. The giver, on the other hand, receives treasures in heaven that "moth and rust do not destroy" (Mt 6:20). The giver receives Timothy's "firm foundation for the coming age" (1 Tim 6:19). What a beautiful arrangement. The giver sees a need, responds out of obedience and joy, and not only reestablishes who his or her god is but receives an eternal reward for this act of faithfulness. I believe God awaits every day to grant unfathomable blessings on those who will give obediently and abundantly. Here again is the joy of Christian fundraising. Done properly, it brings blessings on all those who are asked. When people respond to requests for support, they are laying up for themselves treasures in heaven. Eternal rewards for God's people are the results of good Christian fundraising.

What implications are there here for our development programs? I believe this teaching should guide us in our use of acknowledgments, in our use of premiums, in how we handle naming opportunities for capital projects, in the assumptions behind our major donor programs and so forth. While the world around us sees nothing wrong with public rewards and honors for big givers, we must be led in a different direction according to the ethics of this kingdom. How do we thank, acknowledge and honor our donors in ways that are in keeping with this understanding of godly rewards for true Christian giving? How do we communicate this truth to our donors in such a way that they see their giving not as a one-way source of blessing but in ways that they actually are the recipient of the greater blessing? How do we teach people the blessedness of giving? In short, how do we participate in the church's responsibility to train stewards? Is that not surely a major objective of our work? I believe that these are the questions we must be asking and the issues we must be discussing if we are to build truly Christian fundraising programs.

The Role of the Spirit

A third teaching is one that is built more on a systematic understanding of Scripture's teaching than on specific verses. It has to do with the motivation for giving. The field of Christian fundraising is inundated with seminars, books, newsletters and consultants who will help us write the "effective appeal letter." We are told if we use the right words, build an emotionally compelling case, use a specific number of sentences in each paragraph and a certain arrangement of paragraphs in every letter, address our envelopes in certain ways and mail our letters at certain times, we will increase our responses by x percent. Major gift presenters tell us just the right words to use and how to "close the deal." Everyone is helping us to motivate our people to give—out of guilt, out of allegiance, out of pity, as an act of conscience or just to get us to go away. In almost every case, the motivation to give is up to us; that is *our* job. If we will just say the right things in the right ways, people will give.

We need to ask ourselves in the face of all of this, why then do we ask our donors to pray in consideration of their giving? Is this perhaps one more place where we have painted a Christian veneer over a wholly secular understanding of the motivation to give? Can we on the one hand believe we are responsible for the motivation of gifts and on the other hand ask our donors to make their giving a prayerful decision? Clearly we cannot hold these two positions simultaneously. We must either accept the worldly view that our role as fundraisers is to motivate, or we acknowledge the powerful role of the Holy Spirit through prayer that we ask of our donors and stop placing on our shoulders the responsibility to move people to give.

There is ample evidence in Scripture to show that all of the decisions in our lives should be influenced by the power of God's Spirit working in us. This work of guiding, directing and granting wisdom is the defining mark of the work of the Holy Spirit. Above we have seen the importance of giving in terms of our singular devotion to God alone. Again we must acknowledge here, in the loudest of voices, that giving is primarily a spiritual matter. Even more pointedly, giving is an act of obedient worship. If we ask our people to pray, we must conclude that the Holy Spirit is the one, true and only right motivator of gifts from our people. Once we have acknowledged and accepted that fact, our entire reason for existence changes radically. No longer are we tasked with motivating giving. No longer need we sweat over the exact right wording to push the right buttons of our donors or parishioners in our appeal letters—and perhaps the term "appeal letter" can be a much-needed casualty in this new fundraising program.

Again I must be careful to clarify my position. I am not saying that letters should not be carefully written, that they should not present the case, the need for funding, how the money will be spent and how important gifts are to the institution. I am not saying that major donors should not be visited and asked for "stretch gifts" and that we should not plan out how we will discuss our needs with them. Nor am I saying that our communications should be shoddy or haphazard, or that we should throw all research on successful programs out the window. What I am calling on us to see is that the basic underlying assumption from which we operate in all of these decisions must be that we rely in total on the work of the Holy Spirit to motivate our donors or parishioners to give.

This should be a liberating and empowering realization. Only within this understanding can we go about our work in the highest professional manner, providing our people with the most accurate information about our organization and its needs, keeping them informed and involved, focusing on information, content and an ongoing partnership with them. Only in this context can we really have interactions with our donors that are not all tied to a solicitation and truly be at ease. We all know that successful fundraising is based on the building of good, solid, long-term relationships. This understanding of the Holy Spirit as the motivator of gifts frees us to do that job to its utmost. We will still ask for funds, but we will do so not hoping that our words were right, that the case was sufficiently compelling or that all the objections were overcome. We will ask simply, honestly and confidently, and then we will sit back and watch God do great things through his people.

There is one more aspect to this teaching that I want to cover. Seeing the Holy Spirit as the sole motivator of gifts changes radically our process of budgeting and projecting our income. In some ways, it may make it nonsensical, for we are asked to project the work of the Holy Spirit. Yet we are called to be responsible in our work, and we must plan, budget and make projections. The point I want to make here is that if the Holy Spirit is central to how our donors will give, should he not also be central to our planning process? By that I mean, should not the same "prayerful considerations" we ask of our donors be at the very heart of everything we do as well? And if we trust the Holy Spirit to answer the prayers of our donors and to guide them into making critical financial decisions with regard to their giving to us, should we not assume the same faith posture in our own asking for guidance and wisdom in projecting how our donors might respond? And finally, if the Spirit is moving the organization to step out beyond its normal expectations in trust, should this not be the primary source of direction regardless of how "financially risky" it may appear to the world? Is not the defining mark of the people of the kingdom of God a single-minded commitment to hear and follow the leading of the Spirit?

Let us commit to give over to the work of the Spirit that which is rightfully the Spirit's, and let us join with our donors in seeking after the guidance of the Spirit in all our planning and projecting.

Spiritual Growing and Scriptural Giving

A fourth teaching we must discuss in this process of building a Christian development program is an extension of the third. In chapter eight we discussed Paul's teachings in 2 Corinthians 8. The chapter begins with these powerful words,

> And now, brothers, we want you to know about the grace that God has given the Macedonian churches. Out of the most severe trial, their overflowing joy and their extreme poverty welled up in rich generosity. For I testify that they gave as much as they were able, and even beyond their ability. Entirely on their own they urgently appealed to us for the privilege of sharing in this service to the saints. And they did not do as we expected, but they gave themselves first to the Lord and then to us in keeping with God's will. (vv. 1-5)

If there was ever a place in Scripture where the ethics of the kingdom of God were shown in their most radical form, it is here. What strange combinations we confront: severe trial and overflowing joy, extreme poverty and rich generosity, and a sense of pleading to be allowed the privilege of giving. As we saw in chapter eight, these are marks of the kingdom of God, and we must understand them if we are to be fundraisers in that kingdom.

In Paul's account of the collection from the Macedonian church, he includes a most important point concerning due process. He tells us that, even to his own surprise, these people gave themselves first to the Lord and then to the task of joyful giving. This, according to Paul, is the will of God. It is the right process for his people and the reason for their ability to give richly out of their extreme poverty. We need to reflect on this verse when we ask ourselves, how do we inspire our donors to be better givers? All of us would love to have a few hundred Macedonian churches in our constituencies! Yet in a very real sense, is not part of our job to help our donors become ever more godly givers? If we are serious about this

donor relationship language, are we not to be concerned, perhaps primarily concerned, not so much in what our donors give, but *how* they give
and *why* they give. Should we not seek ways to inspire our donors to be
better and more biblical givers?

If this is so, then we must begin here and acknowledge that the basis
for improving the giving of our donors is to help, support and encourage
them in "giving themselves first to the Lord." Simply put, better disciples
of Jesus Christ are better tithers, better biblical stewards, better partners
for our ministries. And as they increase in the ministry of giving, they
receive the benefits and rewards of faithful and generous giving. What a
great profession to be in! *It should not be a surprise to conclude that the spiritual growth of our donors should be the primary concern of every Christian fundraiser!* It is in this context that we should be planning our annual program
of visitations, letters, phone calls, mailings, publications and solicitations.
This major aspect of our work should drive our donor relations, church
relations, alumni relations and board strategies.

It is only in this understanding of the relationship between spiritual
growth and faithful stewardship that we can fully embrace Christian
fundraising as a ministry. We minister when we help people grow in their
understanding of godly giving. We minister when we design programs
that challenge our donors to more radical discipleship. We minister when
we support our donors through a consistent program of prayer and personal interaction. We minister when we focus first on our donors' relationship with God and only secondarily on their relationship with us, for
we know that faithfulness to the one will result in the necessary benefits
to the other, and both to the glory of God and the work of his kingdom.
This is what it means to minister through our work in the kingdom of
God. How we do that, what it means for every area of our development
programs must become the topic of highest priority for Christian fundraising.

Giving as Our Witness and Worship

Finally, and following on from all that has been said, Paul's understanding of the right place of giving in our lives leads us to the unmistakable
conclusion that giving is more than the exchange of a medium for the
benefit of another. Giving involves us at our most basic level. Godly, sacrificial giving demands our total commitment to Jesus Christ and the ethics of his kingdom. When we give, we are involved in an act of obedience,

an act of faith, an act of discipleship. We return again to the conclusion that, as members of the body of Christ involved in this process, either individually or collectively, giving can only be seen as a pure and true act of worship. I do not think we have considered this point nearly as carefully as we should and must in our Christian fundraising. Giving in response to the urging of the Holy Spirit is our way of being obedient, of returning our thanks and praise to God, of involving ourselves in his work and ultimately of glorifying him.

If giving is such an act, then Christian fundraising is nothing less than the ministry of aiding people in their worship of God. In our asking we must understand this dynamic, for it puts great demands upon us. It shows the importance of our job in ensuring that our asking is absolutely honest, that our projects are worthy of our donor's support, that our use of donated funds are sound, that our motivations are right and that our process is bathed in prayer. This is holy work that demands spiritually mature and godly people to undertake it. It is a ministry that demands that we do not build relationships for the sole purpose that they may result in giving but that we build relationships as ministers in God's kingdom. As ministers we look to the spiritual growth of our donors as the process by which giving can become more and more the act of worship and praise as God meant it to be.

In this way, Christian fundraising is an extension of the ministry of the church. If we divorce ourselves from that tie, we lose our rights as ministers. This is what we must avoid whether we work in the church or in the world of "parachurch" or Christian education. As members of the kingdom of God we are a part of his body, and therefore our work is ministry in his church. As such, we can as ministers see our job in its holistic sense. This is what we learn from Paul and what we must seek to implement in our fundraising programs. Bassler concludes her fine book on the subject with the following words:

> Paul . . . did not suggest that one becomes partner in ministry through one's donations but that requests for money are to be rooted in a prior sense of fellowship and partnership that has been established on other grounds altogether. This means that the basic work of fundraising begins long before any requests are made. The seeds for these requests are planted through every act that creates in the members of the church a sense of mutual trust, shared faith and common goals. It is then that the act of giving can become a joyous celebration of faith, that the givers benefit more than the receivers,

and that the requests for money can be seen by all as a link in the operation of God's grace.[6]

Our Glorious Calling

These five teachings form a clear framework for a new paradigm for Christian fundraising. Imagine for a moment a program built on the understanding of people's need to give to be freed from the bondage of the power of money. Imagine designing a program that took God's promises of rewards seriously and saw the gift of giving as the greatest blessing in the philanthropic transaction. Imagine acknowledging the primary role of the Holy Spirit as the motivator of all our gifts and the peace and courage we would receive in our planning and asking. Imagine a program whose objectives were built around the desire to encourage and challenge donors to a greater and deeper walk with Jesus Christ, to a more committed level of discipleship and a lifestyle that reflected the ethics of the kingdom of God. Imagine taking up our call to be ministers, supporting and encouraging our donors to give faithfully and cheerfully as a holy act of divine worship.

Can we imagine such a program? And if we can, can we imagine God not blessing an institution or church that developed such a program, supplying all of its needs according to his glorious riches in Christ Jesus?

Christian fundraising is a glorious ministry when it is understood in these terms and undertaken in these ways. As pastors, Christian leaders and laity let us reclaim the place of honor due their work. If it is true that we Christians *need* to give as an expression of our allegiance and an act of our worship and praise, then the role of Christian fundraising is a vital part of the work of the church.

The end goal is that in our asking, our giving, our spending and our living we may all be joyful kingdom stewards. What might such a life look like? Let me offer one example at the close of this book. It is the story of a couple who gave the first major gift to help found Eastern Baptist Theological Seminary in Philadelphia. The story of this gift is recorded in a book by Austen K. deBlois where he writes,

Immediately following the announcement contained in this letter, Dr. Gordon H. Baker led in a prayer of thanksgiving. On motion of Doctor Barras, it was voted to accept the gift with the conditions, and to express the grati-

---

[6]Ibid., pp. 134-35.

tude of the Trustees to Almighty God for his goodness, and for the favor that had been bestowed upon the Seminary through the generous gift of unknown friends.

This first great gift to the Seminary was not made without full knowledge on the part of the donors, of the plans and ideals of the Philadelphia group. Consider the facts in the case. A wise and far-seeing Baptist layman, and his equally wise and far-seeing wife had definitely dedicated themselves and their wealth to the upbuilding of the kingdom of Jesus Christ, whom they loved with single-hearted devotion and served with undeviating loyalty. They were broad-minded and liberal-hearted. They sought no personal renown. They were deeply interested in home missions, in foreign missions, in the redemption of youth, and in Christian education. Their greatness of heart and sweeping range of vision grew out of their perfect faith in the primary principles of the Gospel of Grace. They were not willing to donate their God-given riches to any raw or radical enterprises of humanitarian liberalists.

The correspondence that passed between these two gracious givers and Dr. James A. Maxwell, their dear friend, evinces a rare combination of the elements of shrewd common sense and princely generosity. As they considered that their property came directly from God, they were willing to dispose of their wealth in accordance with His guidance, and not to spend it unwisely or on unproductive objects. They watched very carefully every move in the evolution of the Seminary purpose, and were better acquainted than were some of the Trustees themselves with the progress, and as well with the difficulties, of the enterprise.

It was the intention of the Board in Philadelphia, after the meeting in March, that the use of some church should be obtained, and its rooms used for class purposes during the week. It was hoped that voluntary teachers could be persuaded to give their part-time services in the instruction of students. It was expected that some years would elapse before an adequate endowment could be procured. The Trustees were well aware of all the trying conditions that would have to be overcome before the Seminary could manage to compete successfully with the strength and resources of the existing institutions. This situation was changed, almost miraculously, in the twinkling of an eye, by the munificent gift of the two unnamed donors.

Writing long after the event, Doctor Baker thus describes the effect of Doctor Maxwell's announcement: "I shall never forget the moment when that gift was announced. A holy hush fell on the meeting. Our first act was to engage in prayers of thanksgiving and dedication. There was profound gratitude in all our hearts, and with it a sense of grave responsibility that prevented any outward demonstration of joy. We knew that God had called us to a great task, that He had put into our hands a sacred trust; and we were determined by His help to give a good account of our stewardship, and to produce a theological seminary worthy of the name of Christ and of our great denomination."[7]

May God grant to each of us such a vision and a passion to live our lives in the true reality of our human existence, that of stewards in the kingdom of the triune God of grace.

---

[7]Austen K. deBlois, *The Making of Ministers* (Philadelphia: Judson Press, 1936), pp. 25-26.

Bibliography

Anderson, Ray. "Christopraxis: Christ's Ministry for the World." In *Christ in our Place*. Exeter, U.K.: Paternoster Press, 1989.

Augustine. *The Confessions of St. Augustine*. Oxford: John Henry Parker, 1838.

Bacchiocchi, Samuele. *Immortality or Resurrection?* Berrien Springs, Mich.: Biblical Perspectives, 1997.

Barna, George. *The Second Coming of the Church*. Nashville: Word, 1997.

— — —. *Virtual America*. Ventura, Calif.: Regal Books, 1994.

Barth, Karl. "The Task of Ministry." In *The Word of God and the Word of Man*. London: Hodder and Stoughton, 1928.

———. *The Church Dogmatics*, IV/1. Edinburgh, U.K.: T & T Clark, 1956.

Bassler, Jouette. *God and Mammon: Asking for Money in the New Testament*. Nashville: Abingdon Press, 1991.

Berkhof, Hendrikus. *Christian Faith*. Grand Rapids, Mich.: Eerdmans, 1979.

Bloesch, Donald. *Holy Scripture*. Downers Grove, Ill.: InterVarsity Press, 1994.

———. *A Theology of Word and Spirit*. Downers Grove, Ill.: InterVarsity Press, 1992.

Bruce, F. F. *The Gospel of John*. Grand Rapids, Mich.: Eerdmans, 1983.

Brunner, Emil. *The Divine Imperative*. London: Lutterworth Press, 1942.

Calvin, John. *Institutes of the Christian Religion*. Philadelphia: Westminster Press, 1960.

Dearborn, Timothy. "God, Grace and Salvation." In *Christ in Our Place*. Exeter, U.K.: Paternoster Press, 1989.

deBlois, Austen K. *The Making of Ministers*. Philadelphia: Judson Press, 1936.

Edersheim, Alfred. *The Temple: Its Ministry and Services*. Peabody, Mass.: Hendrickson Publishers, 1994.

Foster, Richard. *The Challenge of the Disciplined Life*. San Francisco: HarperCollins, 1989.

Green, David. "One Nation, After All." *U.S. News and World Report*, March 16, 1998.

Grenz, Stanley. *A Primer on Postmodernism*. Grand Rapids, Mich.: Eerdmans, 1996.

Gunton, Colin. *The Promise of Trinitarian Theology*. Edinburgh, U.K.: T & T Clark, 1991.

Gutiérrez, Gustavo. "Liberation Theology and the Future of the Poor." In *Liberating the Future: God, Mammon and Theology*. Edited by Jeorg Rieger. Minneapolis: Fortress, 1998.

Hall, Douglas John, *The Steward*. Grand Rapids, Mich.: Eerdmans, 1990.

Hart, Trevor. *Faith Thinking*. London: SPCK, 1995.

Hershberger, Ervin N. *Seeing Christ in the Tabernacle*. Meyersdale: Choice Books, 1995.

Kant, Immanuel. *Religion Within the Limits of Reason Alone*. New York: Harper & Row, 1960.

Kinney, John. "1998 Mitchell Lecture." Eastern Baptist Theological Seminary, February 1998.

Kraybill, Donald. *The Upside Down Kingdom*. Basingstoke, U.K.: Marshall, Morgan & Scott, 1978.

Moltmann, Jürgen. *God in Creation*. London: SCM Press, 1985.

————. *The Way of Jesus Christ*. London: SCM Press, 1990.

Mowry LaCugna, Catherine. *God for Us: The Trinity and Christian Life*. New York: HarperCollins; Edinburgh, U.K.: T & T Clark, 1991.

Myers, David. "Money and Misery." In *The Consuming Passion*. Edited Rodney Clapp. Downers Grove: InterVarsity Press, 1998.

Newell, Roger. "Participation and Atonement." In *Christ in Our Place*. Exeter, U.K.: Paternoster Press, 1989.

Oden, Thomas. *The Living God*. San Francisco: HarperCollins, 1961.

Peters, Ted. *God as Trinity: Rationality and Temporality in Divine Life*. Louisville, Ky.: Westminster John Knox Press, 1993.

Polanyi, Michael. *Personal Knowledge*. New York: Routledge Kegan Paul, 1958.

Rieger, Jeorg. *Liberating the Future: God, Mammon and Theology*. Minneapolis: Fortress, 1998.

Rodin, Scott. *Evil and Theodicy in the Theology of Karl Barth*. New York: Peter Lang, 1997.

Sherrard, Philip. "Sacred Cosmology and the Ecological Crisis," *Green Cross*, fall 1996.

Shaw, Vera. "The Ecology of Eden." *Green Cross*, winter 1995.

Sider, Ronald. *Rich Christians in an Age of Hunger*. Dallas: Word, 1997.

Sine, Tom. *Taking Discipleship Seriously*. Valley Forge, Penn.: Judson Press, 1985.

Torrance, James. *Worship, Community, and the Triune God of Grace*. Carlisle, U.K.: Paternoster, 1996.

Torrance, Thomas. *The Trinitarian Faith*. Edinburgh, U.K.: T & T Clark, 1988.

Van Dyke, Fred, David Mahan, Joseph Sheldon, and Raymond Brand. *Redeeming Creation: The Biblical Basis for Environmental Stewardship*. Downers Grove, Ill.: InterVarsity Press, 1996.

Van Leeuwen, Ray C. "Christ's Resurrection and the Creation's Vindication," in *The Environment and the Christian*. Grand Rapids, Mich.: Baker, 1991.

————. "Enjoying Creation—Within Limits." In *The Midas Trap*. Wheaton, Ill.: Victor, 1990.

Veith, Gene Edward. "A Postmodern Scandal." *World*, February 21, 1998.

Wood Lynn, Robert. "Faith and Money." *Inside Information*, spring 1997.

Wuthnow, Robert. *God and Mammon in America*. New York: Free Press, 1994.

Subject Index

abortion, 26, 39

absolute ownership, 80, 102, 120

Adam and Eve, 73, 78, 81, 82, 88, 89, 93, 94, 96, 123, 130, 133, 135, 144, 155, 162

advocate, 180, 182

American dream, 148

analogia entis, 37, 38

analogia fidei, 38

Anselm of Canterbury, 50

asking, 7, 13, 14, 26, 27, 66, 71, 99, 169, 172, 194, 201, 206, 208, 210, 213, 214

Athanasius, 50

Augustine, 50, 72

autonomy, 37

baptism, 156, 180

Barth, Karl, 21, 37, 38, 85, 87, 97, 100

Bassler, Jouette, 168, 171, 207, 213

biomedical ethics, 26

birth-to-death reality, 124, 148

Bloesch, Donald, 51, 56

body, 45, 46, 71, 74-78, 111, 115, 117, 119, 129, 156, 157, 177, 191, 196, 198, 213

body of Christ, 45, 46, 71, 117, 119, 177, 191, 196, 198, 213

Bonhoeffer, Dietrich, 152, 153

Brand, Raymond, 30, 73, 107

capital punishment, 26

Carlin, George, 125, 126

Chalcedonian formula, 107

cheerful giver, giving, 16, 66, 159, 173, 206

children, 5, 10, 12, 20-23, 26, 27, 29, 32, 47, 60, 64, 65, 72, 74, 77, 78, 80, 82, 83, 87, 92, 98, 101, 105, 108, 109, 110, 113, 116-18, 123, 124, 127, 128, 130, 133, 136-42, 150, 151, 154-57, 162, 166, 176, 178-81, 185, 186, 195, 198, 199, 202

Christian deism, 91

Christian education, 182, 186, 187, 190, 192, 197, 213, 215

Christian ethics, 11-13, 16-22, 36, 47, 58, 75, 101

Christian fundraisers, fundraising, 5, 9, 168, 174, 194, 195, 198, 201, 203, 205, 206, 208, 212-14

Christian giving, 16, 145, 146, 206-8

Christian institutions, 167, 197-99, 201

Christian unity, 25

Christocentric epistemology, 21, 31, 56, 58, 86

church, 7, 9, 10, 16-19, 21, 24-29, 31, 32, 34, 35, 37, 38, 41, 43-46, 49, 51, 52, 55, 56, 58-60, 65-67, 69, 77, 78, 79, 90-92, 94, 98, 105, 107-9, 112, 119, 120, 121, 123, 127-33, 135, 137, 138, 141, 145, 146, 150, 152, 154, 156, 157, 164, 166, 167, 169, 171, 174-77, 181-94, 197-99, 201, 202, 206, 208, 211, 212-15

of Jesus Christ, 24, 58, 183, 185, 201

leadership, 190

as steward, 181, 191

citizenship, 130, 136, 137, 167, 169, 196-99

continuity, 37

control, 29, 30, 63, 74, 80, 102, 112, 114, 116-18, 130, 135, 144, 161, 177, 182, 191, 205

Copernicus, Nicolaus, 38, 51, 52

cosmological knowledge, 34

counterfeit ethics, 13

covenant, 63-65, 72-74, 77, 82, 85, 89, 90, 95, 100, 101, 105, 110, 111, 113, 178

creation, 17, 23, 26, 27, 30, 33-35, 37, 41, 42, 57, 59-66, 69-73, 75-96, 98-104, 106, 107, 111, 115, 117, 119-22, 129, 133, 144, 145, 158, 160, 161, 163, 164-67, 172, 175, 178, 180-82, 184, 185, 188, 190

cross, 38, 59, 64, 84, 89, 90, 113, 120, 123, 129, 138, 139, 155, 157-59, 201

Day of Atonement, 110

death, 68, 76, 89, 91, 92, 95, 97, 99, 103, 106-10, 115-17, 120, 122, 124-27, 136, 147-49, 151-61, 163, 165, 166, 168, 169, 171, 174, 178, 181, 183, 185, 186, 188, 189, 192, 197

death-to-life, 158, 165, 166, 168, 183, 186, 188

Descartes, René, 38, 52, 53

discipleship, 12, 16, 68, 73, 76, 114, 120, 121, 128, 182, 184, 185, 192, 196, 197, 202, 212-14

discrimination, 26

doctrine of creation, 70, 91

doctrine of God, 13, 21, 27, 31, 44, 65

dominance, 66, 67, 82, 96, 100, 205

domination, 30, 97, 144

dominion, 66, 73, 80-82, 94, 99, 144, 145

doxology, 11, 82

dual citizenships, 201

dying and rising, 156

dying to sin, 38, 155, 157, 160, 161, 163, 164

dynamism, 38

Eden, 78, 82-85, 96, 101, 102, 112, 116, 123,
　　134, 136, 144, 154, 155, 164, 178
Enlightenment, 37, 38, 40, 51, 54, 89, 199
environment, 29, 54, 76, 80-82, 87, 91, 143,
　　144, 161, 182
epistemology, 21, 24, 25, 31, 32, 37, 47, 50, 56,
　　58, 59, 63, 85, 86
eternity, 46, 53, 77, 84, 92, 106, 154
euthanasia, 26, 39
evangelical repentance, 112
evangelism, 74, 197, 202
evil, 10, 26, 43, 75, 86-90, 93, 95-97, 99, 106,
　　108, 113, 116, 121-23, 144, 152, 153, 155,
　　157, 181, 190, 205
existential knowledge, 34
experience, 9, 23-25, 33-36, 39, 40, 43, 46, 49,
　　54, 61, 69, 90, 123, 126, 127, 161, 175, 176,
　　179, 197
exploitation, 30, 66, 76, 82, 116, 122, 144

Fall, the, 26, 30, 34, 35, 37, 46, 64, 70, 72, 73,
　　75, 80, 82, 84, 85, 86, 87, 89, 90, 92, 93,
　　97-101, 105, 112, 120, 135, 154, 155, 174,
　　183, 189, 192, 197
fallen humanity, 37, 95, 119, 129
false start, 15-17, 19-21, 25-27
family, 5, 7, 42, 70, 79, 124, 125, 132, 149,
　　174-76, 178, 179, 180, 193
fides quaerens intellectum, 50, 51
finitum non capax infiniti, 38, 44
first death, 155
flesh, 41-43, 45, 59, 69, 75, 77, 79, 95, 97, 104,
　　106, 109, 116, 176-78, 183
freedom, 10, 40, 43, 61-65, 73, 80, 82, 85, 87,
　　88, 95, 126, 132, 150, 157-59, 161-64,
　　166-68, 188, 193
　　freedom for, 88, 158, 159, 161
　　freedom from, 126, 158, 159, 161, 163

Galileo, 51, 52
general revelation, 33-36
giving, 7, 10, 14, 16, 26, 28, 29, 39, 47, 59, 60,
　　66, 68, 71, 73, 81, 88, 94, 95, 139, 141, 145,
　　146, 152, 162, 163, 168, 170-74, 179, 180,
　　184, 186-88, 194, 201, 206-14
glorification, 64, 75, 80, 188
glory of God, 33, 35, 66, 71, 72, 92, 98, 184,
　　212
good and evil, 88, 89, 106
Great Commandment, 68, 142
Great Commission, 68, 131

Green, David, 131

Hall, Douglas John, 28, 29, 47, 118, 160
Harnack, Adolf von, 37
high priest, 109-11, 115, 119, 188
holiness, 68, 95, 96
homosexuality, 25, 26, 39
human sexuality, 26, 45, 77
humanity come of age, 36

idealism, 93
idolatry, 33, 36, 123, 143, 159, 204
image of God, 34-37, 70, 72, 74, 77, 78, 80, 96,
　　101, 177, 178
immanence, 62, 63
imperatives, 16, 18, 19, 22, 46, 53, 55, 61, 198
incarnation, 23, 40-44, 59, 64, 98, 103-6, 108,
　　109, 129, 154, 188
indicatives, 19, 22, 25, 55, 61
infinite qualitative distinction, 37
institutional schizophrenia, 202
inviting stewardship, 186, 192

justice, 26, 67, 68, 91, 95, 164, 167, 180, 182

Kant, Immanuel, 37, 53, 54
kingdom builders, 125, 135, 148, 150, 163,
　　170, 175, 177, 183, 189, 195, 197
kingdom building, 126, 140, 141, 147, 148,
　　155, 159, 160, 163, 165, 166, 169, 181,
　　183-86, 189
kingdom of God, 5, 7, 10-12, 17, 20, 29, 38,
　　42-44, 47, 69, 71, 84, 115-18, 120, 122-24,
　　129-31, 133, 134, 136, 137-40, 142, 143, 146,
　　152, 153, 155-58, 161, 163, 164, 168, 171,
　　173, 180, 183, 184, 189, 193, 194-201, 203-5,
　　211-14
　　knowledge of, 21-24, 34-40, 47-49, 55, 56,
　　59, 61, 63, 65, 82, 86, 88, 94, 96, 101

legal repentance, 112
Levitical priesthood, 110
liberal Protestantism, 37, 38
liberation theology, 91
life-givers, 82, 97, 160
logic, 34, 35, 40, 44, 49, 50, 62
lordship, 49, 96, 97, 101, 135, 136, 141, 144,
　　145, 150, 152, 155, 157, 161, 166, 167, 181,
　　183, 184, 197
love, 9, 34, 42, 43, 46-48, 56, 60-65, 67-69,
　　71-73, 75, 78, 79, 80, 82, 83, 85, 87, 88, 95,
　　96, 98, 103, 105, 113, 138, 139, 142, 156,
　　162, 163, 166, 167, 170, 180, 183, 196, 204,

205, 211

Macedonian collection, 171
Mahan, David, 30, 73
mammon, 128, 204, 205
marriage, 45, 79, 124, 176-79, 183
materialism, 9, 16, 18, 30, 159
mind, 23, 29, 51-53, 74-76, 78, 115, 117, 147,
    148, 161, 173, 204
money, 9, 14, 16, 18, 26, 29, 43, 79, 103, 129,
    130, 143, 159, 165, 167, 168, 187, 190, 194,
    195, 203-6, 210, 213, 214
moral example, 105, 106
multiculturalism, 26
Myers, David, 125
myth of the two kingdoms, 29

neighbor, 17, 20, 59, 68, 72, 93, 101, 107,
    115-19, 121, 125, 127, 133, 139-44, 162, 163,
    165-67, 172, 175, 178, 180, 182, 191
nephesh, 75, 129
Newton, Isaac, 38
Nicaea, 45
Niebuhr, Richard, 73
nominalism, 74, 93
nothingness, 86, 95

obedience, 11, 56, 65, 82, 88, 104, 112, 113,
    117, 120, 134, 145, 146, 152-54, 157, 161,
    178, 182, 188, 189, 206, 208, 212
objectivism, 53, 56
one flesh, 45, 77, 79, 97, 176-78, 183
ontology, 37, 86
oppression, 26
owner, ownership, 20, 26, 27, 28, 30, 31, 56,
    63, 64, 80, 83, 102, 113, 114, 116, 120, 135,
    138, 146, 150, 172, 173, 179

panentheistic, 63
parents, 124, 126, 175, 178-81
participation, 11, 40, 46-48, 68, 70, 71, 113-19,
    121, 154, 155, 156, 158, 165-67, 172, 183,
    191, 192
participatory worship, 166, 192
pastor, 10, 66, 145, 183-85, 187, 189, 190, 192
perichoresis, 45
perichoretic, 45, 79
personal transformation, 187, 191, 192
philosophical knowledge, 34
pluralism, 26, 36, 54
possessions, 17, 62, 66, 124, 126, 127, 135,
    138, 141, 148, 150, 165, 190
postmodern, 36, 37, 40, 54-56, 62, 98, 131,

132, 136
power, 20, 30, 33, 34, 40, 45, 51, 52, 59, 61, 62,
    65, 69, 71, 80, 82, 88, 89, 95-98, 100-102,
    106, 109, 114, 116, 119, 120, 122, 123,
    126-28, 135, 142, 143, 145, 150, 154, 160-62,
    165, 166, 182, 184, 189, 191, 192, 204, 205,
    209, 214
preaching, 137, 166, 186-89, 191, 192, 197
problem of evil, 26

racism, 26, 98
reason, 10, 23-25, 34, 35, 37-42, 45, 48-54, 61,
    62, 75, 84, 85, 93, 98, 109, 111, 119, 121,
    127, 131, 134, 135, 152, 154, 157, 165, 166,
    178, 191, 198, 200, 209, 211
reconciliation, 64, 104, 105, 107, 109, 111, 116,
    119, 123, 133, 161, 162, 166, 167, 182
regeneration, 59
relativism, 53, 56, 63, 131, 197
revealed faith, 21, 23, 54
rewards, 125, 138, 173, 188, 206-8, 212, 214
rich young ruler, 16, 39, 138, 168, 169, 205
Rieger, Jeorg, 128
righteousness, 11, 67-69, 92, 95, 112, 119,
    155-57, 171, 207
Ritschl, Albrecht, 37
rule over, 66, 81, 82, 164, 180

salvation, 12, 38, 42, 44, 68, 76, 92, 93, 100,
    104, 106-8, 112, 114, 119, 129, 130, 134, 154,
    155, 158
sanctification, 59
Schleiermacher, Friedrich, 37
Scripture, 4, 20, 23, 29, 44, 45, 49-51, 70, 72,
    80, 89, 92, 93, 107-9, 111, 114, 130, 138, 145,
    146, 148, 153, 155, 168, 174, 176, 195, 204,
    206-9, 211
secondary death, 152
self-revelation, 11, 23, 40-42, 44, 46, 61, 77, 82
self-stewardship, 30
Sermon on the Mount, 170
servanthood, 96, 97, 104, 105, 115, 117, 118,
    137, 184
Sheldon, Joseph, 30, 73
sin, 7, 18, 23, 30, 34, 35, 37-39, 53, 61, 68, 70,
    73, 75, 78, 80, 82-86, 91-95, 97-101, 103,
    106, 107, 109, 111, 112, 114, 115, 119-21,
    123, 126, 129, 130, 133, 135, 138, 144, 145,
    153-66, 175, 178, 181, 183, 196
Sine, Tom, 196-97
Solomon, 146-49
spirit, 11, 21, 22, 40, 44-47, 52, 55, 59, 67-69,
    71, 74, 75, 77, 80, 98, 101, 106, 112-16, 126,

129, 135, 137, 146, 155, 156, 162, 166, 168,
    180, 182, 189, 191, 192, 196, 197, 202, 204,
    206, 208-11, 213, 214
spiritual kingdom, 127, 128, 130, 131, 134,
    135, 139, 144, 145, 146, 150, 169, 184, 192
subdue, 62, 66, 72, 81, 82, 94, 144, 164, 180
success, 59, 60, 66, 100, 102, 130, 137, 138,
    141, 145, 148, 155, 159, 178, 179, 183-85,
    192, 199-201
suffering, 26, 60, 119

temple, 110, 111
theology from above, 107
theology from below, 105
theology of the steward, 10, 11, 16, 19, 20, 25,
    27, 30, 47, 49, 56, 58, 65, 86, 103, 120, 132, 165
tithing, 16, 28, 207
transcendence, 37, 62-64, 153
transformation, 25, 66, 129, 133, 154, 162,
    163, 165, 166, 168, 170, 171, 187-92
trinitarian worship, 166
triune God, 7, 10, 19-22, 32, 41, 44, 58, 60, 63,
    67, 69, 72, 75, 77-79, 83, 98, 101, 106, 107,

117, 119-21, 123, 127, 133, 135, 136, 138,
    139, 142, 143, 150, 151, 153, 156, 161, 162,
    165, 172, 174, 177, 178, 181, 186, 188-90,
    195, 216

universal truth, 56, 131

Van Dyke, Fred, 30, 73
Van Leeuwen, Ray, 126, 163, 165
Veith, Gene Edward, 132
via negativa, 34
vicarious humanity of Christ, 108, 153, 154
vocation, 16, 18, 28, 47, 59, 65, 74, 114, 117,
    161, 162, 166, 168, 190-92

waste, 30, 76
wholeness, 10, 54, 74, 75, 88, 98, 117, 164, 167,
    172, 174, 175, 177, 179
Word of God, 41, 182, 191
worldly kingdom, 29, 125, 127, 128, 137, 145,
    173
wrath of God, 33, 68
Wuthnow, Robert, 18, 129, 130, 159, 206

Scripture Index

Genesis
1--3, *84*
1:26, *70*
1:27-28, *72*
2, *96*
2:24, *77*
3, *95*

Proverbs
3:5, *193*
28:27, *206*

Ecclesiastes
1:12-18, *147*
2:1-11, *147-48*
2:17-23, *148*

Isaiah
58:7, *174*

Jeremiah
17:11, *174*

Malachi
3:10, *206*

Matthew
6:1, *207*
6:1-4, *170*
6:19-21, *170*
6:20, *208*
6:24, *204*
6:25-34, *170-71*
6:33, *47*
7:7-11, *171*
19, *205*
28:18, *157*

Luke
6:38, *207*
19:34, *172*

John
1:2-3, *70*
1:14, *41*
1:18, *43*
3:16, *43-44*
8:32, *42*
8:36, *159*

14:6, *42*
14:10, *46*
15:4, *46*
16:33, *193*
17, *44-46*
17:21, *139*

Acts
20:35, *174, 208*

Romans
1:18-20, *33*
1:23, *34*
5:8, *64*
5:15-17, *92*
6:3-4, *156*
6:6-7, *156*
8:22, *80*

1 Corinthians
6:15-16, *77*
6:19-20, *155*

2 Corinthians
5:19, *108*
8:1-5, *211*
8:2, *171*
9:7, *174*
9:13, *168*

Galatians
2:20, *160*
3:26-28, *118*

Ephesians
1:4, *64*
2:4-6, *156*
2:5, *64*
2:6, *46, 64*

Philippians
1:21, *160*
4:16-17, *207*

Colossians
1:15-20, *165*
1:16-17, *70*
3:3-4, *157*
3:9-11, *118*

1 Timothy
6:10, *174, 205*
6:18-19, *207*
6:19, *208*

Hebrews
1:1-2, *70*
1:1-3, *108*
2:7-9, *117*
2:8, *157*
4:14-16, *111*
7:24-25, *157*
7:27, *157*
9:11, *111*

9:12, *111*
9:15, *111*
9:24, *111*
9:26, *111, 157*
10:10, *111, 157*

James
1:27, *174*
5:3, *174*

1 Peter
2:24, *156*

Revelation
13:8, *64*

FALLEN IS NOT
NORMAL 123

MAMMONITES 128

PROTESTANT ERROR 129

4 LEVELS 144, 29f, 72

CALL TO KINGDOM 17

THE GOD QUESTION 25

analogy of being 37

WHERE DO WE START? 40

THE KINGDOM 42

A/4/B 43

TWO CHOICES 45

THE PRINCIPLE OF LOVE 47f

WORLDVIEW 44f, 76

TRANSCENDENT / IMMANENT 62

UN NE CESSARY / UNKNOWABLE 64

TRI THEISM 67

SOCIAL GOSPEL WEAKNESS 68

"MINE" 75

"NAKED" 78